LONDON JEWRY AND LONDON POLITICS 1889–1986

GEOFFREY ALDERMAN

ROUTLEDGE
London and New York

First published in 1989 by
Routledge
11 New Fetter Lane, London EC4P 4EE
29 West 35th Street, New York NY 10001

Printed in Great Britain by
T J Press (Padstow), Padstow, Cornwall

British Library Cataloguing in Publication Data

Alderman, Geoffrey, *1944*–
London Jewry and London politics 1889–1986
1. London. Local government. Role of
Jews, 1889–1986
I. Title
352.0421

ISBN 0-415-02204-5

Library of Congress Cataloging in Publication Data

Alderman, Geoffrey–
London Jewry and London politics, 1889–1986/Geoffrey Alderman
p.   cm.
Bibliography: p.
Includes index.
ISBN 0-415-02204-5
1. Jews – England – London – Politics and government. 2. London
(England) – Politics and government. 3. London (England) – ethnic
relations. I. Title.
DS135.E55L662   1989
323.1'1924'04213 – dc19   88 – 28653

CONTENTS

PREFACE

In 1985 I accepted an invitation from the European Science Foundation to contribute a short study of the relationship between the London Jewish community and the London County Council to an ambitious multi-national project investigating the impact of ethnic and religious minorities on European urban communities in the nineteenth and twentieth centuries. The present volume grew out of that study, and I should like first of all to record my thanks to the Foundation and in particular to Professor K. B. Nowlan for his critical and enthusiastic encouragement and support of my endeavours.

For permission to consult and make reference to archival material in their possession I must also place on record my thanks to the Board of Deputies of British Jews (especially David Massel, the Board's executive director), the British Library, the Central Zionist Archives of the World Zionist Organisation Jerusalem, the Federation of Synagogues London, the Greater London Record Office, the Guildhall Library London, Hansib Publications, the House of Lords Record Office, the London Board of Jewish Religious Education (especially its secretary, David Lerner), the Jewish Welfare Board (especially its executive director, Melvyn Carlowe), the Mocatta Library (University College London), the Public Record Office, Tower Hamlets Central Library Stepney, and the Rothschild Archive London.

I have benefited from conversations with the following individuals, who kindly put their time at my disposal and answered my queries: the late Dr S. Chazen; Mr J. L. Cymerman; Mrs Gladys Dimson; Councillor Ellis Hillman; Dr Bernard Homa; Mr Henry Morris; Mr A. B. Olivestone; Mr Martin Savitt;

Mr Harold Sebag-Montefiore; Mr Thomas Reif; Mr Ansel Wong. In addition, several individuals agreed to provide information on a non-attributable basis. Mr K. Livingstone, MP, was unable to grant me an interview owing to 'constituency and parliamentary work', and Lord Mishcon wrote to say that he had 'no useful comments to make' on certain points I put to him relating to his period as a member of the London County Council.

Following previous practice, I apply the word 'Jew' and its derivatives to anyone who considered or considers him or herself to be Jewish, or who was or is so regarded.

The research upon which this book is based has been most generously funded by the British Academy (Larger Personal Research Grant), the Economic and Social Research Council (under reference number EOO 23 2283), the Leverhulme Trust, the Marc Fitch Fund, and the Wolfson Foundation. Publication has been assisted by grants from Mr Harry Djanogly (through the good offices of Mr Dennis Roberts), the Anglo-Jewish Association (through the good offices of Mr John Gratwick, OBE), Barclays Bank Hackney, and the National Westminster Bank.

Dennis Roberts, the Chairman of the Finance Committee of Royal Holloway and Bedford New College, has been a tremendous source of strength and encouragement throughout this project, and has taken a personal interest in its welfare above and beyond the call of duty. On the academic side the same must be said of Professor Trevor Smith, of Queen Mary College.

Above all, I must thank my Research Assistants, Dr Robert Fitzgerald (1985-7) and Dr Sharman Kadish (1988), for their many labours in producing the raw materials from which the text has been constructed. They have saved me from many errors both of fact and of interpretation. For those which remain I alone am responsible.

Geoffrey Alderman
Royal Holloway and Bedford New College
University of London
April 1988

Chapter One

LONDON JEWRY AND LONDON GOVERNMENT BEFORE 1889

It is a remarkable fact that although the entry of Jews into the municipal politics of England, and specifically of London, preceded their full entry into national political life, the involvement of Jews in English municipal politics has hitherto escaped scholarly attention. Professor Gartner, in his pioneering study of the settlement and reception of Jewish immigrants in England between 1870 and 1914, manages to mention some of the organs of local government charged with responsibility for health, sanitation, and education in the metropolis, but leaves unexplored the relationship between them and the London Jewish community; in particular, the impact upon the Jewish immigrants of the reforms of London government in the late nineteenth century is largely ignored.[1] Dr Holmes's standard work on antisemitism in British society tells us very little indeed of the municipal dimension, while Dr Lipman's history of the Jewish Board of Guardians, though acknowledging that the reform of London government had important repercussions upon the work of the Board, simply does not trace these consequences.[2]

Similar criticisms could be made of the growing number of specialist studies of modern Anglo-Jewish history, in which municipal politics, if they feature at all, do so as a fringe activity.[3] But those who have written about local government in London are equally guilty of ignoring what might be termed the ethnic dimension. True, Dr Thompson's study of London politics between 1885 and 1914 devotes a few pages to the Jewish community, but in a tangential way that contrives to paint the Jews of the East End as little more than an exotic backcloth.[4] In his indispensable account of the London Municipal Society, Dr Young confines his treatment of Jewish aspects to a biographical note of Sir Herbert Jessel (1866–1950), though in fact Jessel's contact with the Jewish community of which he was nominally a part was minimal.[5] The two standard histories of the London County Council pass over the Jewish presence in silence.[6]

These omissions alone would justify a study of the Jewish impact upon the municipal politics of London, an impact which has been both distinguished and distinctive. Although the growth of very significant Jewish communities in the provincial cities of Victorian England provided ambitious Jews with new avenues for political advancement and (hence) social acceptance and assimilation, a majority of British Jews live and have always lived in London.[7] The epic struggle of a handful of wealthy Jews to obtain political emancipation (strictly speaking, the right to be elected to and to sit in Parliament as professing Jews) culminated in the passage, in 1858, of two bills, one amending the Oaths Act, the other allowing each of the Houses of Parliament to decide for itself the form of oath to be administered to a Jew.[8] This victory grew out of the determination of the banker Lionel de Rothschild (1808–79) to represent the City of London in the Liberal interest.

Rothschild's eventual triumph owed a great deal to the support of the Corporation of the City of London, but its achievement had been immeasurably assisted by the previous exertions of Sir David Salomons (1797–1873), a founder of the Westminster Bank, in campaigning for the entry of professing Jews into municipal life. This campaign, too, had inevitably centred upon the City of London, in which several hundred Jewish electors, concentrated mainly in the Aldgate, Portsoken, Billingsgate, and Tower wards, constituted a political force in their own right, and were wealthy enough to demand an input into City affairs. We know that as early as 1818 one London vestry had decided to admit proxies in order to enable Jews to vote whenever parish elections fell on Jewish holy days.[9] In 1830 the Common Council permitted Jews to become Freemen of the City. One consequence of this was that they could become members of the City Livery Companies, and Salomons at once applied to become a member of the Coopers' Company. In 1835 he was elected one of the two City Sheriffs, obliging Parliament to legislate to enable him to enter office without having to take a Christian form of oath (Sheriff's Declaration Act, 1835).[10]

2

That same year (in which, incidentally, Parliament relieved Jewish voters also of the necessity of swearing a Christian oath as a condition of exercising the franchise), Salomons was elected an Alderman for the Aldgate ward, a result declared void because of his insistence on taking the oath of office as a professing Jew. Thus began a decade of expensive litigation and frustrating political activity.[11] In 1837 an amendment to extend the benefit of the Municipal Corporations Declaration Bill (introduced to relieve Quakers and Moravians of the necessity for oath-swearing) to all citizens was defeated by sixteen votes in the Commons. But it was also in 1837 that Moses Montefiore attained the shrievalty of the City, and was knighted by Queen Victoria into the bargain, and that year also saw the foundation of the University of London, admission to which was to be without religious discrimination.

The key to the removal of such discrimination in relation to the City Aldermanries (and so, ultimately, to the office of Lord Mayor) lay within the Conservative Party. During the late 1830s and 1840s the election of Jews to municipal office outside London became almost commonplace. In 1838 A. Abrahams was elected as a councillor at Southampton, and in 1841 E. Emanuel became a councillor at Portsmouth; in 1839 David Barnett had become a founder member of the Corporation of Birmingham, where, from mid-century, Jews were well represented among the Poor Law Guardians.[12] In 1839, too, Salomons served as Sheriff of Kent, and in 1842–3 E. Lousada acted in a similar capacity in Devon. In 1838 Salomons himself, Sir Moses Montefiore, and J. M. Montefiore had all served in the office of Commissioner of the Peace in Kent and Sussex.

In November 1843, in the course of two impassioned letters, Salomons laid these facts before Sir Robert Peel, the Conservative Prime Minister returned to office in 1841.[13] Peel, mindful no doubt of the weight of reactionary opinion that he himself had to contend with from within his own party, was slow to act. But the election (and subsequent disqualification) of Salomons as Alderman for the Portsoken ward (autumn 1844) forced the pace of change. On 22 February 1845 Peel formally requested Lord Chancellor Lyndhurst to draft the necessary legislation to allow professing Jews to hold any and every municipal office.[14] The Jewish Municipal Relief Act became law on 31 July.

These events marked the successful close of the campaign for

Jewish political emancipation in its local-government phase, and they formed the essential prelude to the campaigns of Salomons and Rothschild for full parliamentary equality. In 1847 Salomons was at last admitted as a City Alderman (for the Cordwainer ward); the tenure of this post meant that, by the simple progression of time, Salomons would become the first Jewish Lord Mayor of London, in 1855. Two years later a Jew (I. L. Levy) was elected Mayor of Rochester. Meanwhile (1846) Benjamin S. Phillips had become the first Jew to gain election to the Common Council of the City of London. In 1865 Phillips (1811–89) became the City's second Lord Mayor of the Jewish persuasion, a position which his son, George Faudel-Phillips, held thirty years later. Another Jew, Henry Isaacs, held the office of Lord Mayor in 1889.[15]

The position of the Jews of the City of London in relation to the City Corporation provided opportunities for communal influence, but these were rarely used. One such occasion was at the time of the pogroms in Russia that followed the assassination of Tsar Alexander II. In February 1882 the Mansion House, the official residence of the Lord Mayor, was the scene of a great public meeting to protest against the anti-Jewish atrocities in Russia; a Mansion House Relief Fund was established, and the sum of £108,759 was collected to assist Jewish refugees both in England and on the Continent.[16]

But this was very much an emergency situation that evoked widespread sympathy in Britain and which was, moreover, above party-political considerations; the Fund benefited immeasurably from having the imprimatur of the City fathers, but its proceeds were not used to improve the lot of Jews already settled in Britain. Indeed, the Jews of the City never used their position to influence the application of City resources for purely communal benefit. Any thought of doing so would have run counter to some of the most basic attitudes of those who led the Anglo-Jewish community at this time, and a consideration of these attitudes helps explain why Anglo-Jewry made so little use of the organs of London government prior to the establishment of the London County Council.

Until the 1880s Anglo-Jewry did not possess a manual working class of the relative size or (after the 1867 Reform Act) of the electoral influence that was to be found in either the metropolis or any of the industrial towns of Victorian England. At the end of the

Napoleonic Wars Anglo-Jewry numbered between 20,000 and 30,000 people, the majority living in the capital, where Jews had originally settled following the Readmission permitted by Oliver Cromwell. At the top of the social scale were the wealthy Jews, engaged in wholesale commerce, banking and stockbroking, and the diamond trade. Below them were to be found shopkeepers, silversmiths, and watchmakers, and below them a class of Jewish artisans. At the bottom of the social scale were the Jewish pedlars and old-clothes dealers, some of whom (as receivers of stolen property) were known to be members of the criminal fraternity.

The existence of a Jewish pauper class caused deep anxiety among the Anglo-Jewish gentry, the more so as the French Wars had triggered a wave of xenophobia in England, leading to attacks on Jews and Jewish property. At this time, therefore, communal leaders were anxious to prevent the Jewish poor from becoming a burden on the English public purse, even though Jewish parishioners, like their Gentile counterparts, contributed to the poor rate. Thus when, in 1795, discussions had taken place with the government on the possibility of establishing a Jewish Poor Fund, communal spokesmen were quite happy to have the fund financed by a special tax on Jews – not instead of payment of the poor rate but in addition to it; the scheme failed because of communal fears that, if successful, it would attract even greater numbers of poor Jews from abroad.[17]

On the eve of the Russian pogroms, the number of Jews living in Britain had grown to perhaps 60,000, of whom 46,000 or so lived in London.[18] The statistician Joseph Jacobs then estimated that about 35,000 of these London Jews were professional people, merchants, shopkeepers, and petty traders; the rest comprised servants, assistants, and over 10,000 paupers, most of whom were maintained not by the Boards of Guardians elected under the provisions of the Poor Law Amendment Act of 1834, but by a quite different body, the Jewish Board of Guardians, established by the leading Ashkenazi synagogues (i.e. following the German and Polish ritual) in London on 16 March 1859.[19] The statutory Boards of Guardians maintained the grim workhouses, entry into which was so dreaded by the Victorian poor. Jacobs found instances of a handful of Jews who were workhouse inmates in the 1870s; but the splitting of families, the near impossibility of observing Jewish dietary laws, the Sabbath, and other holy days, as well as the well-known brutality of the workhouse system, acted by themselves as powerful deterrents.[20] The outdoor relief afforded by the Jewish Board of Guardians was infinitely preferable; besides, its existence gave tangible expression to the importance placed by Judaism on the giving of charity, and secured the maintenance of the view that, if Britain was to continue as a haven of refuge for persecuted Jews, the Jewish poor should not become a burden on the state.[21]

Although, therefore, it might have been supposed that the political emancipation of Anglo-Jewry, and the attainment of full civil equality, would have led to greater involvement in municipal government, pre-eminently in London, this did not happen. Where Jews were elected onto local-government bodies, they were elected as individuals, not as Jews and certainly not in order to further Jewish interests – for until the second half of the nineteenth century there were none to be furthered. The well-to-do Jews of the City and – increasingly – the West End of London neither needed nor wanted the assistance of local government in the ordering of communal affairs; the poor Jews of east London were content to rely on their more affluent co-religionists. The apparatus of the Poor Law was felt to be no concern of the Jews.

Nor was there any enthusiasm for the creation of a Jewish presence on the complex mosaic of parish vestries and other (generally self-elected) bodies which, together with the justices of the peace, governed London outside the limits of the City Corporation. In 1855 Parliament attempted to bring some order into this confusion by passing the Metropolis Management Act. Henceforth, the vestries, or groups of vestries known as district boards, together with the Corporation, elected representatives onto a new London-wide authority, the Metropolitan Board of Works, whose responsibilities extended mainly to the provision of sewers and the maintenance and improvement of London's streets.[22] The Metropolitan Board was also, with the passage of time, given totally inadequate (and cumbersome) powers of slum clearance, principally under Disraeli's Artisans' Dwellings Act of 1875.[23] The responsibilities of the vestries and district boards extended to street maintenance, sanitation, and housing within their own areas, and their powers were considerably widened by the Sanitary Act of 1866.

Some vestries worked well to improve standards of health and reduce chronic overcrowding; most, however, were noted for their staunch conservatism and not infrequent corruption.[24] Composed, for the most part, of local landlords and tradesmen, their major preoccupation was, inevitably, with the size of the local rate. In 1855 the total local-government electorate in the area covered by the Metropolitan Board of Works numbered about 195,000 – less than one-third of the total adult male population of London. The qualification for the franchise (payment of the poor rate) ensured that the electorate for the district authorities in London remained small and affluent. In practice, moreover, 'there was generally little public interest in the elections and many of them remained mere formalities'.[25]

Jewish interest in the workings of these bodies was bound to be peripheral. But the anti-Jewish proclivities of some vestries acted as a powerful alienating force, especially once the immigration into east London of Russian and other eastern European Jews gathered momentum in the 1880s. The *East London Observer* of 29 March 1884, reporting on the choice of candidates for the posts of Overseers of the Poor for St-George's-in-the-East, quoted one vestryman as observing that 'there were men on the Vestry capable and willing to hold office. Why did they not elect them instead of a Jew?' A colleague declared 'I would not sit on the Board with a blasted Jew.' According to one local elector, 'the Catholic Church and the Jews [are] being made the subject of intolerant remarks and base attacks ... we entreat you in all seriousness and with some urgency as brothers-in-faith to attend the nominations ... and the elections ... for the sake of preserving civic and religious freedom'.[26]

Jews did seek membership of the London vestries, and were successful in vestry elections. In the early 1860s the Reverend Professor D. W. Marks, minister of the West London Reform Synagogue, was a member of the vestry of St Marylebone; a Mr Levy, an owner of lodging houses and tenements in Southwark, was at about the same time a vestryman of St George's, Southwark; Herbert Jessel, elected as Conservative MP for St Pancras South in 1896, began his very long association with the City of Westminster (on the Council of which he served from its inception, in 1899, until 1948) on the vestry of St George's, Hanover Square, in 1897.[27] But no Jewish vestryman adopted a Jewish profile. Jewish involvement with the Metropolitan Board of Works was also minimal. It is possible that a couple of members of the Metropolitan Board may have been Jewish.[28] The Board itself went largely unnoticed by the Jewish community, but this is hardly surprising. So far as the Jewish community was concerned, the Metropolitan Board's inauguration and early years were overshadowed by the emancipation controversy. Its many worthwhile endeavours, such as the construction of an entirely new sewerage system for London, and a host of street improvements, were of no specifically Jewish interest.

It is, in this connection, worth observing that when, in the 1860s, the Jewish Board of Guardians began to concern itself with the living conditions of the Jewish poor, and in ways in which these might be improved, its reluctance to use the existing machinery of local government was not due entirely to the wish not to involve 'the state'. On 20 April 1865 the young architect and communal worker Nathan Joseph addressed to the Board of Guardians' Honorary Secretary (the banker and future Conservative MP Lionel Louis Cohen) an impassioned plea for the Board to take steps to ensure the sanitary improvement of the dwellings of the Jewish poor. Among the problems which Joseph considered most acute were defective or non-existent drainage, the absence of supplies of drinking water, poor ventilation, and the accumulation of refuse. Some of these defects were the landlords' responsibility, others were immediately or by default the responsibility of the vestries and district boards, and the City Corporation.

But although the City could generally be relied upon to carry out its duties conscientiously, the vestries and district boards could not. The Board of Guardians therefore appointed its own sanitary inspector, George Parsons (recommended by the City Medical Officer of Health), to inspect houses and press the landlords and local authorities to discharge their obligations. During the cholera epidemic of 1866 the Board of Guardians also took it upon itself to provide twenty-seven standpipes for the supply of pure water.[29] Not until the passage of the Cross Act of 1875 did the Metropolitan Board of Works itself acquire the power, outside the City, to compulsorily purchase and demolish houses it considered to be insanitary; even then, it had no power to provide alternative accommodation for those made homeless in this way. Although its powers were subsequently enlarged (notably by the 1885 Housing of the Working Classes Act) they were still inadequate and, in any case, by this time the days of the Metropolitan Board were clearly numbered.

The very necessary activities of the Metropolitan Board never excited the public imagination, neither did they inspire public confidence nor (perhaps unfairly) do they appear to have engendered municipal pride. In part this was, no doubt, due to the system of election to the Metropolitan Board itself. The members of the Board were not directly elected by the ratepayers, and membership of it was certainly no avenue to higher public office. The system of indirect election meant that it could, in some instances, take local electors no less than twelve years to oust and replace a single Board member![30] Moreover, almost from the outset of its life, the Board was dogged by allegations of financial mismanagement and corruption; these culminated, in 1887, in a Royal Commission which found that two members of the Board and several officers had been indulging in malpractices, the object of which was their own financial profit.

Ironically, a prominent Jew did play a part in bringing these facts to light, for the campaign for a Royal Commission had been triggered by a series of revelations that flowed from the pens of Harry Marks (1855–1916) and W. R. Lawson, and which were published in the *Financial News* in October 1886; Harry Marks, who was elected to the first London County Council in 1889 and to Parliament, as Conservative MP for St-George's-in-the-East (Stepney) in 1895, was a son of Professor D. W. Marks, and owned and edited the newspaper in which the allegations appeared.[31]

From these developments the public reputation of the Metropolitan Board never recovered. The revelations of proven financial skulduggery served, moreover, to give an additional sense of urgency to the resolution of two other, wider problems. The first of these concerned London itself. The geographical extent of the jurisdiction of the Metropolitan Board of Works was identical with that enjoyed by the Commissioners of Sewers from 1848. Although the functions of the Metropolitan Board were subsequently enlarged (to include, notably, inspection of London's gas supply in 1860, and control of the fire brigade in 1866), the area of jurisdiction was never modified to keep pace with the rapid growth of the metropolis in mid-century. Worse still, the Metropolis Management Act had left intact the jurisdictions of the Lords

Lieutenant of Middlesex, Surrey, and Tower Hamlets, and the administrative functions of the Justices of the Peace of Middlesex and the other counties. The Corporation of the City of Westminster continued to be appointed by the Dean and Chapter of the Abbey.[32]

During the 1860s and 1870s there was much public debate concerning the future reform of London government. Broadly speaking, although there was a great deal of agreement that London needed a unified administration, and the removal of the many separate and occasionally conflicting jurisdictions, there was no agreement as to the method by which this unified administration was to be brought into existence. The vested interests of the City Corporation were adamant that, if this was to happen, it would be by enlargement of the Corporation, not by its supersession. In 1884 the Corporation spent over £14,000 (and engaged in a variety of underhand activities) in ensuring that a bill introduced by the Liberal government, to absorb (but preserve) the City within a new London-wide authority, never reached the statute book.[33]

The bill had the strong support of the London Municipal Reform League, founded in 1881 by J. F. B. Firth, a barrister who later became a Liberal MP and deputy-chairman of the first LCC. No Jew was ever prominent in the affairs of the League, but one of its bitterest opponents, and a champion of City autonomy, was the stockbroker Benjamin Cohen (1844–1909; brother to Lionel), president of the Jewish Board of Guardians from 1887 to 1900 and Conservative MP for East Islington between 1892 and 1906. Like Firth, Benjamin Cohen was a founder-member of the LCC, on which he sat as one of the City representatives from 1889 to 1901; during this time he acquired a reputation as one of the Council's severest critics.[34]

We have already noted, in relation to Jewish municipal freedoms, that a measure opposed by Tory interests was eventually passed by a Conservative government. Political emancipation came, in 1858, during the minority Conservative administration of the Earl of Derby and Benjamin Disraeli. So it was with London government: reform was achieved by a Conservative minister, Charles Thomson Ritchie. It was, appropriately, carried through by a backstairs method that amply repaid the political manipulations of the City fathers four years previously.

Ritchie, the MP for St-George's-in-the-East, was a Tory Radical, one of a growing number of Conservatives who sat for inner London constituencies and who saw the future well-being of Conservatism in distinctly urban terms. In 1886 he was put in charge of the Local Government Board by the Marquis of Salisbury, then entering upon his second term as Prime Minister. As part of a policy of 'Tory Democracy', Ritchie set about the reform of county government, determined to sweep away the rule of the shires by the old landed magistracy, and replace it with a system of elected county councils. He himself had in 1884 moved the rejection of the Liberal bill to reform London government. But now, taking advantage of the tide of public opinion running strongly against the Metropolitan Board of Works, he announced that London itself, within the area of the Board, was to be elevated to the status of a county. True, the City and (for ten more years) the vestries and district boards were to be left intact, and the Metropolitan Police were to remain under the control of the Home Secretary. None the less, Ritchie explained in the Commons:

> We propose to take London as defined under the Metropolis Management Act out of the counties of Middlesex, Surrey and Kent, and we propose to create it a County of London by itself, with a Lord Lieutenant, a Bench of Magistrates, and a County Council of its own.... We propose that the Council shall be directly elected by the ratepayers, as in all other counties and boroughs; that the franchise shall be the same; and that it shall consist, as in all other cases, of elected and selected members; the elected members sitting for three years, and the selected members [aldermen] for six, one half of the number retiring every three years. It will take over the licensing powers and all the duties of the Metropolitan Board of Works, which will cease to exist.[35]

The elections to the first London County Council took place on 17 January 1889, and its 118 elected members met for the first time on 31 January, at the offices of the Metropolitan Board of Works in Spring Gardens, off Trafalgar Square.

What did London Jewry make of these events? The last years of the Metropolitan Board of Works had coincided with a fundamental change in the size and social and political composition of the capital's Jewish community. In the Pale of Settlement in

Russia and Poland, the assassination of Tsar Alexander II in 1881 had resulted in a wave of officially inspired pogroms. These attacks were renewed and intensified between 1882 and 1889, when the economically oppressed Russian peasantry found an outlet for their discontent in anti-Jewish violence. There was a further wave of pogroms between 1902 and 1906. In the mid-nineteenth century there had been a constant trickle of Jewish refugees coming to Britain from Russia; the trickle now became a flood.

At the outset, few of these Jews thought in terms of permanent settlement in England; England was merely a stopping point on the way to America, a point of arrival at Grimsby or Tilbury, a cross-country train journey, and then a point of departure at Liverpool. Sometimes, however, the refugee's cash ran out. More often, a sojourn in England that was intended to be temporary became a permanent settlement. The artisans and craftsmen, tailors, dressmakers, glaziers, and furniture makers who came from the Pale of Settlement found that they could eke out a living by working exceedingly long hours and living (as immigrants in England have always lived) in the poorest and most squalid parts of the great cities. In England, moreover, there was an established and well-to-do Jewish community, which had clearly managed to make its way in a Gentile society. Here, too, there were evident opportunities for economic betterment and political advancement.

Between 1881 and 1914 about 150,000 Jews from eastern Europe settled in the British Isles.[36] Most found their way to London. Merely from a demographic viewpoint this amounted to a revolution. Between 1851 and 1881 London's Jewish population had grown from about 20,000 to 45,000 – a rate of about 4 per cent per annum.[37] But between 1881 and 1900 London's Jewish population expanded to approximately 135,000 – an annual growth rate of 10 per cent; of these, it was estimated in 1899 that roughly 120,000 were living in the East End.[38]

Some of the less immediate (but no less profound) consequences of these developments will be explored in due course. Here it is necessary to observe not merely that the existing London Jewish community was swamped by the newcomers, but that, as a result, the political – and party political – centre of gravity of that existing community was violently disturbed.

To begin with, the immigrant presence strained beyond all expectations the resources of the Jewish Board of Guardians. In its formative years the Board had to cater for the needs of between 5,000 and 10,000 Jewish poor, some of whom might have required only occasional relief. The policies pursued by the Board were generous, certainly when compared with those of typical Poor Law Guardians. Those who formulated the policies of the Board at this time did not, in general, regard Jewish poverty as a 'crime', for they knew that most of the problems faced by the Jewish poor were not the result of deliberate idleness, but stemmed largely from the fact of immigration. So long as this immigration was maintained within reasonable bounds, the schemes of cash and medical relief, loans and apprenticeships could – it was hoped – eventually lift most of the Jewish poor beyond the level at which they would need to call upon the services of the Board; only the hopeless cases would remain, and they could be passed on to the Poor Law Guardians.

In short, prior to 1881 the Board of Guardians, reflecting the views of the Anglo-Jewish gentry that financed it, viewed the problems of the Jewish poor as finite, and looked forward to a time not too far distant when these problems would, to all intents and purposes, disappear; there was all the more reason, therefore, for generosity and open-mindedness. The mass immigrations that began in the 1880s, however, 'rendered all these calculations abortive'.[39] In 1880 the number of applications for relief processed by the Board was less than 2,500; by 1894 this number had more than doubled, and (measured over the entire period 1881–1914) the number increased by between 100 and 200 per cent.[40] The Board advertised in the Jewish press in eastern Europe that Jews who sought to escape persecution by coming to Britain would face many hardships, and would not obtain relief during the first six months of residence (when they needed it most). Those refugees who did reach Britain were encouraged to continue their journeys to America or South Africa, and some were persuaded to return whence they had come.

However, even if such extreme measures did result in fewer Jewish immigrants coming to or staying permanently in London, it did not alter the fact that the size of the community of Jewish poor to be found in the metropolis after 1881 was beyond the resources of the Board of Guardians to deal with by itself; in London, the scope and nature of the problems of the Jewish poor were henceforth no longer 'containable' within the Jewish community, which, unwittingly perhaps, had to look to the organs of local government of the capital for help in their solution.

From this point of view, therefore, the establishment of the London County Council (LCC) and, under the London Government Act of 1899 (another Conservative measure), of twenty-eight metropolitan boroughs, was bound to assume in the eyes of London Jewry an importance that had not attended the formation of the Metropolitan Board of Works. Whilst it was true that the LCC possessed at its inauguration very few powers beyond those of the old Metropolitan Board (one significant new power was that of appointing a team of medical officers), its formation 'was followed by a complete change of atmosphere in London government', symbolized by the election as its first chairman of Lord Rosebery (who had married into the Rothschilds).[41]

The LCC attracted from the outset men – and later women – of high calibre, who benefited from the status membership of it bestowed, and who used it as a springboard for careers in national politics. Elections to the LCC were national events, the more so as the original fifty-seven LCC constituencies, each returning two councillors (four additional councillors were returned by the City of London) were identical with the divisions used for elections to Parliament, and, since the LCC elections took place every three years, they could be regarded as a barometer of the political mood of the capital, and, perhaps, as a pointer to forthcoming General Elections.

The legislation that authorized the setting up of the LCC was hardly noticed in the Jewish press, and of the six Jewish MPs then in the Commons (three Liberals, two Liberal Unionists, and one Conservative) only the Unionist Sir Julian Goldsmid (St Pancras South) spoke in the debates.[42] Jewish interest in London politics was, however, stimulated that year (1888) by other developments. The most pressing was the establishment, by both Houses of Parliament, of inquiries into the problems attendant upon the influx of Jewish pauper refugees into the country – the Select Committee of the House of Commons on Alien Immigration, and of the House of Lords on the Sweating System. The Lords' inquiry came to the conclusion that 'undue stress has been laid on the injurious effect on wages caused by foreign immigration, inasmuch as we find that the evils complained of obtain in trades which do not appear to be affected by foreign immigration'. The

Commons' Select Committee felt that the immigrants were 'generally very dirty and uncleanly in their habits', but declared none the less that they showed themselves to be 'quick at learning, moral, frugal and thrifty and inoffensive as citizens'.[43]

These parliamentary investigations did not result in any curb on the influx of Jewish immigrants; their only practical result was that the Board of Trade instituted annual returns of the immigrant flow. None the less inasmuch as they had centred largely upon the situation in London, the Jewish community of the metropolis found itself under a most unwelcome spotlight. Jewish immigration into east London had come at a time of economic depression and serious unemployment (there were riots by the unemployed in 1886 and 1887) and had, in truth, aggravated a housing shortage that was already bad. The alien population of what became the London Borough of Stepney increased from 15,898 in 1881 to 54,310 by 1901, but during the same period the number of habitable dwellings in the area fell from 35,300 to 31,500.[44]

The Jewish influx could not be held responsible for the manner in which slums were built, and since the Jews themselves largely occupied these insanitary dwellings, they could hardly be accused of forcing the already resident population to live in inferior accommodation. Steps taken by the Jewish authorities to improve conditions were widely acknowledged as having beneficial effects upon the whole neighbourhood. For example, the old Metropolitan Board of Works had in general been precluded from building upon sites it had cleared compulsorily under the 1875 Act. In 1883 the Metropolitan Board cleared an area around Flower and Dean Streets, Whitechapel, which had been notorious for its rookeries, disease, and criminality. But it was only in 1885, with the formation of the Four Per Cent Industrial Dwellings Company, that a buyer was found for the site, on which the famous Charlotte de Rothschild Dwellings were constructed.[45]

The initiative in forming the Company had been taken by Nathan Mayer de Rothschild (raised to the peerage later that year), and its other directors comprised some of the leading figures of the Anglo-Jewish elite, such as Lionel Cohen, president of the Board of Guardians, and the banker Samuel Montagu, who in December 1885 was to become Liberal MP for Whitechapel. Rothschild Buildings (as they were known) were by no means intended solely for Jewish occupation. But they attracted, and were bound to attract, an overwhelmingly Jewish tenantry. They were the largest of a series of 'model' tenement blocks in the area (another was Nathaniel Dwellings, completed by the Four Per Cent Company in 1892) which had by 1894 transformed the locality of the Ripper murders into one of poor but respectable Jewish inhabitants.

The foundation of the Company originated in an inquiry undertaken by the United Synagogue some four years before Parliament turned its attention to the Jewish immigrant presence, and was indeed a political gesture, intended in some measure to defuse what was already regarded in Anglo-Jewish circles as a serious political problem. The immigrant presence threatened even then to trigger a new anti-Jewish agitation, less than thirty years after the successful campaign for political equality. If Jews – however unjustly and unjustifiably – were accused of causing a housing crisis in the East End, then Jewish money would be well spent in alleviating the situation. But, as with poor relief, it was doubtful whether Jewish philanthropy alone was capable of solving the problem.

The subject of education provided a further crop of difficulties. At the time of the passage of the 1870 Education Act, the provision of a specifically Jewish full-time education in London was dominated by the Jews' Free School (JFS), situated in Bell Lane, Spitalfields. Founded in 1817, and sustained largely by Rothschild money, the JFS had originally been intended to provide merely a religious education for the children of poor Jews, in order (it was said) to help combat the activities of Christian missionaries, but also to counteract the attractions of the criminal life.[46] Although government grants for educational purposes were inaugurated in 1833 (but only to religious bodies), it was not until 1853 that the Treasury agreed to provide money for Jewish schools, and then only on condition that such schools admitted children of all faiths, and allowed non-Jewish parents to withdraw their children from those lessons devoted to Jewish religious instruction.[47]

By 1880 the JFS had no less than 1,600 boys on its roll, and 1,000 girls, taught by a staff of seventy (including pupil teachers). There were also in the capital at that time two Jews' Infants Schools (1,240 pupils), the Spanish and Portuguese School in Heneage Lane (350), the Stepney Jewish School (392), the Westminster Jews' Free School (358), and a number of smaller establishments, such as the Bayswater Jewish Schools. Between them all these schools catered for about 5,600 children.[48] There was no prospect that the community itself would be able to build additional schools that would have been necessary to accommodate the offspring of the immigrants that began to arrive at this time.

The gap in educational provision was made good by the 'state' schools set up following the passage of the Act of 1870. In brief, this measure replaced the old system of government grants for school buildings (but not for their upkeep) with a system of school boards, in both municipal boroughs and county parishes. The London School Board, whose fifty-five members were elected by male and female ratepayer suffrage (and the secret ballot), was empowered to levy a rate, and to use the proceeds thereof to build and maintain schools, catering for children between the ages of 5 and 13, wherever, in its view, the voluntary system was deficient. In the East End this deficiency was self-evident. The first Board school in the area was the Old Castle Street School, which by 1882 had 1,273 children on its books, of whom 95 per cent were Jewish. It has been estimated that in 1894 there were in London 15,964 Jewish children, of whom just over half attended Board schools; by 1901 the proportion of Jewish children in the capital attending Board schools was over 60 per cent.[49]

The religious education in Board schools was meant to be non-denominational Christian. Parents of Jewish pupils could however withdraw their children from such classes; these children received instruction in Judaism from teachers employed first by the Jewish Association for the Diffusion of Religious Knowledge (established 1860) and later (from 1894) by the Jewish Religious Education Board.[50] In practice, however, Board schools with very large Jewish proportions on their books were run as 'Jewish' schools:

> In the East End of London [wrote the historian of the School
> Board] there are many schools in which the majority of
> children are Jews. At these schools arrangements are made for
> the Jewish children to be taught by teachers of their own faith.
> ... Jewish teachers are naturally appointed to these schools as
> far as possible.[51]

Thus by 1882 the Old Castle Street school had a Jewish headmaster and several Jewish teachers.[52] Schools such as this would observe the Jewish holy days and close early on Fridays during the winter months, to facilitate Sabbath observance.

Professor Gartner has rightly observed that 'as the distinction between Jewish and State schools gradually dissolved, it made little difference to Jewish parents where they sent their children to school. State schools gradually made common cause to educate Jewish children in Jewish areas.'[53] It followed, therefore, that in these localities the Jewish community should want to play a much more active part in the running of Board schools; this, in turn, implied some Jewish involvement in the London School Board itself.

During its entire existence, however, the Board had only three Jewish members, and of these only one was elected. On 16 February 1888 Claude Goldsmid Montefiore was co-opted onto the Board to represent Tower Hamlets, which of course included the Jewish East End. Montefiore (1858–1938), a great nephew of the redoubtable Sir Moses, and related also to the Rothschilds, had taken a First in Classics at Oxford, but at the time of his joining the London School Board he had not yet made that break with religious orthodoxy which was to lead him, by stages, to become the 'prophet' of Liberal Judaism. In 1888 he was closely associated with the Jews' Infants Schools, and his co-option was regarded as a recognition of the importance of Jewish interests in the London educational system:

> The event is one which may reasonably be regarded not only as a recognition of Mr Montefiore's worth and ability, but as due satisfaction to the just claims of the [Jewish] community that so important a body as the London Jews should hitherto have remained unrepresented at the School Board.[54]

Montefiore's tenure of the Tower Hamlets seat lasted only a few months, until the Board itself was re-elected *en masse* in November. The *Jewish Chronicle* hoped that his presence on the Board might have hastened the funding of Jewish voluntary schools from the rates.[55] This principle – supporting voluntary denominational schools out of local taxation – was itself highly contentious, and Montefiore was, in truth, in no position to advance it. He seems to have regarded his period on the Board merely as a way into 'the stream of public life'.[56] He was an intellectual, not a politician, and when he had to face a popular election he lost.[57]

A token Jewish presence on the School Board was none the less maintained – just – through the election, for Marylebone, of

Herbert Henry Raphael (1859–1924), a barrister who was to become a founder-member of the LCC in 1889 and Liberal MP for South Derbyshire from 1906 to 1918. In January 1891 Raphael was joined by Sir Philip Magnus (1842–1933), who had in the 1860s acted as a minister at the West London Reform Synagogue, and who subsequently became a lecturer in applied mathematics at University College London.[58] Magnus was busy making his reputation as an expert in further and technical education, and represented the University of London in Parliament from 1906 to 1921, in the Unionist interest. His place on the School Board, as a co-opted member for Tower Hamlets, may well have been intended to fill the gap created by the defeat of Montefiore (to whom he had once acted as tutor). But his official connection with non-orthodox Judaism must surely have ruled him out as a fit person to voice the concerns and defend the interests of the thousands of strictly orthodox parents in his constituency. Of Raphael's involvement in the activities of London Jewry we know little. He was at one time president of the Home for Jewish Incurables; the fact that his funeral took place on a Saturday, in a church at Capel, near Folkestone, might be regarded as evidence of an attachment to the religion of his ancestors even more slender than that of Philip Magnus.

Magnus did not stand for election to the School Board in November 1891. Raphael did so, but was defeated; Magnus and, for good measure, the Revd Dr D. W. Marks, were among those who supported his Anglican rivals in the constituency, including the Revd J. R. Diggle.[59] At first glance this alignment of Jews and Tory Anglicans seems curious, and still more curious when we realize that other Anglicans at Marylebone had the support of Chief Rabbi Hermann Adler and Benjamin Cohen, and that at Chelsea the *Jewish Chronicle* supported a Roman Catholic.[60] In fact, such support was logical and consistent, and a comprehension of it will help our understanding of both Jewish political attitudes in general at this time, and of the approach of London Jewry to the politics of the LCC.

The restriction of the School Board and LCC franchises to ratepayers would probably have excluded most of the recently-arrived Jewish immigrants, but this hardly mattered at this time, because, as unnaturalized aliens, such immigrants could not in any case have exercised the vote. In the 1880s and 1890s, Jewish votes in

London were cast by the comparatively affluent middle- and lower-middle-class native-born Jews, and those who could afford the naturalization fee. In mid-century this Jewish vote had been cast largely in the Liberal interest, because the Liberal Party had consistently supported emancipation, whereas the ranks of Conservatism had included Anglican diehards who opposed emancipation to the last. But in the decade following the commencement of Disraeli's great ministry of 1874–80, Jewish support for Liberalism had been substantially eroded.

In part, the responsibility for this turn of events lay with Gladstone, whose insensitivity to Jewish concerns at the time of the Bulgarian crisis (1876–8) was matched only by his refusal to be moved by the plight of Russian Jews a few years later.[61] But the political realignment of the Anglo-Jewish electorate was also part of a wider socio-political movement. At the time of the emancipation controversy the Conservative Party had been the party of the Land and the Established Church; by 1900 it had become the party of Big Business, and in 1912 felt able to appoint, as its leader, an industrialist who was also a Presbyterian (Andrew Bonar Law). Alarmed by the collectivist leanings of a newer generation of radical Liberals in the 1870s and 1880s, the propertied classes whose support had been crucial to the formation of the Liberal Party in mid-century began to desert to the Conservative camp.[62] Although the momentous and, as it turned out, irreversible split in the Liberal Party in 1886 had taken place over the issue of Gladstone's policy of Home Rule for Ireland, this was, in truth, merely the occasion, and the pretext.

As long ago as 1877 the *Annual Register* had prophesied that the time would come 'when the two great sections of Liberalism should fall definitely apart, and fuse on one side with the great Radical body ... [and] on the other, with its natural opposite, the Conservatism of the time'. This process reached its climax in the second half of the 1880s, and the Anglo-Jewish middle classes could hardly fail to be affected by it. After 1886 no Rothschild was elected to the House of Commons under the auspices of the Liberal Party. In 1880, eight of the thirteen Jewish parliamentary candidates were Liberals, and four Jewish Liberal MPs were elected, as against one Conservative; in 1900, eleven of the twenty-three Jewish candidates were Unionists, of whom seven were elected as against three Liberals.

Although Nathan Marcus Adler, Chief Rabbi from 1845 to 1891, was very careful never to enter the arena of party politics, his son Hermann, 'Delegate' Chief Rabbi from 1879 and Chief Rabbi in his own right from 1891 to his death in 1911, was a pillar of the establishment and a staunch supporter of the Conservative Party. So – by 1888 – was Professor Marks.[63] But there is much evidence to suggest that this move to the right affected Jewish voters as well as Jewish leaders. Although the long tenure (1885–1900) of the Whitechapel parliamentary constituency by Sir Samuel Montagu, a staunch Gladstonian, might suggest that the Jews of the East End were likewise Liberal in political sentiment at this time, the Whitechapel–Montagu connection was (as I have argued elsewhere) in a class of its own.[64] First, most Jews living in White- chapel at the end of the nineteenth century did not possess the vote; its registered electorate of 5,004 in 1900 amounted to only 6.4 per cent of its total population.[65] Second, Montagu's position as a strictly orthodox Yiddish-speaking Jewish philanthropist formed the basis of a unique bond between him and those he represented. The neighbouring constituency of St George's (whose alien pro- portion in 1901 amounted to 28.8 per cent) only went Liberal once (1892) in the period 1885–1900; and when Harry Marks won the seat for the Conservatives in 1895 the Jewish vote (about 350) was cast almost wholly for him.[66] At Limehouse at the same election the Jewish Conservative Harry Samuel had the support of 'nearly all the local Jews'.[67] In 1900 a Jewish resident of Stepney declared that its west ward, 'packed with Jews ... [was] a hot-bed of Toryism'.[68]

In the specific context of the politics of the London School Board there was another reason why Jewry should have supported the Tory–Anglican connection. The Education Act of 1870 had been framed, in part, to meet the wishes of extreme Radical and Liberal nonconformists, who had campaigned and continued to campaign for a nationwide system of free, compulsory, secular education. The school boards were at liberty to decide for them- selves whether or not religious instruction should be given in schools under their control (subject, of course, to the parental right of withdrawal); in London the formulation of Professor T. Huxley was adopted, that 'the Bible shall be read and there shall be given ... explanations and ... instruction therefrom ... provided always ... that no attempt be made ... to attach children to any particular denomination'.[69] Although the Act of 1870 did not institute a system of free education, school boards were empowered to pay the fees of the children of poor parents, irrespective of whether those children attended board or voluntary denominational schools.

As we have seen, these provisos and their attendant safeguards suited the needs of London Jewry, but they did not meet with the approval of Liberal nonconformists, who objected to paying a local education rate to support schools in which 'suspect' or, worse still, non-Christian religious instruction might be given.[70] In Birmingham, under the influence of militant nonconformity, the School Board refused to activate clause 25 of the 1870 Act, which authorized but did not compel it to pay school fees. The London School Board, though dominated for most of its existence by the 'Progressives' (a loose alliance of Liberal nonconformist businessmen and clerics, temperance reformers, trade unionists, and out-and-out secularists) never went this far.[71] But there was always a risk that it might do so and that, perhaps, under Liberal or Progressive control, religious instruction might be banished altogether from the curriculum of Board schools.[72]

There was, therefore, every incentive for London Jewish ratepayers to support the (Anglican Tory) 'Moderates' in School Board elections. In 1885, under the leadership of Mr Diggle, the Moderates gained control of the Board, and they maintained their dominance until 1897. 'Diggleism' meant, in crude terms, that the Board was under the thumb of the Established Church.[73] But the special position of 'Jewish' board schools was maintained and expanded during this period of heavy Jewish settlement in the metropolis. It was for this reason that both lay and religious leaders of Anglo-Jewry were happy to lend their public support to Moderate candidates, whether Anglican or Roman Catholic, and to oppose a Liberal candidate such as Raphael, even though he was Jewish. The *Jewish Chronicle* did not exaggerate too much when it declared in December 1891 that:

> the victory of the Moderates at the School Board Election will have been received by the community with almost unanimous satisfaction ... it is pretty clear that the policy of the Progressists [Progressives] aims at driving the voluntary schools always closer to the wall.[74]

The confidence placed by London Jewry in Conservative–Moderate policies in relation to education was not misplaced. Although the Progressives won control of the School Board during its last seven years (1897–1904), their victory was pre-empted by the passage of the Voluntary Schools Act, in 1897, by Lord Salisbury's Unionist government. This legislation freed voluntary schools from the obligation to pay rates, and increased the money available from the Treasury to support such schools; the seven Jewish schools in the metropolis at once formed themselves into the Jewish Voluntary Schools Association in order to be able to take advantage of this largesse.[75] By the beginning of the twentieth century the Jewish schools, both in London and the provinces, were utterly dependent upon state aid; this circumstance – and the fact that the Conservatives were known to favour state support for religious education – was to have important consequences for the relationship between London Jewry and the party-political system of the capital.

The Progressive–Moderate dichotomy that had developed in the politics of the London School Board was important too for the history of party relationships on the LCC. But to talk of 'parties' in relation to the early history of the LCC is perhaps itself misleading. To begin with, the Council at its inception had no powers or responsibilities in the spheres of elementary or secondary education, and was therefore insulated from the bitter religious divisions that characterized the deliberations of the School Board. Moreover, the Council came into existence at a time of great fluidity in national party politics; the permanent separation of the Liberal Unionists from the Liberal Party could not, at that time, be taken for granted. Although the Liberal Unionists found that they were in broad agreement with Conservatives on many basic issues, they still thought of themselves as Liberals; the official Conservative intervention in the School Board elections of 1894 brought forth a vigorous protest from Liberal Unionists in the capital.[76]

The prehistory of the LCC defined to some extent the party groupings that evolved within it. Much of the debate about the reform of London government in the 1870s and 1880s had centred, as we have observed, on the role and future of the City Corporation. The Progressives were deeply suspicious of the power and influence of the City, which survived the Act of 1888 and which boasted (and still boasts) its own police force. There was no LCC control of the Metropolitan Police. Progressives therefore demanded such control, a sentiment in which Gladstone, along with the Liberal radicals Joseph Chamberlain and Charles Dilke, concurred.[77] The vestries and district boards also survived after 1888. Progressives wished to see these swept away, along with the City, so that the LCC would indeed become 'one Central Representative Body for the whole of London'.[78]

When, in 1899, Lord Salisbury's government replaced the vestries and district boards with twenty-eight London boroughs, each with its own Mayor (the LCC never had a Mayor), Progressives regarded the reform as proof of the determination of the Conservatives to contain the County Council within a subordinate status, using the City and the Boroughs as countervailing powers and alternative sources of authority and, in this way, dividing and ruling the capital of the Empire, denying it what the Liberal MP for Poplar, Sydney Buxton, unashamedly called 'municipal home rule'.[79]

The matter was not simply one of civic dignity. Under Fabian influence, the Progressives espoused a policy of municipal Socialism, and campaigned for LCC control of London's markets and of its water, gas, and electricity undertakings, for the establishment of a municipal bank, and for the operation of tramway and Thames steamboat services by the County Council (two enterprises that did, amid great controversy, see the light of day).[80] Progressives complained that the LCC could not raise loans without parliamentary consent, but they also looked to Parliament to give the Council greater powers to deal with the housing situation. Furthermore, responding to pressure from London's trade unions, Progressives argued that it was right and proper for the LCC to insist that all those firms who contracted with it should observe minimum conditions of work and rates of pay for their employees and that the resources of the Council should be used to stamp out the evils of the sweating system, which were particularly rampant in the East End.[81]

In terms of national politics most Progressives were Liberals, and certainly, except in the minds of Tory diehards (of whom, by the end of the nineteenth century, Lord Rothschild was one), Progressivism was not Socialism. Socialists argued that municipal trading should be carried out 'at cost'; Progressives declared that the profits derived from such trading should (or could) be used to keep down rates. This difference of approach was fundamental, but it did not deter Socialists from marching under the Progressive banner.[82] The ethos of the Progressive alliance was, in any case, underpinned by the thought that collective municipal action was basically a good thing:

> collective municipal action, [Buxton explained] is the best hope for the future; by these means alone can be obtained for all, those social advantages and conveniences which very few are able to obtain for themselves ... by collective municipal action mainly, can a greater diffusion of wealth, and the advantages springing from wealth, be brought about without undue pressure or injustice on any class or on any individuals.[83]

Those who hoped that London might be governed without reference to party considerations were, therefore, bound to be disappointed. In 1889, following the first elections to the LCC, the Progressives had a majority of twenty-eight seats. Although their organization in the Council Chamber was rudimentary, under the inspiration of J. B. Firth they used this majority to ensure that all eighteen aldermen whom the Council had to appoint were of the Progressive persuasion. In these early days there was some free voting; but from 1892 (when the Progressive majority increased by ten) an organized whipping system held sway.

The fact and experience of this tight Progressive hegemony stung London's Conservatives into action – but not *as* Conservatives. The Moderate Party, as it was known, was defined at the outset mainly in terms of its opposition (more or less) to the Progressive programme. Moderates were anxious to protect the interests of ratepayers, and to see that ratepayers' money was not squandered in costly and over-ambitious schemes. Moderates believed in private enterprise and in the protection of private freedoms and privileges. They believed, or at all events had by the mid-1890s come to believe, that a single authority for London, susceptible to Progressive control, must never come about. They also saw grave dangers in a situation in which the LCC was controlled by a political faction so clearly opposed to Conservatism. By 1894 the misgivings of those Moderates who grieved at the importation of party-political considerations into

London government had been largely overcome. In the summer of that year the London Municipal Society was founded, 'the most important step the Conservative Party has taken for many a long day'.[84] This new venture was within the space of a few months given the seal of approval of Lord Salisbury himself, who in a speech at the Queen's Hall on 7 November declared that Conservatives 'must not be shy of using all our political power and machinery (cheers) for the purpose of importing sound principles into the government of London'.[85]

> From a loosely clustered group of moderately-minded members, with no policy but a vague watering down of their opponents' strong medicine, there developed a well-knit . . . party with . . . a clear and declared allegiance to the national Conservative party.[86]

At the County elections the following year the Moderates improved their position so much that Progressive control of the Council for the next three years was only possible through the votes of the aldermen appointed previously. In 1898 the Progressives did better; in 1901 their majority increased to fifty-four, and in 1904 it still stood at forty-seven seats. But between 1904 and 1907, and for reasons which will be examined in due course, the Progressive popular vote collapsed. The Moderates – now called Municipal Reformers – captured the LCC at the 1907 election, and remained in control of it for the next twenty-seven years.

Chapter Two

LONDON JEWRY IN THE PROGRESSIVE ERA

There are two ways of measuring Jewish involvement in LCC elections during the Progressive era. Neither will give a complete (let alone accurate) assessment. We may use aggregate data based upon the election statistics, concentrating especially on those constituencies which are known to have contained significant numbers of Jewish electors. The difficulties here are numerous. To begin with, there were of course no such things as separate electoral rolls for ethnic groups. Furthermore, and as was noted in the previous chapter, aliens were legally debarred from voting.[1]

To what extent this statutory prohibition was enforced in practice is impossible to say. Writing to Theodor Herzl in September 1900 the Secretary of the English Zionist Federation had to confess that, from an electoral point of view, Zionist influence in Whitechapel was not great, because 'so many of our friends are not naturalized'.[2] Some aliens, however, undoubtedly found their way onto the electoral register; in 1914 there were apparently only a handful of non-Jewish names on the parliamentary register for Rothschild Buildings.[3] Yiddish newspapers circulating in the East End before the First World War usually devoted some space to elections for the LCC; the *Idisher Ekspres*, in particular, thought it worthwhile to exhort its readers to vote for Progressive candidates – and at a time when we know few immigrant Jews could afford the £5 naturalization fee.[4]

Even at parliamentary elections the precise number of Jewish electors in the East End cannot be exactly calculated. A contemporary estimate of 1,500 Jewish electors in the Whitechapel parliamentary constituency in 1895 would appear to be accurate; of these, the Conservatives claimed half.[5] According to the 1901 census, aliens accounted for 31.8 per cent of Whitechapel's population, and in 1900 its registered parliamentary electorate (5,004) formed only 6.4 per cent of its total inhabitants.[6] The electorate for LCC elections was larger than for parliamentary elections at this time, mainly on account of the female voters enfranchized for county-council purposes by the legislation of 1888. In 1900 the county-council electorate in Whitechapel was 5,962, or just over 19 per cent more than the parliamentary electorate.[7] If we apply this percentage increase to the 1895 Jewish estimate we arrive at a Jewish county-council electorate of roughly 1,785, or about 28 per cent of the total.[8] By 1900, when the total number of county-council voters in Whitechapel had fallen by 6.3 per cent (just over 400), the Jewish proportion must certainly have grown, perhaps to as much as a third of the whole. At that time the number of Jewish parliamentary voters in the neighbouring constituency of St-George's-in-the-East was approximately 350, or about 10 per cent of the total.[9] Applying the same calculation as before, the number of Jewish electors for LCC purposes works out at around 418.

The evidence of parliamentary elections and of census material suggests that, between them, Whitechapel and St George's contained the largest numbers of Jews and Jewish electors in London in the pre-1914 period, with smaller but growing communities (growing, that is, both absolutely and proportionately) in Stepney, Mile End, Limehouse, and parts of Bethnal Green and Hackney. Whitechapel returned two Progressive councillors at every LCC election between 1889 and 1913 except 1895 and 1904 (in 1895 one Moderate was returned, and in 1904 one Jewish Independent). St George's was less consistent, but failed to return at least one Progressive only in 1895. Mile End was Progressive at every election except 1895 and 1907. Limehouse returned Moderates only in 1907 and 1910. The two Bethnal Green seats were Progressive throughout this period. Hackney South only failed to return two Progressives in 1913, and Hackney Central only in 1889, 1907, and 1913; Hackney North alone showed some consistent Moderate loyalty, returning one Moderate in 1889, 1892, and 1898, and two Moderates or Municipal Reformers in 1895 and from 1907 onwards.

Does this mean that, prima facie, the Jewish county-council electorates of east London must be deemed to have been

Progressively inclined? The answer is almost certainly in the negative. Low turnouts were (and have remained), alas, a central feature of London municipal politics. At the first LCC election the turnout was a mere 38.3 per cent, though if the calculation is confined to those divisions that were contested the percentage rises to 50 per cent. This proportion was more or less maintained during the 1890s, but in 1901 (contested divisions only) fell to 40.8 per cent; only in 1907 did turnout again exceed half the electorate (55.5 per cent in contested seats).

In 1910 turnout stood at 50.2 per cent, and at 52 per cent in 1913; never again in the history of the LCC was the proportion voting to reach, let alone exceed, half the total number of registered electors in those seats in which contests took place.[10] It is the case that, certainly in the pre-1914 period, much higher turnouts were to be found in some constituencies, including those with significant Jewish electorates. In 1907 the Whitechapel turnout was as high as 64.8 per cent, and at St George's it was 63.1 per cent.[11] But we are still dealing with very small numbers in absolute terms – 3,646 and 2,998 voters respectively. To candidates anxious for votes the importance of turnout could scarcely be exaggerated; hence, Jewish votes, like Irish Catholic votes, were worth some special attention. But we would be in serious error if we attempted to read the loyalties of Jewish voters (let alone of Jewish inhabitants) from the crude breakdown of votes cast in any particular constituency. The most that can be done is to reach some tentative conclusions, perhaps supported by contemporary qualitative evidence.

We are, however, on much more solid ground when we examine the credentials of those who were elected to the LCC. The principal English-language Jewish newspapers of the period, the *Jewish Chronicle* and the *Jewish World,* recorded most Jewish candidates standing at LCC elections; their lists can be checked against and supplemented by reports in the *Idisher Ekspres,* which commenced publication in 1896. The resulting information, though probably not complete, can none the less be regarded as reasonably authoritative; it is summarized in the Appendix. Two aspects are outstanding.

The first is that during the period 1889–1913 (and, indeed, throughout the history of the LCC) the Jewish community was consistently overrepresented. Jews formed a fraction of 1 per cent of the population of the LCC area, but provided over 5 per cent of the councillors; in 1910 the proportion was over 10 per cent. This overrepresentation, which mirrored that to be found in the Westminster Parliament, was almost certainly a function of Jewish overrepresentation in those socio-economic groups from which councillors – and MPs – were drawn.[12] Secondly, and no less remarkably, over the period 1889–1913 as a whole the Jewish presence on the LCC was divided almost equally between the Progressives and the Moderates; only in 1889 and 1907 were there serious political imbalances.

The seven Jews elected to the LCC in 1889 were all men of substance and standing in the community at large and also (with the exception of H. H. Raphael) in Anglo-Jewry. Five of them were or were to become Members of Parliament. Benjamin Cohen was (as expected) returned unopposed for the Moderates in the City of London, and Harry Marks won a seat for the Moderates at Marylebone East. Of the five Jewish Progressives, two were furniture makers: Nathan Moss, who sat for Hoxton until 1898, and Horatio Myer, a leading light of the fashionable Bayswater Synagogue, who was returned for Kennington in the first LCC and sat as MP for Lambeth North from 1906 to 1910. The stockbroker Arthur Leon was Progressive member for Limehouse 1889–1907 and for St Pancras North 1910–19, and the barrister Herbert Raphael sat for the Progressives at St Pancras West, 1889–92.

In none of these elections had Jewish voters played any special part, nor had the Jewish identity of the candidates had any distinctive impact. But at Whitechapel the banker Stuart Samuel won a seat for the Progressives after a contest in which his uncle, Samuel Montagu, had campaigned unashamedly for him.[13] Stuart Samuel came top of the poll, obtaining 1,523 votes as against 1,477 for his successful Progressive running mate, C. Tarling. The only other candidate at Whitechapel in 1889 who obtained at least 1,000 votes was Morris Abrahams, well-known locally as the highly successful manager (1871–94) of the Pavilion Theatre, which catered for a largely Jewish clientele.[14] Abrahams, who was heavily involved also in social work (Jewish and non-Jewish) in the East End, did not stand in 1892, but three years later, helped by a split in the Progressive camp, was elected as the only Moderate to sit for Whitechapel in the period under review.

Abrahams retired in 1898, and Stuart Samuel did not stand for the LCC in or after 1892, though he continued to 'nurse' the constituency, for which he became MP in succession to his uncle in 1900. However, the unique impact that a Jewish presence might have, as evidenced by the fortunes of Samuel and Abrahams, became during the 1890s a subject of intense local interest. In its early years the elections to the LCC were always held on the first Saturday in March. Orthodox Jews could vote after the close of the Sabbath or, if they were not too fussy, they could ask the returning officer to mark their ballot papers for them. Neither expedient was considered totally satisfactory. In 1892 Montagu tried unsuccessfully to interest the Board of Deputies in pressing for LCC elections not to be held on the Sabbath at all, and in March 1897, when a county-council by-election was about to be held at Whitechapel, the Moderate councillor and Conservative MP E. A. Goulding 'expressed the hope that, in view of the fact that the majority of the inhabitants of this constituency were of the Jewish religion, the polling would not take place on a Saturday'.[15]

The 1897 contest provided the political parties with a dramatic illustration of the impact of the Jewish presence upon the municipal politics of east London. Abrahams' 1895 victory at Whitechapel clearly pointed to a dilution of the Progressive/Liberal dominance. For the by-election (caused by the resignation of Thomas Catmur) a Jewish Progressive of sufficient stature could not be found. Montagu did the next best thing, by importing Harry Lawson, formerly councillor for St Pancras West 1889–92, and Liberal MP for Cirencester 1892–5, who, though a Christian himself, was the grandson of Joseph Levy, founder of the *Daily Telegraph*.[16] While Montagu lent the full weight of his prestige among Jewish workmen to the Lawson candidature, Lady Montagu marshalled the female vote in her capacity as president of the Whitechapel Women's Liberal Association, and W. C. Steadman, the Progressive councillor for Stepney, used the good offices of the Revd J. F. Stern, minister of the Stepney Synagogue, to address (at the synagogue premises) a meeting of the East London Jewish Communal League on the virtues of having in control of the LCC a regime sympathetic to trade unionism.[17]

Not to be outdone, the Moderate candidate, Ernest Meinertzhagen (not Jewish), secured the active support of Harry Marks and Morris Abrahams, and, a week before the poll, of Lord Rothschild, who was persuaded to address a meeting in the division in the hope of counteracting 'the undoubted influence with the Hebrew voters which Sir Samuel Montagu has in regard to Mr Lawson'. Addressing a gathering of over 1,000 persons, Lord Rothschild attacked the extravagance of LCC housing schemes in the area:

> Those who lived in Whitechapel knew what small private efforts had done for them in securing better dwellings, and he was proud to say that the architect who had built some of those dwellings [such as Rothschild Buildings] had been consulted on the subject by the London County Council.[18]

Predictably, Meinertzhagen gained the support of the local Ratepayers' Association and, it was claimed, of the Irish Catholic voters, reckoned to number between 400 and 500.[19]

A meeting of the Whitechapel and Spitalfields Costermongers' and Street Sellers' Union assured Lawson of its support, perhaps because of the LCC's efforts to buy Spitalfields Market.[20] The overall theme of the election was indeed the Progressive record at Spring Gardens, and central to the debate – as Rothschild had sensed – was the housing issue. No matter how admirable the record of the Four Per Cent and other philanthropic ventures in this field, local people looked to the Council rather than to private enterprise to provide the necessary volume of new housing needed. The chairman of the Council's Housing of the Working Classes Committee was none other than Arthur Leon, and his announcement, in late February, that the long-awaited Bell Lane clearances could go ahead, was in truth the major feature of the by-election.[21] Lawson romped to victory with a majority of 503 votes. We cannot be certain what part the Jewish electorate, by itself, played in this result. We can be sure that both sides felt it was of central importance. By common agreement the poll had therefore been held on a Thursday.

If the Jewish voters of Whitechapel had indeed played a part in Lawson's victory, it was (as events in 1904 were to emphasize) more likely to have been an expression of their Jewishness, and of their devotion to Montagu, rather than as a reflection of any special Jewish tendency in the Progressive direction. In one respect, however, Progressive policies did dovetail neatly with Jewish interests. Though Montagu identified himself with the efforts of the Anglo-Jewish grandees to deal with the housing question, he did not share the reluctance to be found in some

Jewish circles to using the resources of local government to solve such problems; in short, the Progressive enthusiasm for building working-class dwellings 'on the rates' met with his enthusiastic approval.

In its Progressive phase the major point of contact between London Jewry and the LCC was on the housing issue. It was, indeed, the Jewish community that spurred the Council to act, at least as far as the East End was concerned. In a forthright letter of support for P. M. Martineau, who represented St George's for the Progressives from 1889 to 1895, David Schloss, honorary secretary of the Sanitary Committee of the Jewish Board of Guardians, had in January 1889 waxed lyrical in praise of Martineau's helpful attitude as a St George's vestryman in regard to representations from the Board concerning sanitary defects.[22] The Board had, in company with local Poor Law Guardians and the Whitechapel District Board, made forceful representations to the Metropolitan Board of Works concerning gross overcrowding in an area adjoining Bell Lane, Spitalfields, but to no avail.[23] Now full use could be made of Jewish representation on the LCC – in particular the presence of Stuart Samuel on the Council's Housing of the Working Classes Committee – to press for improvements.[24]

The problem of Bell Lane was one of a number inherited from the Metropolitan Board of Works and, though notorious, it was considered less urgent than that of Boundary Street, between Bethnal Green and Shoreditch, the clearance and reconstruction of which was commenced in 1890 and not completed until 1900.[25] Under the Housing of the Working Classes Act of 1890 local authorities were enabled to acquire land, if necessary by compulsion, for housing purposes, but the houses so erected had to be sold to the private sector; this obligation was not removed until 1909. Moreover, even the powers to order the demolition of insanitary dwellings and the clearance of sites were hedged about with restrictions. In August 1889 an LCC sub-committee appointed to investigate Bell Lane reported that they had not found 'that any considerable amount of squalor or disease prevailed. For this, the peculiar conditions under which the Jews, who form the majority of the inhabitants, live, as well as the numerous charitable dwellings, are doubtless responsible.'[26]

The cost of a clearance scheme was, in 1890, judged to be prohibitive. But, under the impetus of David Schloss, the Board of

Guardians began a sustained campaign, aimed initially at the District Boards of Works, particularly that of Whitechapel. The Guardians' Annual Report for 1888-9 used the evidence given to the parliamentary select committees in 1888 as a springboard for this purpose. At first the attention of the Whitechapel Board was drawn to inadequate toilet facilities in many of the houses in its area. Later the Guardians concentrated on refuse collection. In 1889 the Guardians' Sanitary Committee observed that some of the blame for sub-standard housing was due to the fact that local authorities were 'more or less lax' in their efforts to ensure high standards.[27] The following year the Guardians were able to report that in the period 1884-90 the proportion of houses visited (in the five districts of the City, Whitechapel, Bethnal Green, St George's, and Mile End) in which unsatisfactory toilet facilities had been found had fallen from 93 per cent to just 2 per cent. 'In one respect, at any rate [the Guardians noted] the effects of the [Sanitary] Committee's action are clearly manifest. The reluctance of the local authorities to enforce this obligation imposed by the law, of providing a flush of water to closets, is being at length overcome.'[28]

Within a short time of the establishment of the LCC, therefore, the Jewish Board of Guardians had begun to forge with it a close relationship in the central fields of public health and housing; the Guardians had indeed transformed themselves into a pressure group of a special sort, one upon which the Council relied for the collection of data which, as yet, it had neither the experience nor the expertise to collect for itself. The small number of Jewish councillors had spread themselves widely upon the Council's committee structure; following the 1892 elections Arthur Leon became vice-chairman of the Public Health and Housing Committee, and chairman the following year; this Committee also included Nathan Moss.[29]

It was, perhaps, the expectation of a sympathetic response that emboldened the Board of Guardians to press the County Council in two particular areas in the 1890s. The first concerned the evils of the sweating system, the subject of the Lords' inquiry of 1888. The passage of the Public Health (London) Act of 1891 (partly in response to the findings of the inquiry) gave the LCC some powers to deal with insanitary conditions and overcrowding in workshops; it was to Schloss that the Council's Public Health and Housing Committee looked to provide information on the basis of which action could be taken.[30] In 1893 he was able to report that 'a good deal' was being done 'to avoid the gross over-crowding of the workers, formerly so prevalent', and that 'in some instances' steps had been taken 'to provide less inefficient ventilation'.[31]

In his 1893 report Schloss had demonstrated statistically that the districts of Whitechapel and Mile End contained the smallest percentage of homes found to be in a satisfactory sanitary condition in those areas of London with which the Board of Guardians concerned itself. In so declaring, he was saying nothing that the Board had not said before:

> For many years [the *Jewish Chronicle* explained] the East End parishes have been sadly lagging behind in putting into force the powers given them by the law, and they need continual prodding from outside to exercise even moderate vigilance in setting the houses of their districts in order. Quite elementary sanitary requirements are often unprovided and there is, generally, a lack of that regard for public health which modern hygiene demands; there is particularly a deficiency of inspection.[32]

On this occasion, however, the pleas of the Jewish authorities for more inspectors and better standards of inspection did not fall on deaf ears. In May 1894 the LCC's Public Health and Housing Committee, citing the Schloss document, instructed the Council's Medical Officer of Health, Dr Shirley Murphy, to report on the sanitary conditions and administration of Whitechapel, and Mile End Old Town. Murphy's conclusions fully supported those of Schloss.[33] One almost immediate result of this initiative was that the Whitechapel District Board was persuaded to appoint two additional sanitary inspectors.[34] Another was that the widely believed myth that the presence of large numbers of Jewish immigrants was a primary cause of bad housing was publicly and authoritatively exploded, in spite of the evident though privately expressed desire of the Whitechapel District Board to blame inefficient sanitation merely upon the presence of Polish Jews in the neighbourhood.[35]

Schloss used the public attention thus generated to impress once again upon the LCC the claims of the Bell Lane rookeries.[36] But the political stalemate that resulted from the municipal elections of 1895 prevented action, and, as we have seen, it was not until the unique circumstances of the Whitechapel by-election that the Council was constrained to act, having at last secured the co-operation and financial contribution of the freeholder, Sir Algernon Osborn.[37] By this time, and largely through the efforts of the Four Per Cent Company, the East End Dwellings Company, and local businessmen, many of the forbidding, interconnecting courts and alleyways whose condition had so exercised the minds of east London social workers, had disappeared. The LCC's own Boundary Street scheme, opened by the Prince of Wales in 1900, swept away 'the Nichol', the slum-habitation of the criminal classes, made still more notorious in Arthur Morrison's novel *A Child of the Jago*, published in 1896.[38]

In 1898, following their impressive gains at the March elections, the Progressives announced a new initiative to deal with the still-acute housing shortage – made worse, indeed, by the slum clearances of the previous decade, which had rarely rehoused all those whom they had initially displaced. The 1890 Housing Act had relaxed previous statutory requirements as to compensation, and had given the Home Secretary the power to suspend, in whole or in part, the obligation previously laid upon a local authority to rehouse on the same site; dwellings built by an authority under this Act had to be maintained by it. The Progressives now proposed to take advantage of this legislation to acquire new sites for the purpose of erecting working-class dwellings, and to carry out all the clearances involved 'at the sole cost of the Council' – that is, such charges would not be recouped from the rent of the dwellings so erected.[39]

Predictably, Benjamin Cohen attacked this policy as a restriction upon private enterprise:

> Dwelling companies [he told the Council] could do the
> housing of the working classes in suitable tenements in refined
> quarters at reasonable rents and yet pay a fair return to their
> shareholders, and yet it appeared the Council was unable to do
> this without charging the rates. That there would be a charge
> on the rates could hardly be denied.[40]

The Progressives did not deny it; almost as soon as the policy had been approved the Housing of the Working Classes Committee asked for and obtained supplemental estimates totalling over £4,000 to finance the erection, by the Council, of dwellings in the

Boundary Street area and Limehouse.[41]

Samuel Montagu did not decry this approach, but he had already become critical of the policy of rehousing within the same districts those who lived in the most congested parts of the East End. He had also reached the conclusion that one way of combating the antisemitic movements that were already evident in the East End was to disperse the Jewish refugees to outer London and, if possible, away from the capital altogether. In December 1898 he approached the LCC with a most generous offer of the gift of twenty-five acres of land at Edmonton on which the Council could build working-class dwellings, on condition that White-chapel residents would be given preference when those who were to occupy the dwellings were chosen.[42]

On a legal technicality this offer had to be refused, because the LCC was at that time unable to acquire land outside its own borders – a difficulty that was remedied in the Housing Act of 1900. In 1902 the offer was renewed, but with an alternative, which the Council accepted, of £10,000 with which to build, on its White Hart Lane estate, Tottenham, a special housing complex for Whitechapel residents, 'without distinction of race or creed'.[43] This scheme – a block of 122 houses known as Tower Gardens – was completed in 1907.[44] It constituted one of the last major housing programmes carried out by the LCC before the Great War; for the Municipal Reform victory of 1907 brought the larger White Hart Lane project, and the Progressive policy of building council houses, to an abrupt end.[45]

In other respects, too, the policies followed by the Progressive regime were of benefit to the Jewish masses of the East End. We have already noted the contact between the Council and the Board of Guardians on the issue of sweating. In the matter of the general enforcement of a minimum wage, the Council under the Progressives was prepared to lend a sympathetic ear to the garment workers of east London in their campaigns.[46] As far as its own contractors were concerned, the Council was in a position to act. In 1897, following suggestions made by a deputation from the International Tailors', Machinists' and Pressers' Union (formed by the Jewish Social Democrat Lewis Lyons in 1890), the Council agreed to take steps to ensure 'that the full amount of wages reached the actual workers, and were not intercepted by middle-men under a system of subletting, and that no deductions for

sewings [cotton and other sundries supplied by the employer] ...
were made by contractors from the prices fixed by the Council'.[47]
Under the influence of trade-union and other sympathetic councillors, the Council approved a schedule of minimum prices to be
paid by its contractors for the making up of garments. John Burns,
the working-class Liberal MP for Battersea, told the Council that
the matter

> affected the industrial residuum of our big city, and an
> industrial residuum whose difficulties are accentuated by the
> fact that they speak in a different language to ours, and it is
> only through a body like the London County Council that
> they can be helped in the matter. ... The Council's decision not
> to have any of its clothing done under home work conditions
> had probably effected one of the most influential changes in
> the East End of London.[48]

The Progressive Council also interested itself in the administration of markets, especially Spitalfields Market, which by the
1890s had already acquired a distinctly Jewish atmosphere.
Spitalfields Market was then a private monopoly. In 1893 Samuel
Montagu had brought in a bill to sweep away this monopoly and
in the same year the Council's Public Control Committee had
voiced the desirability of the LCC acquiring existing markets in
the public interest.[49] In 1899, acting on numerous petitions presented to it, the Council promoted a bill to enable it to acquire
Spitalfields Market compulsorily. Opposition from the City Corporation thwarted this proposal, and a similar one the following
year. In 1902 the Council's bill was successful, but only after the
addition, under Conservative pressure, of a clause giving Stepney
Borough Council the right to buy the market after a period of ten
years. Faced with this prospect the LCC decided not to act on its
powers, and the market thus came into the ownership of the City
Corporation.[50]

On other matters, too, of comparatively minor public importance but of some concern to London Jewry, the Progressive administration proved sympathetic and constructive. One such was
the provision of special arrangements for delinquent Jewish boys
at the Council's Mayford school, prior to the construction of the
Jewish 'Industrial' school at Hayes.[51] In 1905 the Council's
Education Committee agreed to provide training facilities in con-

nection with the proposed school for delinquent Jewish girls at Stamford Hill – Montefiore House, opened in 1905.[52] In 1901 the LCC's Public Health Department was able to help refute allegations that the Jewish presence in certain East End areas constituted a health hazard; Dr Murphy, the Medical Officer of Health, pointed out that in the neighbourhood of Buckchurch Lane (St-George's-in-the-East) 'the low death rate from all causes is interesting, because the population is almost wholly a Jewish population'.[53]

In February 1903 the Council's Housing Department was able to disprove a statement made in the House of Commons by the Unionist MP for Bethnal Green South-West, Samuel Forde-Ridley, that the new Boundary Street estate was 'now already nearly half full of aliens, who live under conditions we would not like to see our working classes subjected to'; in fact, of 1,044 tenements only 27 per cent were occupied by Jews and aliens, and there was found to be only one case of infringement of the Council's overcrowding regulations.[54]

The need for the Jewish community to be able to cite irrefutable statistical evidence of this sort was of particular importance at this time because of the rise of political antisemitism in the East End and at Westminster. In east London the General Election of October 1900 had been marked by the return to Parliament of a group of Conservative MPs who had made the issue of restriction of 'alien' – that is, Jewish – immigration the central feature of their campaigns. This group included, in addition to Forde-Ridley, Thomas Dewar at St George's, Claude Hay at Hoxton, Harry S. Samuel (a Jew) at Limehouse, and Major William Evans-Gordon, the leader of the group, at Stepney; at Whitechapel the restrictionist David Hope Kyd had come, with the support of Lord Rothschild, to within seventy-one votes of beating Stuart Samuel. In May 1901 Evans-Gordon and his friends established the British Brothers' League, a highly vocal pressure group whose efforts were rewarded with the establishment of the Royal Commission on Alien Immigration in 1902 and the passage of the Aliens Act in 1905, the first statutory restriction on immigration in modern British history.[55]

The willingness of some Jewish leaders to associate themselves with the restrictionist campaign was a function partly of political opportunism and loyalty and partly of fear: the presence of Jewish pauper refugees, and the agitation to which it had given rise, threatened (so it was said) to endanger the safety of the entire Anglo-Jewish community, especially since the poor Jews tended to be much less hostile to Socialism than their bourgeois co-religionists. The British Brothers' League could boast all-party backing. Among the Liberals who supported it was Sydney Buxton at Poplar, and by 1905 the strength of constituency feeling was so intense that even such Progressive champions of Jewish rights as Bertram Straus (Jewish, elected to the LCC for Mile End in 1898 and as Liberal MP for Mile End in 1906) felt obliged to ask Sir Henry Campbell-Bannerman, leader of the Liberal Party in the Commons, not to oppose the second reading of the Aliens Bill.[56]

The anti-alienists did not ignore the organs of municipal government in their campaign. In February 1895 the Conservative MP Sir Howard Vincent, a leading restrictionist whose exertions in this direction predated those of Evans-Gordon, advised his party leader, Lord Salisbury, that by espousing a policy of restriction the party would be helping the Moderates to win control of the LCC.[57] Salisbury had himself introduced a bill in 1894; restriction became official Unionist policy, though not yet with the highest priority. Inasmuch as the Moderates gained two seats from the Progressives at Mile End in March 1895, two at St George's, and one (Abrahams' victory) at Whitechapel, and almost captured control of the LCC as a result, this stratagem undoubtedly had some merit in it. At the time of the election of the first Borough Council at Stepney the Moderates included in their manifesto the 'opinion that steps should be taken without further delay to restrict the constant influx of pauper aliens into this country, and more particularly into the already overcrowded districts in the East End of London'.[58] The Moderates won control of Stepney and, over London as a whole, gained control of twenty of the twenty-eight borough councils.

Had this Moderate success extended to the County Council itself in 1901, parliamentary action might have been taken sooner, and with greater effect than turned out to be the case with the 1905 Act; the aliens 'problem' was, after all, a London problem, and a demand from London's own local government for action would have carried great weight. Perhaps for this reason the *Jewish Chronicle*, for the first time, instructed its readers on the importance of the forthcoming contest for control of the Council's affairs. Noting that Jewish representation on the LCC had 'not hitherto been what it ought', the paper opined that:

> There should be something attractive in the Council's sanitation work to a member of a race in whose religious laws sanitation plays so prominent a part. The chance of joining a body which has for one of its functions the solution of the terrible over-crowding question cannot be a matter of indifference to any Jew who has the capacity and the leisure to serve a constituency.

> We, as Jews, with the East End congestion perpetually weighing upon us, have a double interest. In taking a hand in this matter, Jewish Councillors would not only be seeking the welfare of this ... city ... but they would have the satisfaction of effecting something for Anglo-Jewry too, while showing their Gentile fellow-citizens that the community is not blind to the difficulties with which the Jewish colony in the East End are prominently associated. If such considerations apply in the first place to Jewish candidates, they apply with equal force to the whole body of Jewish electors.[59]

As we have seen, Jewish representation on the LCC increased only marginally compared with 1898. In St George's and Stepney the Progressives lost seats (one in each division), and there was some loss of support (but not of seats) in Limehouse, but these results were very much against the East End trend: in Whitechapel the Progressive share of the poll increased from 51 to 64.2 per cent, and an increase of over 18 per cent in the Progressive vote at Hackney North led to the capture of the remaining Moderate seat there; London-wide the Progressives had a massive majority of 54 seats – their largest ever.

The Jewish contingent on the LCC now comprised two Progressives, Straus and Leon, and two Moderates, the playwright Jocelyn Brandon (Hammersmith) and Alfred Louis Cohen, Sir Benjamin's brother, who had succeeded to the City seat.[60] Alfred Cohen's membership of the LCC lasted but two years, for he died in 1903, but in the autumn of 1901 it fell to him, assisted by Straus, to oppose the only attempt made by the Moderates to persuade the LCC to adopt an official anti-alien line. On 15 October A. T. Williams, a prominent member of the British Brothers' League and of the Stepney council, and also newly-elected to the LCC (for Stepney) moved at a plenary session of the County Council

> that it be referred to the Local Government and Taxation Committee to report upon the whole question of alien immigration in London, the effects upon the districts of London most concerned, and as to what steps can be taken by the Council to procure statutory powers to control or prevent alien immigration in the future.[61]

The motion was ill-advised, on two counts. Although the phrase 'alien immigration' was subsequently amended to 'pauper alien immigrants', the supporters of the motion could not escape the charge that it was, at bottom, anti-Jewish. Moreover, as Cohen was quick to point out, it represented a challenge to the doctrine of free trade, to which all Liberals and many Conservatives were devoted, because 'in a free trade country ... it was not possible to protect labour unless the produce of labour were also protected'.[62] The motion was rejected by a majority which the LCC minutes did not record, but which was described in the newspapers as large.

Anti-alienists made no secret of their belief that the failure to obtain LCC endorsement of their views was a setback. Addressing a meeting of the British Brothers' League at Limehouse Town Hall in November, Williams referred to it, and to the rejection of a restrictionist motion put at a housing conference summoned by Stepney Borough Council, as 'two serious defeats'. The latter he blamed, perhaps correctly, upon the presence of 'several of ... the Jewish persuasion [who] thought that it was an attack on their faith'.[63] On 27 November the restrictionists exacted revenge of a sort, when the Borough Council voted 24 to 10 to disagree with the outcome of the housing conference.[64] But the Progressive majority on the LCC ensured that the prize of LCC endorsement was never within their grasp.

The wider aim of the British Brothers' League, to secure a quick cessation of immigration, was thwarted. The appointment of a Royal Commission defused the issue, and the legislation of 1905, restricted as it was to 'undesirables', and giving as it did a right of appeal to an immigration board, never had the impact that the restrictionists desired. In any case, by 1905 pre-1914 Jewish immigration to Britain had passed its peak. The number of immigrants dropped sharply, from over 11,000 in 1906 to under 4,000 in 1911; the bulk of the new arrivals were admitted without inspection.[65]

In terms of electoral politics, however, the Progressives proved tragically unable to capitalize upon the Jewish support to which they felt they had become entitled. To understand why this was, and to try to form some estimate of the part played by the Jews of London in the Progressive defeat of 1907, we need to examine in detail the Jewish reaction to the great educational reforms which Arthur Balfour's Unionist government enacted in 1902 and 1903. As we do so, we need also to remember that we are dealing, not with one homogeneous Jewish community, but with several sub-sets: a wealthy elite that was already largely Tory; a Jewish middle-class that (under socio-economic and demographic pressures) was increasingly becoming so, and which was, even now, moving away from the City and the East End to Hampstead and Hackney, to Willesden and West Kensington, even to Tottenham and Golders Green, outside the LCC area.[66] The Jewish working classes of inner London could generally be relied upon to support Liberal and Socialist politics, if they had the vote and exercised it, but could easily be deflected by 'Jewish' issues; the lead given them by members of the Jewish Liberal intelligentsia was, therefore, unreliable.

Considerations such as these help explain seemingly contra-dictory postures evinced by different sections of the London Jewish electorate at this time: why, for instance, a gathering of Stepney Jewish workmen (principally cigar makers) during the LCC elections of 1901 could agree to support the Progressive candidates, while a local newspaper, explaining the finer points of the simultaneous contest at Mile End (where Bertram Straus, an undoubted champion of Jewish causes, was defending his Progressive seat) felt confident in informing its readers that 'a good deal will depend on the Catholic and Jewish votes. Rumour gives the benefit of the former to the Progressives, and of the latter to the Moderates.'[67]

The Progressive platform, pre-eminently on the housing question, was bound to be attractive to the Jewish under-class, but once Jews began to be able to afford better housing, and, therefore, to be liable for the personal payment of rates (typically included in their rent), perspectives changed. The housing question itself had, by the early years of the new century, become more complicated as a result of the anti-alien agitation. Even those who supported the building of council houses on the rates wondered whether it was right to allow foreign-born Jews to occupy them. Montagu's generous initiative at Edmonton had already (1899) attracted some precipitate criticism from trade unionists, determined to make the point that council housing should not be used for the benefit of 'only one section of the community'.[68] Hence, no doubt, Sir Samuel's insistence that the dwellings be allocated without reference to race or creed. The growing importance of the trade unions to the Progressive alliance could only heighten radical sensitivities in this regard, and the 'rich Jew' antisemitism of the left that surfaced during the Boer War (1899–1902) was bound to intensify such misgivings.[69] By the time of the 1903 elections to Stepney Borough Council we read of the local Liberal and Radical Association rejecting two would-be candidates simply because they were Jews.[70]

Nor should we suppose that the Jews of the East End were solid in their opposition to *some* immigration control, especially if such control was just sufficient to divide Tory moderates from antisemitic diehards. Straus's sensitivity on this point, and the views of some Jewish Conservatives, have already been noted.[71] The Moderate victory of 1901 at Stepney was that of A. T. Williams, who (as might be expected) pushed a hard restrictionist line. His unsuccessful running mate was Edward Micholls, a wealthy Manchester cotton-spinner, and a Jew. Micholls and Williams issued to the Stepney electors a joint address, which included the following commitment in the matter of the immigration of alien paupers:

> We would support a measure dealing with this question, as we feel that a Nation's first duty is to look after the welfare of its own Citizens, and that these unfortunate immigrants help to increase the poor rate, to lower wages, increase the difficulty of Old Age Pensions, to crowd our already congested streets, and thus make the Housing Question the more difficult.[72]

There is no evidence that Micholls came under special attack from fellow-Jews in the division for holding these views, or that he suffered any withdrawal of Jewish support. The magnificent Progressive victory of 1901 was, indeed, not a little deceptive, at least in east London, for it came just too soon for the anti-alien campaign to register its full impact. By the time of the LCC elections of 1904 this campaign had reached national proportions. At the same time the Progressives had succeeded in rousing the Jewish community to a frenzy of hostility. As with the politics of the London School Board a generation earlier, the twin issues of voluntary schools and religious teaching in state schools provided the *casus belli*.

In 1902 the Unionist government had, by its Education Act, brought the school-board system outside London to an end, and in 1903 the reform was extended to the capital. Local authorities (generally the county councils) became responsible henceforth for the provision of elementary, secondary, and technical education. The Acts of 1902–3 established the principle of local-authority involvement in education, and must be considered one of the foundations of the present-day British educational system.[73] At the time, however, their passage was highly controversial, not so much on account of the demise of the directly elected school boards as because of the powers given to local authorities to assume some control over the voluntary (now known as the 'non-provided') schools. Most of the managers of these schools were nominated by the denominational bodies that owned and were responsible for the maintenance of the school premises, but a minority were appointed by the local authorities, who were responsible for secular instruction and its attendant costs; in return, such non-provided schools received general support from the local rates.

Nonconformist fury at the application of the principle of the use of moneys derived from the local rates to support schools dedicated to denominational religious instruction knew no bounds; there were 'passive resisters' who refused to pay rates on this basis, and, led by Lloyd George, Liberal politicians promised that the Acts of 1902–3 would be repealed. The Jewish reaction was quite different. The Act of 1902 was greeted by the four provincial Jewish schools (Manchester, Birmingham, Liverpool, and Hull) with quiet satisfaction, for they were only too pleased to have the costs of secular education at their establishments paid for by the state, thus enabling their limited endowments to be used to pay better salaries to teachers of religion.[74]

In London the situation was more complex. As far as

elementary education was concerned, financial responsibility rested with the Education Committee of the LCC (on which the County Council itself was in a minority) but management devolved upon the borough councils. The favoured treatment which had been accorded by the London School Board to schools with large Jewish intakes was now felt to be in jeopardy, on account of the anti-alien majorities on some borough councils, notably Stepney:

> the conceding of the school management to the Borough Councils [the *Jewish Chronicle* observed] is a matter which will have to be more closely considered before receiving unqualified approval. It is impossible to deny that there are local feelings at work in some of the boroughs which ... may have undesirable results ... the difficulties that have arisen in certain areas as to the burden cast on the rates by the necessity of providing for Jewish children in Board schools is not to be overlooked in this connection.[75]

The borough councils, not yet three years old, were regarded in Jewish circles as nothing more than 'the old Vestries' in disguise, and the perpetuation of a bland but definitely Christian religious test for teachers appointed at the local-authority schools (where, of course, non-denominational worship was retained) was not regarded as a good omen.[76] The former practice of appointing Jewish headmasters in 'Jewish' Board schools was, indeed, abandoned.[77] Jewish spokesmen conceded at once that the community was bound to benefit from the proposal that the administration of the eight Jewish voluntary schools in London be shared with the LCC; the considerable annual expenditure thus saved could be diverted to improve standards of Hebrew and religious instruction.[78] But one consequence of the new arrangements was that the persons appointed by the County Council to the managing committees of these schools tended to be Christians – such as Alderman Potter, a former Mayor of Stepney, at the Jews' Free School – and although such appointees were acknowledged to be of 'generous sympathies', they did not meet with wholehearted approval in Jewish circles.[79]

There was no doubt that, on balance, Anglo-Jewry supported the legislation of 1903; on its behalf Benjamin Cohen gave the bill a broad and generous welcome in the House of Commons.[80] The relationship of the community with the School Board in its last, Progressive phase had been good; the success of the 1903 legislation was bound therefore to depend upon the manner in which the Progressives at Spring Gardens approached their new and (it must be said) unsolicited responsibilities. But, in spite of the hope expressed in December 1903 by McKinnon Wood, Progressive leader of the LCC, that the transfer of educational responsibilities to the County Council would not lead to the intrusion of religious or sectarian questions into the forthcoming council elections, the LCC contest of March 1904 was very heavily impregnated with the smoke and fire of the Nonconformist crusade against Balfour's enactments.[81]

Whatever moderation the Progressive leadership sought to inject into the educational policy of the Council was counterbalanced by the strength of Nonconformist feeling that the entire apparatus of the 1903 Act was immoral and unjust. On 28 April 1903 the Progressives committed the Council to a protest against being required by law to levy rates to be applied to the maintenance of denominational schools not under public control: either these schools should be properly and wholly controlled by those who provided the bulk of their funds (in which case no member of the teaching staffs at them should be appointed on a religious basis), or their control and expenditure should revert entirely to the voluntary bodies that had seen fit to establish them.[82] The Liberal Party in Parliament and the Progressive alliance in London were both committed to the repeal of the Conservative legislation.

Such a policy was bound to bring the London Jewish community and the Progressives into conflict. In Whitechapel this was to have a dramatic result. The Progressive party there had already earned for itself a reputation for internecine jealousies and intrigue, which had been partly responsible for Morris Abrahams' victory in 1895. In 1904 the refusal of local Jews to endorse or be a part of the Progressive opposition to the London Education Act resulted in a schism. A champion of the Jewish view was found in the person of Henry Herman Gordon (1873–1939), second son of the Revd A. E. Gordon, Cantor of the Great Synagogue, Duke's Place, Aldgate.[83] Henry Gordon (who had been trained for the ministry) had returned from building railways in India to immerse himself in communal work in the East End and, as a Progressive member of the first Stepney Borough Council, had been in the forefront of the fight against anti-alienism there and more generally in the borough. He was to become one of the most respected Progressive members of the LCC, on which, as a member for Whitechapel and its successor (1919), Whitechapel and St George's, he sat without a break from 1904 to 1922. In 1916 he held the office of Deputy Chairman of the Council.

But in 1904 Gordon was a rebel. With the support of a galaxy of Jewish religious and lay leaders, led by Lord Rothschild and two *dayanim* (judges) of the Chief Rabbi's Ecclesiastical Court (Moses Hyamson and Susman Cohen), and with the support also of the local Catholic clergy, he stood as an Independent candidate on a platform which had as its central plank the sanctity of the 1903 Education Act, which had freed the Jewish and Catholic communities from much of the financial burden of running their local voluntary schools.[84] A militant campaign followed, as unprecedented in the history of the LCC as it was in the annals of Jewish involvement in municipal politics in Britain.

Squeezed on the one side by Gordon and his clerical aides, and on the other by local Tories (who were able to some extent to offset Jewish opposition to immigration control by playing the education card),[85] the Progressives brought in to campaign for them, first, Stuart Samuel, the local MP, and then Henrietta Adler (1868-1950) the elder daughter of the Chief Rabbi.[86] Thus did 'Nettie' Adler begin her long and distinguished association with the London County Council, specializing in educational matters and youth work. Unable, as yet, to stand herself for election, she used the prestige of her name to try to rally Jewish support behind the official Progressive candidates. What her father thought of these activities was not, on this occasion, recorded. But we know that Hermann Adler himself was a Tory, and that Gordon thought seriously enough of Nettie's intervention to issue a statement that he had it 'on the authority of the Chief Rabbi' that Nettie was 'working without his authority and without his consent. She is of an age [Gordon explained] when he cannot interfere with her discretion.'[87]

Nettie had already acquired some experience of East End schools as a manager, under the London School Board, of the Hanbury Street group of schools; she was also a member of the Visiting Committee of the Jewish Board of Guardians and of the

Jewish Religious Education Board. In 1905 she was rewarded for her efforts by being co-opted onto the LCC's Education Committee. In the course of time she acquired an encyclopaedic knowledge of the Jewish East End, and contributed the chapter on 'Jewish life and labour in East London' to the *New Survey of London Life and Labour* published under the auspices of the London School of Economics in 1934. She served as Deputy Chairman of the LCC in 1922–3. She certainly had a much closer relationship with East End Jews than her father, and she certainly met more of them. But in 1904, as the daughter of a Chief Rabbi whom many religious immigrant Jews viewed with suspicion, her imprimatur upon the Progressive nominations did not impress.[88]

Armed, according to one local newspaper, with 'the great bulk of the Jewish and the whole of the Roman Catholic vote', Gordon's position was unassailable.[89] He topped the poll, obtaining 290 votes more than his nearest Progressive rival.[90] At Stepney, where the Moderates already held one seat, they came to within three votes of capturing the other, and at St George's only 255 votes separated the bottom Progressive from the most successful Moderate candidate. These results, as those in Bow and Bromley and Hackney North, where Moderates also did well, were undoubtedly due in part to the immigration question, which was already becoming a housing question. But the impact of the education controversy, and the Jewish desertions from the Progressives on its account, were undeniable. The *East London Observer*, noting that after the declaration of the poll 'the horses were taken from Mr Gordon's carriage, and he was drawn by an enthusiastic crowd through the streets to his house', gave the Progressives the grim warning that if they did not acquiesce in the giving of rate aid to the voluntary schools they would be 'forever blackened'.[91]

And so they were. Nationally, in its opposition to the Acts of 1902 and 1903, the Liberal Party believed that it was backing a winner, though in fact the Liberal revival that culminated in its electoral triumph of January 1906 was grounded in the popularity of its opposition to Tariff Reform and the Unionist disarray over this issue. Liberal opposition to the abortive Aliens Bill of 1904 and to the passage of the Aliens Act of 1905 did it some good in Jewish eyes, but this goodwill was short-lived. In spite of Jewish pleadings, the government of Campbell-Bannerman did not repeal the 1905 legislation, which it recognized as having broad popular backing.[92] The central part played by the Jews in the defeat of Winston Churchill at the Manchester North-West by-election of April 1908 may be said to have signalled the strength of Jewish feeling on this issue, but a secondary matter of which much was made during the Manchester campaign was the attempt of the Liberal government to repeal the Balfour Education Acts; Sir Philip Magnus told the Jews of North-West Manchester that this would result in the placing of intolerable financial burdens on the Jewish voluntary schools, and a correspondent of the *Jewish Chronicle* estimated that in Manchester alone this burden would amount to £2,000 per annum.[93]

In London the dogmatic obstinacy of the Liberals in trying to overturn the Acts of 1902 and 1903 had already reaped a predictable harvest. The central theme of the Liberal Education Bill of 1906 was, in Asquith's words, a refusal 'to recognise what was called the inalienable right of the parent to have his child taught a particular creed at the expense of the State'; accordingly, while a national system of undenominational schools was to be set up, there was to be full public control over the non-provided schools, and the abolition of religious tests for teachers at these schools.[94] Clause 4 of the bill went some way to meeting the special needs of the Roman Catholic and Jewish communities, by stipulating that extended facilities for religious education at a voluntary school could be provided, but only if four-fifths of the parents demanded it; however, this provision was permissive, and not mandatory upon a local authority, a point brought out strongly when a deputation from the Jewish Religious Education Board and the Jewish Voluntary Schools Association saw Birrell, the president of the Board of Education, in May.[95]

The 1906 bill was emasculated in the House of Lords, and then dropped. Jewish hostility to it had been exacerbated by the experience of Progressive interpretation and administration of the 1903 Act. The records of the Council's Education Department testify to the continuous irritation of the Jewish authorities in this regard. One particular source of complaint was the amount of time allowed for Hebrew and religious instruction in the non-provided schools.[96] Another concerned the payment of teachers customarily engaged in Sunday-morning teaching at these schools.[97] In January 1906 the Council's Non-Provided Schools Sub-Committee announced its intention to restrict the intake at the Stepney Jewish School.[98] The following March the Day Schools Sub-Committee refused to recognize the Revd W. Levine as a member of the staff of the Jews' Free School, and in May the Revd N. Goldsten, who had been teaching for eighteen years at the Westminster Jews' Free School but who had no formal teaching qualifications, was summarily dismissed.[99]

It mattered little that some of these decisions could no doubt be justified on the grounds of efficient administration. The publicity which they generated necessarily and adversely affected the Progressive image in Jewish (and Roman Catholic) eyes. Between 1904 and 1907 this image suffered a much more widespread deterioration. The assumption of educational responsibilities by the LCC played havoc with its finances. In 1893 its net debt had been a little over £18 millions, not much worse than the debt it had inherited from the Metropolitan Board of Works; by 1907 the debt exceeded £48 millions. The Moderates, who now dared to call themselves Municipal Reformers, exploited without mercy what they alleged was Progressive unwillingness to protect the ratepayer; the Progressives were declared to be nothing more than Socialists in disguise. To bolster this attack the religious question in education was exploited to the full.

In Whitechapel the Progressives were careful to mend their fences with Henry Gordon. He received the endorsement of Stuart Samuel and only one official Progressive was put up in the division; Gordon's comfortable victory there marked his return to the Progressive fold, but on his terms so far as the education controversy was concerned.[100] Elsewhere in the East End, however, two well-known Jewish Progressives were defeated. At Limehouse Arthur Leon failed by sixty-nine votes to retain his seat, and at Stepney, where a strong ratepayers' association had been formed, the much-respected Jewish businessman and communal worker Carl Stettauer (1859–1913), a founder of the Hampstead Synagogue and a member since 1903 of the Borough Council, lost (resoundingly) for the Progressives their only remaining seat in the division.[101]

It was not only in the core areas of immigrant Jewish settlement that the Municipal Reformers played the anti-alien card. In Hackney Central and Hackney North the Progressives lost all four seats to the Municipal Reformers at the end of a campaign soured by allegations that the Borough Council, then under Municipal

Reform control, was preparing a list of Jewish defaulting ratepayers; there was some truth in this rumour, and, under the pressure of intense local publicity, the Council's Finance Committee reversed what had been a clear decision to single out Jewish absconders for special investigation.[102] To make matters worse, the Municipal Reformers put out a pamphlet declaring that because of high County Council rates, small workshops had to employ foreigners, who accepted lower wages; the clear implication was that immigrant Jews pulled down wage levels.[103]

But although the *Idisher Ekspres* made much of this episode, the reaction of the Jewish establishment was one of almost total silence. Water Rothschild, in a letter to Alderman Billings, the Municipal Reform leader in Hackney who was elected to the LCC for the Central Division, minimized the importance of the issue, pointing instead to 'the spread of Socialistic doctrines and the avowed intentions of Progressives and Socialists to crush out all individual effort'.[104] This reflected a well-rehearsed Rothschild theme – that the Progressives and the Socialists were pursuing identical objectives, and really ought not to be differentiated.[105] It was a charge that the *Ekspres* sought to rebut: 'no-one', it argued 'suspects that Stettauer is a socialist' and, in any case, 'Jews are not afraid of Socialism'.[106] The anarchist *Arbeter Fraint*, which usually did not bother to give coverage to the affairs of the LCC, none the less on this occasion thought it worthwhile to point to the achievements of the LCC under the Progressives; even East End Jewish anarchists, who were wont to eschew the institutions of representative democracy, could not have relished the prospect of a County Council effectively under Tory control.[107]

Yet, if there was a concerted move by enfranchised Jewish workers of the East End to come to the aid of the Progressives in 1907, it was neither recorded in the press nor reflected in the voting figures. Leopold Greenberg, a Liberal and a Zionist, who had in January 1907 become editor of the *Jewish Chronicle* (a position he held until 1931), while lamenting the absence from the new LCC of Stettauer and Leon, admitted that to have the record number of eight Jews on the Council was no bad thing, even if six of them were Municipal Reformers. Among the newcomers were another of Benjamin's brothers, Nathaniel Cohen (City of London), and David Davis (North Kensington), both members of the Board of Deputies, Isadore Salmon (Islington West), a future vice-president of the United Synagogue and of the Board, and Percy Simmons (whom the impact of the education issue and the intervention of two independent Roman Catholic candidates had helped to victory at St George's).[108]

The Municipal Reform victory of 1907 – in aggregate terms practically a mirror-image of the Progressive victory of 1904 – breathed new life into the Jewish opposition to the insistence of the Liberal government that the educational reforms of 1902–3 must be undone. 'The strong professions of sympathy of the victorious party for the voluntary schools', Greenberg confessed to his readers, 'should ease any Jewish anxiety that may exist under this head.'[109] On 15 March (why had these figures not been released two weeks earlier?) he calculated that, if the full cost of religious instruction in the Jewish non-provided schools in London were thrown back onto the community, a sum in the region of £1,727 per annum would have to be found.[110] When, in 1908, the Liberals attempted once more to legislate on the education question, Jewish defenders of rate aid for the voluntary schools found that, for the first time, their views matched those who controlled the County Council.[111]

This was a novel situation. Whether it would extend into other policy areas, and, if so, for how long, remained open questions.

Chapter Three

MUNICIPAL REACTION AND THE RISE OF LABOUR

The Municipal Reform victory of 1907 ushered in twenty-seven years of Conservative rule at County Hall. Elected on a platform of financial retrenchment, the Municipal Reformers lost no time in reversing Progressive spending policies: the controversial Thames steamboat service was brought to an end, the LCC's Works Department was axed, and there was an unsuccessful attempt to privatize the council-owned tramways. But the larger promise made in 1907, to ease the rate burden, could not be kept. Initially this was because of the Council's increasing educational obligations, and the expansion of its trading activities, especially schemes of slum clearance, the cost of which was bound, still, to fall on the rates. More generally, however, it soon became clear that, irrespective of party-political views, Londoners looked to the LCC to offer and maintain a range of public services which neither central government nor borough councils nor private enterprise could or would provide. In the financial year 1913–14 the central rate levied by the Council stood at 5s. 7d.; in 1907 it had only been 3s.[1]

The First World War itself did not add much to Council expenditure – indeed housing and other building works were suspended during hostilities. But after the war successive governments used local authorities as the major tool in house-building programmes. The London borough councils could only build houses within their own areas, but the LCC and the City Corporation were by now no longer bound by such a restriction, and governments of all political varieties were successful in persuading the LCC to undertake major housing programmes. Most notable in this connection were the Coalition government's Act of 1919, the

Conservative (Neville Chamberlain's) Act of 1923, and Acts of 1924 and 1930 passed by Labour governments. The White Hart Lane scheme was revived and expanded. New estates were built at Roehampton, Becontree, and elsewhere, while fresh efforts were made to tackle the slum problem.[2]

Undoubtedly, however, the greatest impact made upon London government by any single piece of inter-war legislation was that occasioned by the passage of Neville Chamberlain's Local Government Act of 1929. Under the provisions of this mammoth statute, the entire apparatus of the Victorian Poor Law was swept away, and the responsibilities and duties of the old poor-law authorities were transferred to the counties and county boroughs. In London this meant the abolition of the twenty-five local Boards of Guardians, and of the Metropolitan Asylums Board; all the workhouses, infirmaries, hospitals, laboratories, and the ambulance service previously run by these bodies became, on 1 April 1930, the responsibility of the LCC. The 1929 Act also charged county councils with new areas of responsibility in the fields of public health, maternity and child welfare, roads, and town and country planning.[3]

As a result of the passage of the Act of 1929, the LCC rate rose, in 1930, to over 7s.[4] Then came the fall of the second Labour government (August 1931) and the defection of the Labour leader, Ramsay Macdonald, to head a National (in practice largely Conservative) administration. The Municipal Reformers responded to the financial crisis by a policy of severe economy that clearly went beyond what was required to meet the national situation; the decision to do away with school prizes in 1931 (saving around £12,000) raised a storm of protest that cut across party-political boundaries.[5] At the 1931 LCC elections the Labour Party had lost seats for the first time sine 1919. This may have lulled the Municipal Reformers (returned to power at County Hall with 83 seats out of 124) into a false sense of security. In 1934 the Labour gains were just sufficient to give them a majority of fourteen seats; Herbert Morrison entered upon the inheritance he had worked so hard and for so long to achieve.

The major theme of inter-war municipal politics in London was thus not the extension of the powers and activities of the LCC, less still the rate burden; these were matters of some controversy, of course, but since both phenomena flourished irrespective of who was in charge at County Hall, no political party could claim to be blameless. The *locus classicus* here was the manner in which the London Passenger Transport Board was established: the idea of unifying the capital's bus and underground railway services under a public corporation was formulated by the second Labour government in 1930 but enacted by the National government in 1933.

The distinguishing characteristic of London politics between the two World Wars was the demise of the old Progressive Party, and its replacement by Labour as the only credible radical alternative to the Conservatives. In the early 1920s the Progressives were still a force to be reckoned with in London politics. Before the First World War there had never been more than three Labour members of the LCC. In 1919 fifteen were elected, and after 1925 there were more than thirty councillors taking the Labour whip. In 1925 the Progressive total had fallen to six; thereafter the London Liberal Federation determined to run candidates as 'Liberals', hoping, perhaps, to capitalize upon the apparent revival of Liberal fortunes nationally now that Lloyd George was in control.[6] The hope was never fulfilled. By 1928 London politics had been recast very firmly in a twin Socialist–Conservative mould. At the LCC elections that year the Liberal total was reduced to five. 'There is no room [the *Daily Telegraph* observed] for a third party in London municipal politics.'[7] The 1931 elections (which predated the fall of the Labour government) witnessed only one Liberal gain. By 1934, the year of Labour's takeover of the LCC, London Liberalism was more or less dead; not a single Liberal was returned as a London County Councillor.

These events were bound to have a dramatic impact on the relationship between the LCC and London Jewry. By 1910 there were more Jewish Municipal Reformers on the LCC than Jewish Progressives. After 1928, however (see Appendix) there were as many Jewish Labourites as Reformers, and after 1934 the Jewish contingent at County Hall was overwhelmingly Labour in composition.

During the First World War there was an electoral truce in London politics, as nationally. In 1916, following the formation of the Coalition government under Lloyd George, a similar arrangement had been entered into in the LCC. The Progressives hoped that this could be continued after the end of hostilities, and that both they and the Municipal Reformers could face the London electorate (now increased to 1,612,000 by virtue of the provisions of the 1918 Representation of the People Act) with an all-party programme. Initially the Municipal Reformers agreed, but the arrangement fell through, following an unsuccessful approach by the Progressives to the London Labour Party to join in a grand post-war coalition.[8]

One of the most revolutionary effects of the 1918 Act was that receipt of poor relief ceased to be a voting disqualification. This, added to the substantial widening of the qualifications for the franchise generally, brought into being in London, as elsewhere, a poorer electorate much more favourably inclined to the Labour viewpoint.[9] Therefore, although there was to be no post-war coalition to govern London, the pressures upon both the Progressives and the Municipal Reformers to come to arrangements that would prevent Labour gaining seats were strong. In two areas of especial interest to the Jewish community this resulted in unopposed returns, which had the effect of prolonging, for a few more years, the presence on the LCC of prominent Jewish Progressives. It was agreed that of the three Hackney divisions the Progressives would be given South Hackney, the Municipal Reformers the North, while Central Hackney returned unopposed one Reformer and one Progressive – Nettie Adler.[10] At Whitechapel a similar arrangement resulted in the return, also unopposed, of Henry Gordon.

In 1918 the Whitechapel and St George's divisions had been amalgamated, creating a constituency which both for parliamentary and local-government purposes was probably more thickly populated with Jewish voters than any other in the country at that time.[11] Gordon's ascendancy over this Jewish electorate was by now considerable. But in 1922, when the former arrangement with the Municipal Reformers was no longer in force, he did not stand. Although the Reformers put up a Jewish candidate – Woolf Joel – of their own, his appeal was not that of Gordon nor of a young Jewish Labour activist, Morris Harold Davis. Davis's running mate, C. J. Kelly, came top of the poll, and Davis himself came only eighty-seven votes short of winning the other seat.

Fearing, with good reason, that Davis would have little difficulty in reversing the result next time, at the end of 1924 the local Conservative Association approached the Progressives with the offer of a pact, 'this being considered the only way of defeating Socialism'.[12] Gordon, by now chairman of the Whitechapel and St George's Liberal Association, replied with a firm rejection.[13] This time (1925) both the Reformers and the Progressives ran Jewish candidates; Adolph Ludlow, honorary secretary to the English Zionist Federation and a prominent local Conservative, came bottom of the poll; Ida Samuel did better for the Progressives, but still obtained fewer than half the 4,187 votes that Davis accumulated, thus inaugurating his own LCC career as well as the long Labour tenure of the Whitechapel stronghold. Miss Samuel was successful in obtaining a seat on the County Council, but not until another six years had elapsed and not in a Jewish constituency; in 1931 she was elected for the Liberal Party at North Lambeth.

Henry Gordon withdrew, it would seem, from an electoral situation that was becoming ever more problematic. Nettie Adler fought almost to the bitter end. The failure of other Jewish candidates to do well in Whitechapel points to the growing popularity of Labourism as a creed that, in an area such as that, was to carry all before it. At Central Hackney it was not the policies of the Socialist left that were to prove insuperable, but the politics of the antisemitic right. To understand how this came about we must briefly trace Nettie Adler's relationship with her Hackney constituency from the date of her first election, in 1910.

In the years immediately preceding the First World War, Hackney was undergoing a fundamental change in its social structure. Just beyond the traditional East End, it was rapidly losing its middle-class image as working-class families, taking advantage of improved public transport, escaped from Stepney and Whitechapel to better-quality rented accommodation now within reasonable commuting distance of their workplaces. By 1910 Hackney South (bordering onto Bethnal Green and Shoreditch) was largely working-class in composition; Hackney North (an area which included Stoke Newington and Stamford Hill) was still predominantly well-to-do.[14] Substantial working-class settlement in the Central division came later than in the South; by 1910, however, and from an electoral point of view, the working classes predominated there too.[15]

This working-class influx helped the Liberal cause only to a very limited extent. At the parliamentary level, Hackney South was securely located within the Liberal camp. However, although Hackney North went Liberal in 1906, by 1910 it had returned to a Conservative allegiance, and that year returned the (Jewish) botanist Oscar Warburg as one of its county councillors.[16] Hackney Central only ceased electing Conservative MPs in 1906. It was fast becoming an area of Jewish settlement; Dalston, at the centre of the division, had had an established Jewish community since the mid-1880s, and although the Hackney synagogue (also in the Central division) dated from 1897, the community that it served had begun to form more than a decade earlier.

At the LCC elections of March 1910 it became for the first time possible (following legislation passed in 1908) for women to stand in the knowledge that, if successful, their election to the Council could not be challenged on the grounds of their sex. At Hackney Central Nettie Adler was adopted as a Progressive candidate. In what might otherwise have been a lacklustre contest (coming hard on the heels of the January General Election), Nettie's candidature provided a centre of interest, for she brought into the division a glittering array of leading Jewish Liberals, including Herbert Samuel and Rufus Isaacs, as well as Sidney Webb and Sir J. W. Benn, the Progressive Leader at County Hall.[17] Nettie's interest in education, and in the role of women in education, and her support for a school-building programme, were well known. She made no secret of her Jewish identity, even to the extent of letting it be known that she would not campaign on the Saturday of the poll.[18] In a poll of 53 per cent (higher than the London average) Nettie and her running mate scored a comfortable victory; she and Susan Lawrence (a Municipal Reformer) became the first women to sit as of right on the London County Council.

During this contest antisemitism was little in evidence. An attempt by one local newspaper to draw attention to the Jewish influx into the area, by pointing to the large number of Jewish children at Sigdon Road School ('now ... entirely controlled by the Jewish calendar') found no support.[19] At County Hall Nettie immersed herself in the general work of the Education and Asylums committees, but she was also supportive of Jewish interests (for example, in relation to arrangements in LCC schools for religious observance).[20] By the time of the 1913 County Council elections her continued presence on the LCC was regarded, from the point of view of London Jewry, as indispensable. Uniquely, the *Jewish Chronicle* advised the Jewish electors of Central Hackney how to vote:

it would be a cause for real regret should she not be again returned for Central Hackney ... and we hope that the Jews in Central Hackney will do their best to return Miss Adler at the top of the poll ... not merely on account of the honoured name she bears, but because of the admirable work she has done for London in general, and Jews in particular.[21]

In spite of the fact that ill health interrupted her campaign, and that her running mate lost his seat and came bottom of the poll, Nettie retained hers by just nine votes.[22]

With the virtual cessation of Jewish immigration, and the gradual dispersal of Jews from the East End, the antisemitism that had been such a feature of Conservative/Municipal Reform politics at the very beginning of the century might have been contained, and perhaps even diluted. The very fact of Jewish settlement in Hackney was a sign of upward social mobility, which Nettie herself documented. In the material which she collected in order to write her contribution to the *New Survey of London Life and Labour*, she prepared a table showing the working- and middle-class proportions among the Jews of east London; the category 'middle-class' was primarily an occupational one, and included professional and clerical workers, shopkeepers, supervisory shop staff, and the self-employed, but it also comprised households enjoying an income of at least £250 per annum, regardless of occupation. Using these definitions, Nettie calculated that in the boroughs of Hackney and Stoke Newington at the end of the 1920s there were almost twice as many middle-class as working-class Jews; even in Stepney and Bethnal Green more than a fifth of the Jews were middle-class by this time.[23]

These figures must be set in the context of the changing balance of Jewish settlement in the LCC area as a whole. In 1903 the statistician S. Rowson had estimated the Jewish population of the County of London as 144,000.[24] Of all the estimates made around that time, this one (based on marriage and burial statistics) would appear to be the most accurate.[25] Within this total well over 80 per cent lived in the boroughs of Stepney, Bethnal Green, and Poplar.[26] In 1929 H. L. Trachtenberg put the Jewish population of the County of London at about 183,000.[27] Of these, according to Nettie Adler's own evidence, only some 46 per cent were still living in the East End boroughs.[28] Put another way, during the period covered by her membership of the LCC the centre of gravity of the Jewish community of the County of London began to move away from the East End, and was ceasing to be located exclusively within the manual working classes. These factors alone ought to have created within London Jewry fertile ground upon which Conservative ideas might have grown. But they did not.

During the First World War the Municipal Reform majority at County Hall was attracted by the popularity of the policies aimed at the foreign-born Jewish population of the capital. In the early years of the century, in spite of the fact that the immigrant Jewish presence in London had been the major target of anti-alienist activity, there had been remarkably little violence against Jews or Jewish property in the metropolis. The outstanding example of physical attacks upon Jews in Britain in the pre-1914 period was the riots of August 1911 in South Wales, where, ironically, Jewish settlement was minute.[29] But the ultra-patriotism and extreme anti-German feeling that swept through the country once war had been declared easily lent itself to exploitation by antisemites.[30] Rich Jews of German origin became the targets of press campaigns, and Jews from Russia and Poland were called upon to volunteer for the British army.

Early in 1916, when it became clear that the proportion of unnaturalized Jews volunteering was small, and after conscription had been introduced for British subjects, Herbert Samuel, the Home Secretary, announced that Russian subjects of suitable age would be required to enlist in the British forces, but that, as an alternative, they could return to Russia to fight for the Tsar; a system of local tribunals was instituted to hear the claims of those wanting exemption. In July 1917 the British and Russian governments signed a Military Service Agreement, one consequence of which was that males of Russian nationality who refused to be conscripted into the British forces were made liable to deportation. At the end of September deportations actually began, but a month later the Bolshevik Revolution took Russia out of the war, and it is most unlikely that Jews so repatriated would ever have seen active service in the Tsarist armies.[31]

During the war the Anglo-Jewish leadership indulged itself in a public display of chauvinism. The *Jewish Chronicle*, choosing not to remember its former condemnations of Tsarist pogroms and British anti-alien legislation, declared (in print and in a banner strung outside its Finsbury Square, London headquarters) that 'England has been all she could be to the Jews; Jews will be all they can be to England'.[32] A Jewish Recruiting Committee was formed in east London under the patronage of the cream of the communal grandees.[33] The 1915 *Yom Kippur* (Day of Atonement) service for the poor at the Pavilion Theatre, Mile End, was interrupted in order to welcome and present a loyal address to the Lord Mayor, while the choir ceased their penitential melodies in order to sing 'Rule Britannia'.[34] The measures which the government took against Russian non-volunteers were welcomed; the fact that it had been a Jewish Home Secretary who had announced them was merely an additional cause for satisfaction.[35]

But within the East End ghetto a rather different attitude prevailed. However just Britain's quarrel with Germany might have seemed, this was not perceived as a Jewish quarrel; for Jew to kill Jew appeared particularly profane.[36] Jews who had fled from Russia and Russian Poland could hardly be expected to volunteer to preserve a regime they heartily detested. To fight against conscription and deportation, and to preserve the right of asylum in Britain, a Foreign Jews Protection Committee was established by a miscellany of Jewish Socialist groups, trade unions, and friendly societies.[37] Its activities aroused bitter local hostility, which was fully supported by the East End press. The *East London Observer* warned:

> If the Government show weakness in their determination and allow themselves to become victims of the 'political refugee' trick, we fear the consequences will be serious. The misbehaviour of any offensive foreign bounder, or the impertinence of a Whitechapel Jew boy, may light the smouldering fires of native feeling.[38]

Long before the conscription issue came to a head, there had been plenty of signs of war-engendered hostility to the Jews. In Stepney in the autumn of 1914 Jews applying for relief under the Poor Law were subjected to discrimination.[39] The sinking by a German submarine of the unarmed *Lusitania* (7 May 1915) led to extensive rioting in east London, in which no attempt appears to have been made by the mobs to distinguish between Germans and Jews. Jews liable for conscription who pleaded before the military tribunals that they should be exempted because they did not wish to fight for the Tsar, or because they feared they would not be able to practise their religion, obviously created a bad public impression.

On 23 January 1917 a meeting at Bethnal Green Town Hall passed a series of resolutions drawing attention to the inequity of aliens being permitted to earn good wages while English conscripts were dying for their country.[40] In the spring, to match the efforts of the Foreign Jews Protection Committee, a Foreign Jews Deportation Committee was set in motion, and MPs were lobbied.[41] Later that year, as we have noted, the Military Service Agreement was signed with Russia, but this measure did not prevent the outbreak of serious disturbances in Bethnal Green in late September.[42]

It was against this background that the Conservatives at County Hall felt justified in undertaking a number of policy initiatives aimed – in fact if not in name – against the community of foreign Jews in London. On 27 October 1914 the Council resolved, as a matter of emergency, that it was 'highly undesirable, in the interests of London, that a large number of alien enemies ... should be allowed free access to all parts of London, and that ... representation ... be made to His Majesty's Government to make the necessary military arrangements to give effect to this view'.[43]

In fact, the government had already (5 August) passed an Aliens Restriction Act. By November the Conservatives had had second thoughts about the difficulties that might be involved in giving practical effect to the October resolution, which was rescinded. The following month, however, the assault upon the rights of aliens was renewed. On 22 December the Council debated a report from its Education Committee, which had wondered whether it was right that children of 'alien enemies' who were not themselves British citizens should have access to the 'central' schools which had been established in 1911; these schools, entry to which was limited and a privilege, gave a four-year training along commercial and technical lines to children specially selected at the age of 11. It was proposed that although alien offspring already at such schools would be allowed to continue their studies, no further entry of alien children into them would be permitted. An attempt by Sir J. W. Benn, supported by Nettie Adler, H. H. Gordon, A. L. Leon, and Percy Harris, to refer back the motion was defeated by forty-four votes to thirty-seven; the proposal became Council policy.[44]

In 1915 this scarcely-disguised attack upon Jewish interests was renewed, this time in the context of a report from the LCC's Stores and Contracts Committee, whose policy not to give contracts to firms controlled by 'enemy aliens', and to remove from its list of companies invited to offer tenders the names of thirty-six such firms, was approved without challenge.[45] In April 1916 the Council resolved, again on the initiative of its Education Committee, to extend the policy with respect to central schools to the eligibility of children in London for LCC scholarships and other awards; henceforth these were not to be available to the children of enemy aliens unless these children were themselves born in Britain.[46]

Until October 1917 these regulations affected significant numbers but not the vast majority of London's Jews; unnaturalized Jews born in Russia and Poland were aliens, but not *enemy* aliens. But with the news of Lenin's seizure of power in Russia, and the subsequent withdrawal of Russia from the Allied war effort, attitudes towards Russian Jewish immigrants hardened in two respects. The Russian peace with Germany (March 1918) was regarded as a betrayal of the Allied cause. More seriously, the advent of the Bolshevik government, committed, apparently, to the notion of world revolution to advance Communism, put all Russian immigrants in Britain under suspicion – at least in the opinion of influential sections of the rightwing press. In April 1919 the High Tory *Morning Post* attacked the Russian-Jewish community *en bloc* as emissaries of Bolshevism; this was a line of argument that had been in evidence during the General Election the previous December.[47]

These accusations were sweeping and far-fetched, but they became harder to dispel because they were shared – publicly – by important sections of the Anglo-Jewish leadership. The promulgation of the Balfour Declaration (2 November 1917) had brought to a head a simmering crisis in relations between the Zionist and anti-Zionist wings of Anglo-Jewry.[48] The anti-Zionists consisted in the main of English-born, culturally assimilated elements, irredeemably opposed to the idea of Jewish nationhood (they thought of themselves as 'Englishmen of the Jewish persuasion'). The immigrant presence in London, giving new life (as it seemed) to antisemitism, had from the start filled them with unease, and the strength of both Zionism and Socialism within the immigrant community were further causes of antipathy. Numerically the anti-Zionists were a small group. But their lack of numbers was to some extent counterbalanced by their prestige and social status. They included no less a figure than the barrister David Lindo Alexander, who in May 1917 had been forced to resign as president of the Board of Deputies partly on the issue of his anti-Zionism.

A week after the Balfour Declaration had been issued, the group announced the formation of the League of British Jews, 'to resist the allegation that Jews constitute a separate Political Entity'.[49] Alexander was a founder-member of the League; its president was the Conservative MP Lionel de Rothschild, and Sir Philip Magnus was a vice-president. In April 1919 ten leading members of the League, including Louis Montagu (the second Lord Swaythling), president of the Federation of Synagogues, appended their signatures to a letter that appeared in the *Morning Post*, accusing the *Jewish Chronicle* and its sister paper, the *Jewish World*, of aiding and abetting the Bolshevik cause.[50] When *The Jewish Peril*, the English translation of the notorious forged *Protocols of the Elders of Zion*, appeared at the beginning of 1920, the *Post* wisely treated it with some reserve. But a few months later the *Post* itself ran a series of articles (later to appear in book form under the title *The Cause of World Unrest*) in which the central theme was the idea of a centuries-old Jewish conspiracy 'to produce revolution, communism, and anarchy'.[51]

Although, therefore, now that the war had ended, no Jew could be classified as an enemy alien, there was a great deal of popular and media pressure tending to brand Jews – or at any rate those not born in Britain or who had not bothered to become naturalized – as potential traitors, unreliable, and untrustworthy. The Conservative majority at County Hall felt that it had to respond to and indeed to be seen to be part of this campaign, in which Jews of Russian or Russo-Polish birth were to be the chief targets.

In November 1917 Nettie Adler took it upon herself to inform Stuart Samuel, newly installed as president of the Board of Deputies in succession to Alexander, that a recommendation was to be put to the LCC's Education Committee from its Elementary

Education Sub-Committee to the effect that in future no scholarships be awarded by the Council except to British-born children whose fathers (or in some circumstances whose mothers) were British-born or naturalized before 1 January 1914, or to foreign-born children of naturalized parents, provided that such naturalization had likewise been effected before January 1914. There was no question here of enemy status, and it was obvious – given the financial impediments to naturalization in the pre-war period – that a very large number of Jewish children were going to be discriminated against.[52] What was equally obvious was that a proportion of these children were to become the objects of discrimination even though they had been born in Britain and were, therefore, British subjects.

Nettie's initiative enabled Stuart Samuel to take some pre-emptive action; he and Charles Emanuel, the Board's secretary, met Cyril Cobb the (Municipal Reform) chairman of the Council's Education Committee and Sir Robert Blair (the LCC's education officer) on 14 November, and tried to convince them that a fairer policy might be to restrict scholarships to children who were British-born provided their fathers had lived in Britain for at least five years before their birth.[53] But though it succeeded in delaying a decision, the lobby failed to have a lasting effect. On 3 March 1918 the LCC resolved that in order to be eligible for Council scholarships candidates would have in future to be British when applying for the award, *and* to have been born, or have fathers who were born, in Britain or the Dominions.[54]

A decade was to pass before this policy was substantially abandoned. Meanwhile, the Municipal Reformers took action which affected Jewish interests much more widely. On 15 April 1919, a week after the *Morning Post* had informed its readers that the Russian Jews were purveyors of Bolshevism, Major E. H. Coumbe, elected the previous month for Stoke Newington but formerly (1907–10) a councillor for Mile End, took the first step towards committing the Council to a policy of not employing aliens.[55] Coumbe's intention was quite explicitly to bar all aliens from employment by the Council, whether or not they were naturalized.

There was clearly some initial resistance within the Council's General Purposes Committee to the adoption of such a draconian edict.[56] However, by the summer of 1920 some of the more squeamish had been won over. On 28 June the General Purposes Committee determined (by eleven votes to ten) to recommend to the full Council that, except in the case of teachers of foreign languages or where the Council resolved otherwise, no persons other than natural-born British subjects be taken into the employ of the LCC.[57] On 6 July this recommendation was adopted by the full Council; Nettie Adler, Henry Gordon, and Percy Harris had been among the thirty-eight councillors to vote for it to be referred back to the General Purposes Committee, but the fifty councillors who supported the policy included four Jewish Municipal Reformers (David Davis, Major H. B. Lewis-Barned, Percy Simmons, and Oscar Warburg).[58]

Three years later the philosophy embodied in this employment policy was taken a stage further. The Council was and continued to be obliged to rehouse those displaced by slum clearance. But under the provisions of a housing regulation approved in June 1923 preference in the general allocation of accommodation on the Council's housing estates was to be given in future to British citizens.[59] This regulation, originally intended (so it was said) to be of a merely temporary nature, soon acquired a permanent place on housing application forms; its effect, quite simply, was to exclude alien applicants 'entirely from consideration for any tenancy in the Council's dwellings'.[60] In Nettie Adler's view this restriction was one factor pushing Jews seeking better housing in the inter-war period to look beyond the boundary of the LCC (specifically to the north-east and north-west of the administrative county).[61]

At the LCC elections of 1925 the Municipal Reformers sought to strengthen the policy adopted in 1923, by holding out the promise that in future no council housing or tenements would be let to aliens at all, even if they happened to be ratepayers.[62] Within Anglo-Jewry those in power at County Hall were now widely regarded as antisemitic. But, as was evident in the case of non-employment of aliens, Jewish opinion was itself split, a fact which no doubt gave comfort and encouragement to the protagonists of anti-alienism in the Council chamber. The housing policy was, without doubt, legal. The 1918 policy on scholarships may well have been illegal.[63] But even where the LCC might have been open to challenge in the courts, very influential leaders of the community queried the wisdom of so doing.

When Joseph Prag, an honorary officer of the United

Synagogue, initiated a debate at the Board of Deputies on the 'blind prejudice' of the LCC, and called for legal action to make 'these London County Council people ... see the wickedness of their ways', he received some support from Stuart Samuel, but only because 'the educational policy of the LCC was driving the pick of Jewish children into the ranks of the socialists and would possibly be the seed of revolutionary tendencies'. Isadore Salmon (vice-chairman of the Council 1924–5 and by now a Conservative MP) offered no support; the Council, he declared, must be compared to a testator, entitled 'to think of his sons before providing for his more distant relations or friends'. Another speaker (Robert Henriques) 'pointed out how necessary it was to exercise tact in cases like this. These were difficult times and there was much prejudice abroad.'[64]

On the housing and employment questions the Board of Deputies did no more than protest. Since the inauguration of the anti-alien employment policy in 1920 the secretary of the Board, Charles Emanuel, had relied heavily upon the services of Nettie Adler not merely as an informant but also as a channel through which pressure might be applied on those who formulated LCC policy.[65] Given her sympathy, and the fact that little was to be obtained from Jewish Municipal Reformers, this strategy was understandable – but hardly calculated to result in reforms. Nettie's own deep and publicly-expressed sense of outrage at the scholarships policy made her a heroine in the eyes of Anglo-Jewry but politically, in Central Hackney, did her much damage. In 1925 the former arrangement between Progressives and Municipal Reformers, under which she had shared the representation of the division with one of the leading Municipal Reformers, William Ray, came to an end. Ray was by this time the vice-chairman of the LCC's Education Committee, 'whose policy [the local paper declared] he had helped to shape'.[66]

Though offered a continuation of the 1922 arrangement, Nettie could not bring herself to share a platform with one whose policies she had come to detest.[67] Unofficially the Board of Deputies lent its name to appeals for assistance in the conduct of her campaign.[68] But this contest – filled with the rhetoric of class warfare – was in truth one that no amount of personal canvassing or charisma could win. She was beaten into fifth place behind the Municipal Reformers and two Labour contestants.

This was not quite the end of her political career in London. In 1928 she again stood for the Progressives. The over-enthusiasm of some Conservatives in their promulgation of anti-Jewish philosophies proved, this time, to be their undoing. At the start of the campaign the *Hackney Gazette* fulminated against the presence in the borough of 30,000 'Jewish and other aliens', turning the area into 'a sort of Middle East', depriving locals of jobs and decent housing.[69] An anonymous but widely-circulated leaflet called upon electors not to vote for the Progressives as 'they are supporting the Jews'.[70] This propaganda was generally acknowledged to have inflicted great damage on the Conservative cause, perhaps by triggering substantial abstentions among potential Jewish supporters of the Municipal Reform programme.[71] Although Ray again topped the poll, his running mate (Lord Cranbrook) was beaten into second place by Nettie, who entered thus upon a final three-year period as a London County Councillor.

In 1931 the Municipal Reformers made certain that their campaign was above reproach; Lord Jessel and Isadore Salmon were brought into the Central Hackney division as guarantors, so to speak, that this was to be so.[72] The Labour Party chose as one of its candidates Dr Bernard Homa, grandson of a famous East End rabbi and already well-known himself in the area. Nettie did not quite come bottom of the poll, but the margin of her defeat was roughly a third greater than in 1925, and, sensing, no doubt, that the credibility of Liberalism in London politics had been ground down between the forces of Toryism and Labourism, she decided not to stand again. Without her, the Liberals of Central Hackney concluded in 1934 that 'it would not be worth while putting up a fight'.[73] In a straight contest with the Reformers, Bernard Homa and his 'Socialist' fellow candidate won a comfortable victory.

The chronicle of Nettie Adler's tenure of the Central Hackney division is, primarily, a testament to the remarkable abilities and political courage of an outstanding Jewess – the first Jewess to achieve national prominence in a political sphere in Britain, and a social worker and educationalist of international repute. But, in the particular socio-economic milieu that Hackney presented in the 1920s and 1930s, it is difficult to avoid the conclusion that her Jewishness, though sometimes an asset, was just as often a source of difficulty and sensitivity. Unlike other Jewish Progressives and

Liberals (for example, Eleanor Nathan on the LCC and her husband Major H. L. Nathan and Barnett Janner at the parliamentary level),[74] Nettie refused to desert to the Labour camp. Progressivism did not win for her the victory of 1928; it was she who won this victory for herself, but in the name of the Progressive cause.

Of the five Progressives returned in 1928, three were Jewish. We must now turn to a very brief examination of the careers of the remaining two, Eleanor Nathan and Percy Harris. Eleanor Joan Nathan (1892–1972) was a daughter of Carl Stettauer. Her marriage (in 1919) to Harry Nathan, elected as Liberal MP for Bethnal Green North-East in 1929 and 1931, inaugurated a partnership of two people strongly committed to the ideal of communal service on behalf of Anglo-Jewry, more especially in the East End. In 1924 Harry Nathan had unsuccessfully fought Whitechapel for the Liberals, conducting a campaign in which his religious affiliation was given great prominence.[75] In June 1926 he was adopted as Liberal candidate at Bethnal Green North-East; his wife won an LCC seat in the same constituency in 1928 and again in 1931.

In this period of her career 'Nellie' Nathan seems to have relied as much on the memory of her father as on the fame of her husband (already a prominent Zionist) in building up local support.[76] Her 1928 victory (she obtained almost twice as many votes as the unsuccessful Labour candidates) was creditable not least because it was one of only three Liberal gains at the election.[77] But Nellie's hold on her Bethnal Green seat must not be put in the same class as Nettie Adler's tenure of Central Hackney. Behind Mrs Nathan's victory in 1928, and Colonel Nathan's parliamentary victory of 1929, there lay a story of popular revolt against the policies of a borough council dominated, at that time, by an uneasy coalition of Labourites and Communists.[78] In November 1928, as the beneficiaries of this revulsion, the Liberals made a clean sweep of every seat on the borough council; one of their first acts was to reverse a decision to name a housing estate after Lenin, and they also ceased placing council advertisements in political newspapers (following complaints that these were nothing more than thinly disguised subsidies to the leftwing press).[79]

At the General Election of 1929 Harry Nathan succeeded in doing what no other Liberal candidate in London managed to achieve, by winning a seat from Labour. The Nathan dominance of Bethnal Green North-East was confirmed in 1931, when Nellie retained her LCC seat in a straight fight with Labour while, later in the year, Harry was comfortably returned as the local National Liberal MP. By this time Nellie had made a reputation for herself as a housing expert; her interventions in County Hall debates on this subject were timely and pertinent.[80] She also acquired considerable expertise in the fields of education and juvenile delinquency. But though she continued to accumulate positions of honour within Anglo-Jewry, she possessed neither the magnetism of Nettie Adler nor the crusading zeal of Miriam Moses, who had in 1931 become 'Independent' (but actually Progressive) Mayor of Stepney in the face of Labour protests.[81]

Nor can it be honestly said that, as a Progressive member of the LCC, Nellie Nathan made any special effort to defend Jewish interests; we do not find her being consulted or used by the Board of Deputies as Nettie Adler had been. The fate of the Nathan hegemony at Bethnal Green North-East was in any case sealed in 1934. In March Nellie lost her LCC seat to Labour by the uncomfortably large margin of 6,410 votes to 4,320. Four months later, reading the omens presented both by this result and by Labour's capture of the County Council, husband and wife defected to the Labour Party.[82] In March 1937 Nellie was returned to the LCC as a Labour member for Wandsworth Central (just a month before Harry became Labour MP for the same division) and it was as a Labour member of the LCC (1937–49) that she became (1947–8) its first woman chairman.[83]

Although Nellie Nathan served in London government until the 1960s (she was a member of the Education Committees of the LCC and the Inner London Education Authority from 1939 to 1967), the last surviving example of the Jewish attachment to Progressivism was provided by Percy Harris (1876–1952) who sat for the neighbouring South-West division of Bethnal Green from 1907 until 1934 and again from 1946 until 1949, and then for the amalgamated Bethnal Green seat from 1949 until just before his death. Percy Harris was an ambitious politician who used his success in local government as a springboard to greater things: he sat as Liberal MP for Harborough during the period 1916–18 and for Bethnal Green South-West between 1922 and 1945. From 1935 he was Liberal Chief Whip in the Commons, and from 1940 Deputy Leader of the Party.

Harris's continued hold of his parliamentary seat even after he had lost the LCC division in 1934 affords a clue to his success. He was, in the truest sense of the phrase, a good constituency MP, and had had the sense to grasp at the outset of his LCC career that housing was and was going to remain the dominant issue in the Bethnal Green neighbourhood. In the 1930s Bethnal Green achieved some notoriety as an area where support for the British Union of Fascists was strong, and one of the BUF's earliest East End branches was established there.[84] Bethnal Green has indeed been identified as a 'locational centre' of East End racism throughout the twentieth century.[85] While these essential truths cannot be doubted, Percy Harris's career is a reminder of the Liberal context in which they must be placed: an area of Fascist strength continued to return a Liberal Member of Parliament, and one, moreover, whose father had been an honorary officer of the New West End Synagogue.[86]

It would be false, however, to conclude from this that Harris was active, either locally or nationally, in promoting Jewish causes or defending Jewish interests. In his pursuit of housing and educational matters he was generally indifferent to any special claims that the Jews of Bethnal Green – or of London – might have had. When, in December 1932, Nettie Adler (now no longer a county councillor and therefore feeling freer, perhaps, to speak her mind) published in the *Jewish Chronicle* an outspoken condemnation of the anti-alien housing policies of the Municipal Reformers, she was supported by fellow Liberals Miriam Moses, Barnett Janner, and Ida Samuel, but from Percy Harris there was total silence.[87] His autobiography contains not a single reference to Jews or Jewish issues.[88] When he died, the *Jewish Chronicle* paid him a fulsome tribute but recorded that his funeral service was held at St Nicholas' Church, Chiswick.[89]

Throughout the 1920s, therefore, while London Jewry was confronted by a suspicious and at times downright hostile administration at County Hall, the Progressive Party could offer it little more than sympathy. Even from Nettie Adler, many of whose efforts were behind the scenes, necessarily shielded from public view, the response was muted; as noted above, her major outburst against Municipal Reform policy came when she was no longer active in LCC politics, and therefore ran no risk of alienating voters less concerned than she with the welfare of the Jewish community. Of the three areas of concern – scholarships, employment, and housing – the Municipal Reformers were only persuaded to make very limited modifications to the first two. That they did so at all was due to the efforts of the Labour Party and, in particular, of one of the first Jewish Labour members of the County Council, Morris ('Morry') Davis, whose extraordinary career coincided with the golden age of Jewish Labourism in London.

The origins of Jewish Labourism, however, predated the formation of the London Labour Party in May 1914.[90] Until the arrival of the immigrants of the 1880s and 1890s, Jewish Socialism in London was confined to a small band of intellectuals and semi-intellectuals, of whom Aaron Lieberman, who founded the very short-lived Hebrew Socialist Union in Spitalfields in 1876, was the best known.[91] A variety of reasons have been put forward for the failure of Lieberman's brainchild. Lieberman's anti-bourgeois and anti-clerical views – indeed his outright atheism – found few supporters within the existing East End Jewish community; the man himself, like many romantics, was hopelessly uncompromising and lacking in realism. Basically, however, although there were plenty of poor Jews in the London of the 1870s, there was really nothing corresponding to the sort of manual working class – or Marxist proletariat – upon whom Socialist teachings might have had some positive effect.

The Jews who came to London in the wake of the Russian pogroms supplied this essential ingredient. In the Pale of Settlement in Russia and Poland there existed at the end of the nineteenth century a flourishing, militant Jewish trade union movement.[92] Many of the unions owed their inception to Socialists, who at a famous meeting in Vilna in October 1897 founded 'The General Jewish Labour Alliance in Russia, Poland and Lithuania'. The Bund, as it was popularly known, was anti-Zionist. Bundists played a prominent part in the Russian Social Democratic Labour Party, and their ideology was thoroughly Marxist.[93]

The organization of a Socialist-Zionist party took somewhat longer to work out. Theodor Herzl's summoning of the first Zionist Congress at Basle on 29 August 1897 was predicated, *inter alia*, upon the view that socio-economic class would have no significant impact upon the movement he had founded. In London, indeed, Herzl found much more support from amongst working-class than bourgeois Jews. In the autumn of 1898 he announced to a packed meeting at the Great Assembly Hall, Mile End, that 'The East End is ours.'[94] In January 1899 the English Zionist Federation was launched, a largely working-class body with middle-class leaders. But in Russia class antagonism within the Russian Zionist Organization resulted in the secession of the proletarian Zionist groups and in the formation, in 1906, of 'Poale Zion', the Jewish Social Democratic Labour Party.[95]

The immigrants who were to comprise the Jewish proletariat in the East End of London and in other areas of settlement, such as Manchester and Leeds, thus brought with them two broad Socialist ethics, Bundist and Zionist. The Bundist strain, strictly-speaking anti-Zionist though often in practice merely non-Zionist, sought to carve out for the Jewish working classes a particular ethnic role within the wider international struggle against capitalism. In London the Bundists found a gifted advocate in the person of Morris Winchevsky (the pseudonym of L. Benzion Novochovitch, who had 'dropped-out' from the famous Vilna Rabbinical Seminary); in April 1885 Winchevsky had established the *Arbeter Fraint* ('Worker's Friend'), 'to spread true socialism among Jewish workers'. In June 1886 publication of this, the major Yiddish Socialist newspaper in Britain, was taken over by the International Workers' Educational Club, whose premises, at 40 Berner Street, off the Commercial Road, became the meeting place for every sort of radically orientated Jewish immigrant in London. Similar clubs were established in the other major centres of Jewish immigrant settlement in Britain.[96]

It was through the medium of the Berner Street Club that the first contacts took place between Jewish workers and English Socialists. The Club was visited by William Morris, Herbert Burrows, Harry Quelch, and H. M. Hyndman, the last three of whom spoke at public meetings of an East End (Jewish) branch of the Social Democratic Federation, organized in the mid-1880s.[97] It must be presumed that links of this sort helped to direct immigrant Jewish Socialists into the mainstream of the British Labour movement, especially since the Social Democratic Federation was one of the founding organizations, in 1900, of the Labour Representation Committee, which in 1906 became the Labour Party. But, colourful though they were, the 'Berner

Streeters' themselves were still a small group, subject to almost ceaseless internal squabbling. In April 1891 the Club, by a vote of twenty-five to twenty-two (the very low numbers voting are themselves significant), decided to embrace an anarchist position; this extended to the *Arbeter Fraint*, sales of which rapidly dwindled. The Club left its Berner Street premises and began 'a period of wandering through the meeting rooms of London'.[98]

For a decade or so thereafter the major contacts between the Jewish and English working-class movements took place at trade-union level. Although there are examples of very small Jewish trade unions existing in London before the 1880s,[99] it was the flood of immigrants at the end of the century that provided a wholly new impetus for union activities. The most impressive area of early growth was that of the Leeds ghetto, where authentic Jewish trade unionism took a firm hold after 1885, and where the Jewish Tailors', Machinists' and Pressers' Union was regularly represented at Trades Union Congresses; this union became an early affiliate of the Labour Representation Committee.[100]

In London, where the work of Jewish trade-union activists was more closely watched over by the leadership of Anglo-Jewry, growth was slower and less impressive. In 1889 the leadership of the East End garment workers was taken over by Lewis Lyons, an English-born machinist who had once been a contributor to the *Arbeter Fraint*. He and some fellow social democrats campaigned against the evils of the sweating system, and in the early summer organized a strike for a twelve-hour day. The strike evinced widespread sympathy and support; non-Jewish trade unions contributed to the strike fund, and so did Lord Rothschild and Samuel Montagu. Montagu's intervention persuaded the masters to agree to the demands of the workers, on condition that the latter did not bring up the question of wages for one year.[101]

This victory was, however, short-lived. With unemployment rife, wages depressed, and new immigrants arriving daily looking for work, a permanent solution to the evils of sweating was to be attained not primarily by trade-union activity but through parliamentary action. This did not take place until the passage of the Liberal government's Trade Boards Act in 1909.

It is of course very likely that the realization that the way ahead in this matter lay through parliamentary activity acted as an encouragement to Jewish workers to involve themselves in Labour politics. Lewis Lyons was a member of the Executive Committee of the London Trades Council which, in 1891, determined to establish its own political party, the Labour Representation League, in order to contest School Board and LCC elections. In 1914 the Executive Committee of the London Labour Party included Joe Fineberg and Dr Marion Phillips, who in 1929 became the first Jewess to be elected to Parliament.[102] But while we must acknowledge the role of the early Jewish trade unions in bringing together immigrant Jews and English Socialists, we must keep the impact of these unions in its true perspective. In 1892 the *Arbeter Fraint* itself estimated that, of some 30,000 immigrant Jewish workers in London, only about 1,200 were members of Jewish unions.[103] Nor, in acknowledging as we must the efforts of both Jewish and non-Jewish Socialists in organizing the Jewish workers of east London, should we seek to argue that the strength of trade unionism reflected also the strength of Jewish Socialism. It did not.

Membership of Jewish Socialist organizations, certainly in the pre-war period, remained very small. In 1907 the Marxist Jacob Lestchinsky observed that the total number of Jewish Socialists in London amounted to no more than about 200, in a community of some 130,000 persons.[104] Prominent in supporting the great East End tailors' and garment workers' strikes of 1906 and 1912 were the anarchists, led by the charismatic Yiddish-speaking Gentile, Rudolf Rocker. But when, at the outbreak of war, Rocker was interned and the *Arbeter Fraint* suppressed, the Jews of east London did not rise up in protest.[105] In 1918 Rocker was repatriated to Germany, and of the colourful brand of East End Jewish anarchism that he had created nothing remained. Indeed, as the immigrant generation became anglicized even the need (often originally linguistic) for separate Jewish trade unions was called into question. The Jewish tailors' unions in London amalgamated with the Tailors' and Garment Workers' Trade Union, and the Leeds Jewish Tailors' Union followed suit in 1915.[106]

Bundism continued (and continues) to have its adherents, and news of the Bolshevik revolution gave it a new relevance. Most Bundists returned to Russia to celebrate the coming of a Socialist state there, and to take part in its defence. Joe Fineberg resigned his position as secretary of the Stepney branch of the British

Socialist Party (BSP) in order to take up employment in Lenin's administration.[107] Others, who stayed in Britain, found for themselves a route from anti- or non-Zionist Socialism, often via the BSP, to the Communist Party of Great Britain. But the Communist Party was not founded until 1920, and although negotiations for the affiliation of the Communists to the Labour Party were eventually to prove abortive (the Communists would not relinquish the option of revolution), this break was still some years away. In 1918 it was possible to believe in Socialism by revolution – if all else failed – and yet be a member of the Labour Party.

In the Jewish East End this was of special importance in helping to build bridges between Jewish and non-Jewish Socialists. Jews and Jewish trade unionists played a crucial role in the establishment of the Stepney Central Labour Party in June 1918.[108] The Party had a Jewish secretary, the formidable Oscar Tobin, Rumanian by birth, a chemist by training, and local organizer of the National Union of Shop Assistants.[109] It was to Tobin's chemist's shop in Harford Street, Mile End, that the young Major Clement Attlee repaired on his discharge from the Army, to learn the politics of the East End and, as it turned out, to take the first steps in his own political career. The formation of the Stepney Central Labour Party, and the entry into that body of the Limehouse Irish, were achievements in themselves, making Tobin 'the East End's most influential political "boss"' at that time.[110] They were also important milestones in the realization of Tobin's greater ambition, Labour control of Stepney Borough Council. In November 1919, never having held a single seat on the Stepney Council, Labour swept to power, wining forty-three seats out of sixty; Attlee became the borough's first Labour Mayor.

Although, therefore, the history of the Jewish presence in the East End during the First World War must be heavily inscribed with words of prejudice and hostility, there was another side to the story. It was during the war that the mass of East End Jewry was won over to the Labour cause. The mutual attraction took place at several distinct levels. The Municipal Reformers were, and (more importantly) were believed to be, anti-Jewish: the policies they initiated in the fields of education and employment were aimed primarily at East End Jews. Because of the electoral arrangements operated at County Council level, and because of their failure to protest more vigorously against these policies, the Progressives, too, were tainted by them.

Labour, by contrast, was absolutely untouched by the ignominy that such measures bestowed. Moreover, while it was certainly the case that, in the pre-war period, some trade unions and trade-union leaders had evinced hostility towards Jewish immigrants[111] (another justification for the existence of Yiddish-speaking, Jewish unions), during the First World War a remarkable transformation had taken place. The War Emergency Workers' National Committee, set up by the Labour Party shortly after the outbreak of hostilities, actively interested itself in cases of anti-Jewish discrimination by East End poor-relief committees.[112] Jewish resistance to enforced conscription in the Tsar's army aroused some sympathy, especially from the Labour movement's pacifist wing.[113] Jewish trade unionists became office-holders in non-Jewish unions and, in this way, came to be selected for municipal elections.

Before 1914 there is only one verifiable instance of a Jew standing for election to a London borough council in the Labour interest, namely the candidature of Lewis Lyons at Stepney in 1912.[114] But in 1919 Jewish Labour candidates were commonplace. The Jewish union activist Isaac Sharp, local secretary to both the Bakers' Union and the Boot and Shoe Operatives, was put up by Stepney Labour Party for the March LCC elections in the combined Mile End and Stepney division; though unsuccessful (there was a straight fight between the two Labour men and two Municipal Reformers, the Progressives having agreed to stand down), Sharp managed to win the backing of the local Yiddish newspaper *Di Tsait*, chiefly on the grounds of his opposition to the LCC's scholarships policy.[115] In November ten of the candidates put up by Labour for the Stepney Borough Council elections were Jews, including Alfred Valentine, formerly a Progressive borough councillor and president of the Whitechapel and Spitalfields Costermongers' Union.[116]

Additionally, after 1918 two special factors operated to bring Labour and Jewry together in east London. The first was Zionism. More important in the long term than the Jewish sections of the Social Democratic Federation was the establishment of the Poale Zion movement in Britain; scarcely less important were the roots that Poale Zion put down in the world of Jewish trade unionists.

By November 1903 two branches of Poale Zion had been formed in London, one under the auspices of the garment workers, the other in connection with the Independent Cabinet Makers' Union.[117] In February 1904 the movement in London opened permanent headquarters in Whitechapel Road.[118]

In the 1880s and 1890s the leaders of Anglo-Jewry saw Jewish Socialism (often equated with and described as atheism) as a stigma, something to be suppressed if possible and, if not, to be belittled and hidden from public view. During the 1914–18 war this attitude changed. Once the Labour Party had entered Asquith's Coalition government in 1915, the Labour proclivities of immigrant Jewry came to be seen as a force for assimilation rather than for separatism. The events of 1917 were a watershed. The ousting of D. L. Alexander from the presidency of the Board of Deputies (see p. 65) marked in some measure the triumph of the immigrant generations over the old Anglo-Jewish gentry; the promulgation of the Balfour Declaration marked (the protests of the gentry notwithstanding) the triumph of Zionism as a major Anglo-Jewish creed. Poale Zion was already at work popularizing Zionism within trade unions and among Labour politicians. It claimed some credit for the insertion (in the War Aims Memorandum approved in December 1917 by a special conference of the Labour Party and the Trades Union Congress) of a paragraph supportive of Jewish claims to settlement in Palestine.[119]

On the eve of the December 1918 General Election Poale Zion issued a manifesto urging Jewish voters to vote Labour.[120] As I have argued elsewhere, the impact of this appeal is difficult to assess, partly because polling took place on a Saturday.[121] In trying to make an assessment of the popularity of Labour Zionism on London municipal politics the difficulties are greater still. The franchise reform of 1918 gave the parliamentary vote to many Jewish immigrants for the first time: the suffrage, hitherto linked to the payment of rates, was bestowed henceforth upon men on the basis of six months' residence and upon women, over 30 years of age, if they were local government electors. At the parliamentary level, there can be little doubt that a new Jewish electorate, substantially Labour in its outlook was ushered into existence.[122]

At local-government level the situation was more complex. The 1918 legislation had extended the right to vote in local elections to those who had for a period of six months occupied premises either as owners or tenants, and to the spouses of those who fulfilled these conditions. This formula excluded those who lived with their parents, women under 30 years of age who were not owners or tenants in their own right, and lodgers in furnished rooms. The great impact made at parliamentary elections in and after 1918 by the limited grant of the franchise to women was not, therefore, replicated at municipal polls, in which women could already participate; at the same time exclusion of those who occupied furnished rooms was bound to act as a bar against many Jewish couples exercising the municipal suffrage.

The differential effects of the 1918 provisions on the size of the local and parliamentary electorates in the LCC area may be deduced from the fact that whereas in 1913–14 a greater proportion of the population of the County of London could vote locally than for Members of Parliament (17.4 per cent compared with 14.9 per cent), by 1919 the position had been reversed: only 37.6 per cent of London's population could vote locally, as against 43.7 per cent at parliamentary elections.[123] In east London differences of a similar order of magnitude are apparent. In Bethnal Green 38.2 per cent could vote for MPs but only 33.7 per cent for borough and county councillors; in Stepney the figures were 30 per cent and 25 per cent; in Hackney they were 36.4 per cent and 35.5 per cent – the much narrower gap here reflecting the comparative affluence of Hackney's inhabitants.

Qualitative evidence suggests that by the early 1920s a substantial portion of the east London Jewish vote was being cast in favour of the Labour Party, to which Poale Zion became formally affiliated in 1920.[124] In November 1922 Whitechapel, the premier Jewish parliamentary constituency, returned for the first time a (Roman Catholic) Labour MP.[125] The previous March Whitechapel and St George's had returned a Labour candidate at the top of the LCC poll; we have already noted how Morry Davis (co-opted onto Stepney Borough Council as an Alderman in 1920) failed by only eighty-seven votes to capture the other LCC Whitechapel seat in the Labour interest. As a result of the December 1923 parliamentary poll, the East End constituencies, with the solitary exception of Bethnal Green South-West, were, according to the *East London Observer*, 'now solid for Labour, and so far as most people can see are likely to remain so'.[126] Fifteen months later the first Jewish Labour candidates were returned to County Hall. By 1934 the Labour contingent comprised over half the Jewish total on the LCC; it was with them that the defence of Jewish interests at County Hall now came increasingly to reside.

Chapter Four

COUNTY HALL UNDER LABOUR: A FRIENDSHIP UNFULFILLED

From 1934 until its supersession by the Greater London Council the LCC was ruled by Labour. The Jewish lobby at County Hall remained, throughout this period, very strongly Labour in composition. The aggregate position is summarized in the Appendix, but these statistics scarcely do justice to the personal impact and importance of the Jewish Labour presence. The period before the Second World War was dominated by Jewish Labourites of moderate disposition, prominent amongst whom were Dan Frankel, Bernard Homa, Santo Jeger, Lewis Silkin, and George Strauss. Frankel (1900–88), a founder of the Stepney Labour Party, represented Mile End on the County Council from 1931 to 1946, and at Westminster between 1935 and 1945; he was also a Stepney borough councillor, and Mayor of Stepney 1928–9. Homa (b.1900) and Jeger (1898–1953) were both popular local general practitioners. Homa's capture of the Central Hackney division in 1934 was noted in the previous chapter; he held this seat until 1949, and from then until 1955 represented Hackney South. In 1951 and again in 1955 Homa tried unsuccessfully to win for Labour the heavily Jewish Hendon South parliamentary constituency.[1]

Santo Wayburn Jeger, whose brother George was Labour MP for Goole, was a founder of the Socialist Medical Association; elected to the Shoreditch Borough Council in 1925 (and Mayor of Shoreditch 1929–30 and 1937–8), he represented Shoreditch on the LCC from 1931 to 1946 and was MP for St Pancras South-East in 1945–50 and for Holborn and St Pancras from 1950 until his death.[2] Lewis Silkin (1889–1972) sat on the County Council for Southwark South-East from 1925 to 1946. George Strauss's membership of the LCC also dated from 1925, and he was Silkin's partner at Southwark South-East from 1932. Both were prominent Labour MPs (Silkin sat for Peckham 1936-50) and colleagues of Herbert Morrison. Silkin, an expert on housing, became one of Morrison's closest confidants at County Hall, was the first Labour chairman of its Housing Committee, and occupied the chair of its Town and Country Planning Committee during the Second World War; Strauss was elected in 1934 the chairman of the LCC's Highways Committee.[3]

As fully identifying members of the Jewish community (though only Homa was practising orthodox) these men were all at one time or another able to be of service to London Jewry in the municipal sphere. None, however, had the charisma or achieved the notoriety of Morry Davis (1894-1985), the Labour leader of Stepney Borough Council 1935-44 and from 1925 until 1945 LCC councillor for Whitechapel and St George's.[4] Davis's extraordinary career and impact can only be understood in the context of his position in the Federation of Synagogues, which during the 1920s was still the largest synagogal body in London, serving the needs of some 12,500 families, most of them still living in the East End. Born in Whitechapel to parents who made a comfortable living from the liquor trade, Davis (who never married) used some of the income derived thereby to launch himself into a communal and political career that was controversial from start to finish. He died a wealthy but disgraced member of the Anglo-Jewish community.[5]

An orthodox Jew, a Socialist, and a Zionist, Davis was also loudmouthed, precocious, intolerant, and 'a crook'.[6] These grave flaws in his character eventually proved to be his undoing, but they were not very apparent in 1925, when he rose to prominence as a leader of the revolt within the Federation against the presidency of Louis Montagu. The immigrant Jews who formed the backbone of the Federation had never forgiven Montagu either for his extreme anti-Bolshevism or for his virulent anti-Zionism; after 1919 he was tolerated mainly out of respect for his father's name and memory. Inquiries into the financial misdeeds of the Federation's secretary, Joseph Blank, brought matters to a head. Montagu took it upon himself to defend Blank, and thus sealed his own fate. On 25 November 1925 Morry Davis moved and carried a resolution at the Federation's Board of Delegates, to the effect that 'despite any rule or minute to the contrary ... at any meeting of the Federation, where any delegate desires to address the meeting in Yiddish, such permission be granted'.[7] Montagu admitted he could not understand Yiddish; his presidency thus came to an end. During 1926 Davis acted as chairman of Federation meetings, while, as a newly-elected treasurer of the Federation's burial society, he was instrumental in voting surplus funds for Zionist charities.

On 20 March 1928 Davis became president of the Federation. This event – the triumph of a popular local figure over a wealthy aristocrat – marked a turning-point in his political career. Once installed as lay leader of the Federation, Davis dispensed with its constitution; never during his entire presidency (sixteen years) was there an election, either for honorary officers or for the Board of Delegates. How was this remarkable feat achieved? To attribute it to apathy is to turn a blind eye to Davis's political skills. Davis pointed the Federation in directions in which its membership had wanted for some time to go. Under his aegis the Federation, freed from the paternalistic restraint of the Swaythling family, became totally committed to the Zionist cause, and generally adopted a much higher and much more assertive profile in the councils of Anglo-Jewry. After the advent of Nazism in Germany, for instance, the Board of Deputies consistently rejected calls for a communal boycott of German goods; but the Federation played a leading part in the formation of a Jewish Representative Council for the Boycott of German Goods and Services, which was inaugurated in November 1933.[8]

So Davis gave the Federation what its members undoubtedly wanted. But there was another side to this picture. Davis inherited from Oscar Tobin the realization that the key to the control of working-class politics in Stepney lay in co-operation with the Irish Roman Catholics; this alliance had been strengthened in the period 1916–22 by the shared hostility of both Jews and Irish in east London to the use made of the Defence of the Realm Act to deport Jews and (in the wake of the Easter 1916 Irish uprising) to imprison Irishmen without trial.[9] Davis cultivated the friendship of the leaders of Stepney's Catholic community, in particular Alderman Jack Sullivan, who nominated him as Mayor of Stepney in 1930, and later Jerry Long, whom Davis nominated as Mayor in 1937; by 1939 one opponent could refer, in truth, to the 'Davis–Long axis' that ran Stepney politics.[10] The need to preserve this alliance led Davis to adopt some strange postures.

Alienated by the anti-religious strain of Communist politics, and doubtless encouraged by the antisemitic tone prevalent in certain sections of the Catholic press, Irish elements in east London tended to support or at least sympathize with the aims of Fascism.[11] In February 1937, perhaps in deference to Irish pressures, Davis and three other Jewish councillors (Jacob Fine, Alfred Greenbaum, and Lewis Tanaman) voted to allow the British Union of Fascists to hold a meeting in Limehouse Town Hall.[12] During the tense atmosphere of 1936, when Fascist activity culminated in the legendary Battle of Cable Street (4 October), one of the most remarkable champions of Jewish rights locally had been the then Mayor, Helena Roberts. Councillor Roberts was Jewish by birth but Christian by conversion; in proportion as she sought to obtain a more even-handed approach by the police, so Davis seems to have taken umbrage against her – to the extent, in July 1938, of using a procedural device to prevent her proposing a committee of inquiry into allegations of police brutality against anti-Fascists.[13]

By the summer of 1938 the Stepney Labour Party was split on pro- and anti-Davis lines; at the same time voices within the Federation of Synagogues (including that of Bernard Homa) began to be raised against him.[14] But Davis appeared immovable. He and his three allies of February 1937 brought an action for libel against the *Jewish Chronicle*, and were gracious enough to accept merely token damages plus costs.[15] Those members of the Federation's General Council who were minded still to oppose him knew that he was accustomed to threaten increases in the rateable values of business premises in the borough; in this way many of his opponents were, it seems, cowed into silence.[16] In June 1939 a motion at the Federation, alleging that its constitution had been violated, was defeated by ninety-nine votes to seventy-eight.[17]

At Stepney Town Hall Davis weathered another storm, whipped up by allegations of inefficiency in relation to the provision of air-raid shelters, for which he (as official 'Air Raid Precautions Controller') was responsible.[18] Not only were the allegations well-founded; they were accompanied by strong rumours of bribery and corruption.[19] In October 1940 Herbert Morrison, now Minister of Home Security in Churchill's wartime coalition government, bowed to local pressure by stripping Davis of his Civil Defence role and appointing in his stead a Controller directly responsible to central government.[20]

The wartime emergency and the exodus of Jews from east London gave Davis absolute control of the Federation's affairs; at the same time it destroyed the environment in which his regime had flourished. The wartime anti-Communism of the Catholic priesthood in the East End drove a wedge between Jews and Irish, which inevitably affected the political stability of the Davis regime.[21] Yet this regime, battered and bruised though it was by the end of 1940, survived another four years. It was terminated, not by any political act, but through Davis's own criminal folly. In August 1944 he was involved in a bizarre incident in which he tried to avoid prosecution for alleged non-payment of a railway fare by making a false statement in order to procure the issue of a forged National Identity Card. Neither his position as Labour Leader on Stepney Council nor evidence as to his good character from Henry Berry, vice-chairman of the LCC, and Walter Edwards, the Labour MP for Stepney, could save him from a six months' prison sentence (24 November 1944).[22] There could have been no more appropriate end to his communal and political careers.

The Davis era had a profound effect upon the character of east London politics in the inter-war period, and upon the Jewish perception of those politics; in particular, it played an important part in forcing those Jews who were repelled by it or who were victims of it into support for the Communist party. But although, within the Federation, grave misgivings were voiced, neither the man, Morry Davis, nor the methods to which he and his friends resorted were ever publicly condemned by the communal organizations of Anglo-Jewry. Partly this was no doubt because of an instinctive reluctance to wash dirty linen in public; Davis held important positions, and if his character and his methods repulsed rather than attracted there was no denying that he supported a wide variety of communal and Zionist charities and causes. In the 1930s Anglo-Jewry was, understandably, much more concerned with events in Germany and Palestine than with the affairs of Stepney. But partly the reluctance to condemn arose from the fact that Davis, whatever his faults, could on occasion be of supreme service to the community, sparing no effort to help others without wishing to take any credit for himself. In no sphere was this trait more evident than in his work within the LCC.

Within a few weeks of his election to the Council in 1925, Davis entered into a correspondence with the Board of Deputies on the question of the LCC's policy on scholarships for aliens.[23] The chances of this policy being modified did not at that time appear good; indeed, an attempt by Percy Harris, Nettie Adler, and others the previous year to have the regulation of 1918 relaxed had been defeated, even though, with the passage of time, the number of children adversely affected by it had naturally diminished.[24] In that year the number of such children amounted to only twenty-six, but the argument of William Ray, that to have given scholarships to these children (most of whom came from east London) would have meant excluding 'British' children, carried the day.[25]

The diminishing impact of the scholarships policy was used by Jewish Conservatives such as Isadore Salmon as an argument in favour of silence.[26] Davis was not impressed and, as a member of the Board of Deputies, and using some of the most blatant cases of hardship and injustice in which the policy had resulted, he began a campaign to swing official Anglo-Jewish opinion into a less docile frame of mind.[27] In January 1927 the Board agreed to send a deputation to the LCC to discuss the matter.[28] Meanwhile, evidence collected from other major education authorities in England revealed that only in Manchester was a policy similar to that of the LCC in force; even the government, in giving scholarships on the results of school examinations conducted by Oxford and Cambridge universities, did so without regard to place of birth.[29]

Although Davis and his allies (prominent among whom was Lewis Silkin) were in a minority at County Hall, at the Board of Deputies they were in a position to carry all before them. The continued irritation and anger that the matter aroused, more especially with the East End Jews, thus threatened the position of the leadership, which included Isadore Salmon (a treasurer of the United Synagogue) and Robert Waley Cohen (a vice-president). Towards the end of 1926 it is clear that contact was made with the London Municipal Society with the aim of defusing a situation fraught with danger not so much for London Conservatism as for the ability of anti-Socialist forces and non- and anti-Zionist forces to continue to dominate the Board of Deputies' proceedings.[30]

While the outright rescission of the 1918 regulation could not be contemplated, Conservatives at County Hall were prepared to replace the blanket prohibition encompassed within it by a policy of discretion. It was left to Nettie Adler to persuade Davis and Silkin that this was as much as could be achieved, and that 'there was a distinct risk of opposition, if more had been asked for and pressed'.[31] On 16 June 1928 the LCC's education officer notified the secretary of the Board of Deputies that the Council would be urged to delegate to its Education Committee the power to deal with each scholarship case on its merits, provided such applicants made reasonable efforts to secure naturalization. On 17 July, without discussion, the full Council adopted this policy.[32]

This limited softening of the Municipal Reform position was followed almost at once by another, in relation to employment. The impetus to change here derived largely from the difficulties experienced by the LCC's Education Department as a result of the prohibition on the employment, even in a temporary capacity, of foreign-born teachers, especially teachers of foreign languages.[33] Once again, however, there is evidence that behind-the-scenes contacts between the Board of Deputies and the London Municipal Society played a part in obtaining some redress.[34] In January 1928 the Council's General Purposes Committee determined to recommend that the LCC's policy only to employ natural-born British subjects be amended so as to permit the employment of naturalized subjects as well. On 4 December 1928 the full Council endorsed this proposal.[35]

This reform was of course welcomed by the Jewish community, but its passage had in truth owed little to specifically Jewish pressure; the LCC had merely fallen in with the policy of central government in relation to the civil service, and there was, indeed, some irritation at the Board of Deputies that no further progress in scrapping the scholarships policy was to be contemplated.[36] As with scholarships, the employment policy, as modified, was bound to affect a limited and diminishing number of people. The same could not be said of the housing policy of 1923.

As new LCC housing estates were brought into commission, the severity of this policy became all too evident.[37] In the Borough of Stepney by the early 1930s the alien (i.e. foreign-born and non-naturalized) population still amounted to 30,000 out of a total population of some 219,000.[38] Most of these foreigners were of course Jewish. As a result, the Aliens Committee of the Board of Deputies began to interest itself in the matter, prompted and assisted by Morry Davis, Nettie Adler, Ida Samuel, and Barnett Janner, elected in 1931 as Liberal MP for Whitechapel.[39] The policy of the LCC appeared to be legal.[40] No protest was entered against it. But what is more remarkable is that, even after Labour had gained control at County Hall, and with Lewis Silkin in place as chairman of its Housing and Public Health Committee, the policy (like that relating to scholarships) remained intact.[41] In March 1935, after an unsatisfactory meeting between Silkin and the Stepney Housing Committee, it was left to another Jewish Stepney councillor, Jacob Fine, to give expression to the immorality of a Labour-controlled LCC applying a Conservative policy on housing discrimination; Jerry Long seconded Fine's motion, which was carried unanimously.[42] At County Hall, however, Silkin brushed the Stepney protest aside; from Morry Davis there was not a word of protest.[43]

To understand why even Jewish Labour stalwarts should have been so muted in their response to LCC policies which they had lost no opportunity of condemning but a few years previously, we need to remind ourselves of the wider (though still primarily London-orientated) background against which housing policy had to be measured. To begin with, the advent of Nazism in Germany had created a new Jewish refugee problem, which antisemites were quick to exploit. Between 1933 and 1945 a total of up to 65,000 Jewish refugees from Nazism settled in Britain.[44] The fact that most of the Jews who entered Britain in the 1930s were educated professional people (the earliest victims of Nazi discrimination) did not help matters – indeed it brought about a dangerous new alliance between middle-class and working-class anti-Jewish prejudice.[45] For instance, at County Hall as early as October 1933 a Conservative (Alderman Eric Hall) could be found complaining that German-Jewish refugees, many of whom were alleged to be associated with 'extreme Communistic organisations in Germany', would in time become a burden on Public Assistance Funds.[46] In July 1935, more than a year after Labour had gained control of the LCC, the Council adopted a recommendation of its Public Assistance Committee that the government be asked to make permanent an Order under the 1919 Aliens Act allowing the deportation of destitute aliens.[47]

In north-west London, as we shall see, the presence of Jewish refugees brought to the surface a great deal of latent middle-class hostility to Jews as a whole.[48] In east London this prejudice found its classic outlet in support for Oswald Mosley's British Union of Fascists. The BUF's campaign against Anglo-Jewry became formal policy in the autumn of 1934. It did not contest the 1935 General Election, but put up candidates at the municipal elections two years later. To counter this threat the Board of Deputies developed the technique of supplying anti-Fascist election literature to candidates in the major political parties, who then distributed it as their own. Sidney Salomon, secretary of the Defence Committee of the Board of Deputies, later explained that 'the democratic parties opposing Fascist candidates were given such assistance as was necessary and, in addition, leaflets exposing the Fascist tactics were printed and circulated.... There was nothing to "tie up" the publication of these leaflets with the Defence Committee.'[49]

Politically, though it generated much short-term anger and violence, the BUF's participation in the 1937 LCC elections was an anti-climax. Six candidates were put up in three east London divisions (North-East Bethnal Green, Limehouse, and Shoreditch); not one was successful.[50] None the less, the fact that Fascist candidates were run at all, that the BUF could poll a respectable 23 per cent of the votes in Bethnal Green (with 19 per cent at Limehouse and 14 per cent at Shoreditch), and that the Fascist campaign had concentrated on the activities of Jewish employers, Jewish shopkeepers, Jewish landlords, and Jewish members of the LCC, all combined to reinforce the siege mentality that was already underpinning the Anglo-Jewish response to antisemitic manifestations.[51] For there could be no doubt that Mosley was exploiting grievances which, whether real or not, were genuinely held against the Jewish community of London.

The deep hostility of some Jewish employers towards trade unionism in London was a prime cause of animosity. Mosley's biographer has noted that many of the BUF's most prominent activists came from the furniture trade, where intense competition led to anti-union practices.[52] Commenting upon the poverty of men and women working in the furnishing trades in Bethnal Green, the Fascist *East London Pioneer* explained that

> during the past ten years Jews have obtained a monopoly of the business in East London. Unless the workers accept terms offered them they get no job.... Many voiced open criticism of

the Union. . . . It is paralysed because Jewish bosses employ outside labour whenever workers protest.[53]

This was not just Blackshirt propaganda. In July 1936 the Board of Deputies itself complained to the Jewish proprietor of one firm about physical harassment of members of the National Amalgamated Furnishing Trades Association (NAFTA) at its Tottenham works. The following February the president of the Board, Neville Laski, received from the Revd H. E. Lister, president of the Hackney Wick Workers' Club and Institute, a complaint that the Jewish Board of Guardians had been supplying blackleg labour to a local Jewish-owned firm intent on 'resisting Trade Union organization'. On 20 March the same gentleman supplied a Jewish friendly society with the names of a further two Jewish firms in the furnishing trade that were refusing to grant trade-union recognition; 'there is [he warned] danger of a serious outbreak of Anti-Semitic feeling'. In May the Board of Deputies received an official complaint from NAFTA that a Jewish employer had repudiated an agreement previously made with it. In October a Jewish-owned upholstery firm in Tottenham dismissed employees who had joined the Amalgamated Union of Upholsterers.[54]

In relation to industrial disputes such as these, the Board of Deputies did what it could to dampen the anti-union ardour of such Jewish employers as would listen to it. In particular, the Board used its influence with some of the large, Jewish-owned retail hire-purchase furniture stores to persuade them to compel factory owners to adopt a more generous wages policy and to recognize appropriate trade unions.[55] Beyond that it could not go.[56] But in so far as complaints against Jewish shopkeepers were concerned, the Board acquired some muscle, in the context of the vexed question of Sunday trading.

This matter was not new. In 1911 the then president of the Board, D. L. Alexander, had chaired a protest meeting, estimated at over 6,000, at Mile End in connection with a Sunday Closing of Shops Bill then before Parliament; Jewish MPs were mobilized and, as a result, London and West Ham, together with parts of Leeds, Liverpool, and Manchester, were excluded from the major prohibition proposed in the legislation, which did not, however, reach the statute book.[57] As early as 1871 the Jewish community had obtained for Jewish employers and employees the right to work on Sundays if they did not do so on Saturdays (the Sunday Work of Jews Act). The right to be able to trade on Sunday providing the Jewish Sabbath (roughly sunset Friday to sunset Saturday) was observed was one that was highly prized by orthodox immigrants. By the non- or not-so-orthodox, however, the ability to trade on Sundays as well as Saturdays was, in the course of time, exploited in such a manner as to threaten to bring the community into disrepute.

The Sunday trading problem, as it developed in the inter-war period, was almost exclusively a London problem, and a Jewish problem. The collapse of the Christian Sunday, hedged about with sabbatarian strictures and enforced by means of the Sunday Observance Act of 1677, was slowest in rural areas (in which, to some extent, it still thrives), much faster in towns, and fastest of all in the metropolis where, even by the mid-nineteenth century, several Sunday street markets (including Petticoat Lane) flourished to serve the needs of the many working-class citizens who worked long hours six days a week and who were often not paid until late on Saturday nights.[58] Jews who operated in these markets and their environs could claim in truth that they were fulfilling a general social need as well as the more limited needs of their co-religionists.[59]

In 1930 Parliament had enacted the Hairdressers' and Barbers' Shops (Sunday Closing) Act, to bring such premises within the general prohibition on Sunday trading. Clause 3 of this legislation, inserted at the behest of the Board of Deputies but in the face of overt opposition from non-Jews, made special provision for Jewish barbers and hairdressers, who could operate on Sunday if they closed on Saturday; but the Act omitted to provide machinery for the policing of this concession.[60] It was not long before the LCC's Public Control Committee began to receive complaints that the concession was being abused, and on 12 July 1934 the Committee expressed the view that Clause 3 be repealed.[61] Representations by the Committee to the Board of Deputies led Neville Laski, Barnett Janner, and Bernard Homa (by now a member of the Public Control Committee) to summon a meeting (6 December 1934) of Jewish hairdressers and barbers within the LCC area, in an attempt to put a stop to abuse of the 1930 Act and so avoid legislation.[62]

Although this meeting had been private, the subject had already been aired in the London press and it was not long before Laski and other communal leaders abandoned secrecy in appealing to the hairdressing fraternity to avoid action that could be – and was, indeed, already being – exploited by the Fascists.[63] These appeals appear to have largely fallen upon deaf ears. In any case, by 1935 the hairdressing problem had become subsumed within the much wider issue of Sunday trading generally. A deputation received by the LCC's Public Control Department in December 1935 included representatives not merely from various hairdressing lobbies but also from the National Amalgamated Union of Shop Assistants, who clearly hoped to enlist the sympathy and support of a Labour-controlled County Council in their attempt to have Sunday trading generally within the London area put under much tighter control.[64]

The combined pressures generated by shopworkers, retail traders, and latter-day sabbatarians proved irresistible. In 1936, under the auspices of the Early Closing Association, a Shops (Sunday Trading Restriction) Bill was introduced from the parliamentary backbenches and quickly passed into law; neither the government, nor the LCC, nor the Board of Deputies dared to resist it.[65] Although some London MPs (Percy Harris, George Strauss, Dan Frankel, and James Hall, the non-Jewish Labour MP elected for Whitechapel in 1935) tried to argue the case for sensible Sunday trading, they did so without much backing from within the Jewish community.[66] Strongly influenced by the advice of Bernard Homa, who had warned that action was needed to stem the tide of anti-Jewish feeling, the Board focused exclusively upon the need to protect the interests of those Jews who conscientiously objected on religious grounds to trading on the Jewish Sabbath.[67]

For the Sabbath-observant Jew, the Act eventually provided that, upon registration with the appropriate local authority, trading up to 2 p.m. on Sunday was to be permitted, provided there was no trading from the onset of the Sabbath on Friday and all day Saturday, even after the Sabbath had terminated; doubtful cases could (once evidence had been collected) be referred to a special 'Jewish Tribunal', serviced and funded by the Board of Deputies but technically appointed by the Home Secretary.[68] Sunday trading up to 2 p.m. was also permitted henceforth in respect of customary street markets in the City of London, Bethnal Green, Shoreditch, and Stepney. The 1936 Act (now incorporated within the 1950 Shops Act) was hastily considered and inadequately drafted; it has proved a lawyers' paradise.[69] But in the atmosphere of escalating Fascist propaganda and violence in London in the spring and early summer of 1936, culminating in the Battle of Cable Street there could be no question of opposing it in principle, or of arguing for the repeal of unworkable provisions.

In the aftermath of Cable Street, Neville Laski secretly met Herbert Morrison and Harry Pollitt, secretary of the Communist Party, and accepted their analysis that the Jewish business community had, by its professional conduct, contributed much to anti-Jewish feeling in the East End.[70] In May 1937 Laski was given much the same message by Louis Rabinowitz, Rabbi of the Cricklewood Synagogue, who charged that the 'disgraceful attitude' of Jewish traders towards the 1936 legislation 'forms in my opinion an unanswerable argument in favour of Fascist allegations'.[71] Barnett Janner's deliberate and public wooing of Jewish voters in his unsuccessful attempt to retain Whitechapel for the Liberals at the General Election of 1935 (an attempt to which Morrison and Pollitt had also drawn Laski's attention) had made an equally lasting impression. In October 1936 two prominent Stepney Jews (Alderman Alfred Kershaw and Councillor Fine) were prevailed upon not to allow their names to go forward for nomination as Mayor.[72]

The anti-union proclivities of some Jewish employers, and the cavalier attitude with which some Jewish retailers treated the Sunday trading laws, mirrored the conduct of very many non-Jews as well, of course. But in the charged and difficult atmosphere of the late 1930s the communal leadership did not feel inclined to point any accusing finger at the application of double standards. At the fashionable St John's Wood Synagogue, in May 1939, Neville Laski condemned 'the price-cutting activities of some Jewish traders in the tobacco, grocery, cosmetic, and chemistry businesses', but added that 'it was no use replying ... that there were non-Jewish price-cutters. He knew there were. But Jews must not trade in this way.'[73]

This 'low-profile' policy extended naturally into the housing question. The allegation that Jewish households displaced Gentile families had originally concerned the East End alone, but as Jews moved into Bethnal Green, Hackney, and Stoke

Newington the accusation followed them like a shadow.[74] The obligation to offer housing accommodation to aliens affected by slum-clearance schemes continued to be raised at County Hall, but Jewish agitation at the continued existence of discriminatory provisions in LCC housing policy generally was allowed to subside.[75] After 1935 we hear no more of official or officially-inspired efforts to have this policy rescinded. In the East End Jewish activists, such as Michael Shapiro and 'Tubby' Rosen, were prominent in the Stepney Tenants' Defence League (formed 1937), which soon acquired a reputation for 'direct action' – especially rent strikes – against unscrupulous landlords (many of whom were also Jewish, of course).[76] But the Board of Deputies kept well away from such activity. Similarly, while the Board urged Jews not to do battle with the BUF, a miscellany of synagogues, Jewish trade unions, Socialist societies, and branches of the Workers' Circle Friendly Society came together to establish the Jewish People's Council (July 1936), to pursue a highly popular policy of co-operation with the Communist Party and street confrontation with the Fascists.[77]

During the late 1930s it is clear that the official organs of Anglo-Jewry did not possess the confidence of the Jews of east London. The very transitory phenomenon of Jewish support for Communism – symbolized by the election of the Jew Phil Piratin as the lone Communist Stepney borough councillor (representing the largely Jewish Spitalfields East ward) in 1937 and later as Communist MP for Mile End, in 1945 – was one result of such alienation. In assessing the strength and significance of this identity we must be careful to distinguish between membership of the Communist Party and support for particular Communists and pieces of Communist policy. I have calculated elsewhere that about half of Piratin's 1945 vote (roughly 2,500) came from Jews. In Stepney, in 1945, it is possible that as much as a third of the Communist membership was Jewish.[78]

But this support was grounded in the common struggle of the western allies and the USSR against Hitler, and the memories of Communist leadership in the anti-Fascist activities in the East End in the 1930s; for the Communist Party alone had taken the BUF seriously from the start, and the Communist Party alone appeared to have possessed the organizational expertise and determination necessary to fight Fascism and at the same time to deal with the social evils (pre-eminently housing) upon which Fascism fed.[79] The high profile adopted by Jewish Communists (such as Sam Elsbury and David Cohen) who organized many East End trade-union branches in the 1920s and 1930s also paid dividends; Communists were seen as people who evinced a genuine concern for Jewish needs, and who matched words with deeds.[80] 'It is not the Jews who made the East End "Red"', William Zuckerman noted in 1937, 'but the East End, which during the last generation ... made the Jew "Red".'[81] The essential truth of Piratin's later explanation, that 'Only the Communist Party stood out as the forthright opponent of fascism', is reflected in the observations of Basil Henriques, warden of the Bernhard Baron Jewish Settlement, and J. J. Mallon, warden of Toynbee Hall.[82] Jews supported Communism at this time because to do so was a visible and practical sign of self-help and of rebellion against an over-docile communal leadership. While Dan Frankel urged Jews to keep away from Fascist meetings, and generally to exercise restraint, even East End Jewish businessmen gave money to the Communist Party to help combat the Fascist menace.[83] As a result of this 'infatuation', Jewish support for the party was forthcoming in spite of its anti-Zionist stance.[84]

But we should note in this connection that the appeal of Zionism itself was emotional rather than political. D. Cesarani, the historian of inter-war Zionism in Britain, has concluded that, certainly during the 1930s, 'Zionism was in a state of collapse in the East End.' 'Zionism in England [he declares] flourished hardly anywhere once the initial enthusiasm which followed the Balfour Declaration gave way to the sober reality of fund-raising and political work for Palestine in an economic and political climate that favoured neither.'[85] The failure of the Zionist card that Barnett Janner played as the unsuccessful Liberal candidate in the Whitechapel by-election of November–December 1930 was indeed a straw in the wind.[86] Explaining the situation to Lloyd George during that contest, Gareth Jones (his political aide) told him that 'the Jews would like to hear something brief and personal about Palestine... they do *not* want the Government policy [the cessation of Jewish immigration to the Holy Land] to be attacked at length.... Many of them are not keen Zionists.'[87] A correspondent told the *Young Zionist* in December 1932 that among Jewish working-class young people Zionism 'has made no headway. The tendency in the best part of our Jewish working class . . . is to join the Communist Party.'[88] Writing of the period June 1936 Joe Jacobs, then secretary of the Stepney Communist Party, observed that 'The Jews in East London were not yet in favour of Zionism. That is not to say that many Jews were not Zionists. The majority did not see this as a solution to their problems. They saw themselves as British Jews.'[89] Zionism did indeed come to have political significance for London Jewry, but not until after the commencement of the Second World War.

There was, however, one other factor that played, in the East End, a crucial role in pushing Jews into temporary support for Communism, namely the chronic divisions in the Stepney Labour Party resulting from Morry Davis's leadership of the party at borough council level. In the Stepney Council chamber Davis could count on the support of his Irish friends in dealing with those (like Tubby Rosen) who dared to criticize his policies on air-raid precautions.[90] But it was precisely because the Irish were so fiercely anti-Communist that Communist criticisms of the Davis regime went down so well with Jewish audiences. Irish support for Franco during the Spanish Civil War (1936–9) marked a watershed in the Jewish-Irish dialogue in east London. On the whole, East-End Jewry adopted a position sympathetic to the Spanish Republicans, whom the Irish viewed as anti-Catholic. The neutrality of the Irish Free State during the Second World War strengthened the Jewish view that the Irish had no desire to fight international Fascism.

Growing criticisms of Davis's communal leadership forced him to rely ever more closely upon Irish support; but in so doing he distanced himself still further from his Jewish clientele. That he still had reserves of political strength was not in doubt. It was Davis himself who moved a resolution at an Extraordinary Meeting of the Stepney Borough Council in November 1943 condemning Herbert Morrison's decision to release Oswald Mosley from detention.[91] At the Board of Deputies Davis continued to prove himself useful in a variety of ways as a member of the LCC: in dealing with problems arising from the establishment of a Christian missionary school in Hackney, for example, and in attending to the dietary requirements of Jewish children attending LCC schools that had been evacuated.[92] His hold on the Stepney Labour Party was so strong, indeed, that he managed to be re-elected

Labour Leader on the Borough Council even as he awaited his trial during the second half of 1944.

None the less, Morrison's repudiation of Davis's authority in the matter of air-raid precautions, and Davis's own outspoken criticism of both Morrison and Attlee over the release of Mosley, had probably scuppered any ambition he might have had of further advancement at County Hall, let alone of preferment to a safe Labour seat at Westminster. Nor, in the short term, was the image of Labour in east London much improved by his removal through imprisonment.[93] It took several years for the Stepney Labour Party to recover from this tragedy. As it tried to do so it was caught between the resurgence of Fascism in east London in the late 1940s (with Mosley's Union Movement) and popular hostility to Jews occasioned by events in Palestine during the last years of the Mandate. In 1947 Stepney Borough Council voted to withhold its approval of a meeting to condemn Fascism and antisemitism, while Hackney Borough Council (also Labour controlled) threw out a Communist resolution demanding that antisemitism be made illegal.[94]

In 1948 and 1949 the Board of Deputies, through its Defence Committee, made strenuous efforts to prevent LCC schools being used for Union Movement meetings, but met with little sympathy and less co-operation, even (it would appear) from Jewish Labour members of the Council.[95] Meanwhile, local Communists reaped a predictable harvest, capturing ten seats on the Stepney Borough Council in 1946; seven of these were won by Jewish candidates, and all ten victories were registered in Jewish wards.[96] In the same year Jack Gaster, son of the late Rabbi Dr Moses Gaster (*Haham*, or religious head, of the Spanish and Portuguese Jews), was elected as one of the two Communist councillors on the LCC for the Mile End division.[97]

The importance of the East End to the Anglo-Jewish experience in the 1930s cannot be doubted. But it should not be over-emphasized. In particular, it would be a mistake to suppose that the whole of London Jewry took a leftward political turn at this time. To begin with, the East End – indeed east London as a whole – was already beginning to lose its centrality in the life of the community. The extensive bombing to which this area was subjected during the Second World War greatly accelerated a process that was, in truth, already under way. By 1930 Stepney's

Jewish population had fallen to about 95,000 (of which over 70 per cent were British-born); during the 1930s the Jewish total fell by over a third, and between 1940 and 1945 the total declined still further from about 60,000 (representing 45 per cent of the total population of the borough) to between 25,000 and 30,000.[98]

In the East End the Federation of Synagogues, of which Morry Davis remained president until the very moment of his conviction, was still the dominant body; but it was dominating a Jewish community in rapid and irreversible decline. In the suburbs the United Synagogue, to which many of the communal grandees belonged, had taken the initiative in establishing a presence to serve the needs of small but growing congregations. Chief among these were Golders Green, Cricklewood, Hendon, Willesden, Hampstead Garden Suburb, Dollis Hill, Finchley, and Edgware to the north-west of the LCC area, and West Ham, Upton Park, Ilford, Becontree, South Tottenham, and Edmonton to the north and north-east. Even in the East End, Nettie Adler had noted how by the end of the 1920s no fewer than 20 per cent of Jewish earners were owners or managers of shops, workshops, and factories; that is, they were no longer members of the manual working classes.[99] This process of *embourgeoisement* was intensified in the suburbs, where upwardly mobile Jewish families moved in an atmosphere very different from that of east London; their reactions to social and political problems were correspondingly dissimilar.

Although antisemitism was commonplace in east London in the 1930s, much of it tended to remain at street or street-corner level: crude, regimented, often physical, and exploited always by the BUF, but having little positive impact at the level of formal municipal politics. *The Times* had seen fit to declare in October 1936 that the working-class Gentile cockney evinced towards 'Jews in bulk' an 'uncrystallized dislike'.[100] In fact there was in the East End a great deal of Jewish–Gentile solidarity against Fascism, to say nothing of co-operation in fighting for tenants' rights and, later, for better air-raid protection.[101] However cool relations between Jews and Irish in Stepney had become, the local authority had, after all, formally protested against Mosley's release. But at Hampstead, in 1945, over 2,000 signatures were collected on a petition to Parliament asking 'that aliens of Hampstead be repatriated and that, meanwhile, they could be housed in army or prisoner-of-war camps'.[102]

The petition, which received national publicity, was repudiated by the Hampstead Borough Council, but it carried the signature of the Mayor, Councillor S. A. Boyd, and it was later excused on the ground that the borough was 'feeling the presence of so many foreigners somewhat oppressive because of the housing short-age'.[103] In 1939 only about 15,000 Jewish refugees lived in the boroughs of Hampstead and Hendon (which included Golders Green).[104] The *Hampstead and Highgate Express* was certainly exaggerating when it claimed, in 1943, that a quarter of Hampstead's population of 80,000 were refugees.[105] None the less the very fact of overestimation reflected much local hostility that was at once anti-Jewish as well as xenophobic in origin. In 1940 the *Hampstead and Highgate Express* welcomed internment of aliens as 'a blessing in disguise'; in 1943 and 1944 both this news-paper (whose 'Heathman' column was particularly antisemitic) and the Jewish press agreed on the severity of prejudice against the refugees, which was definitely linked to a local housing crisis.[106] In June 1944 the *Kilburn Times* reported two local clergymen as advocating that the Jewish population of the area be limited to 1 per cent of the total.[107]

The official Jewish response to developments such as these (observable in provincial centres as well as London) was weak and defensive. A handbook, in English and German, issued jointly by the Board of Deputies and the German Jewish Aid Committee in January 1939, warned refugees not to make themselves con-spicious, not to talk 'in a loud voice', and not to take part in any political activities.[108] Gordon Liverman, chairman of the Board's Defence Committee, privately condemned 'the thoughtless be-haviour of so many ... [refugees] in areas where they are concentrated, namely Golders Green, Hampstead, North London, etc.'.[109] In June 1940 the Board's Aliens Committee, on the advice of its Public Relations Officer, went so far as to instruct refugees to spy on one another.[110]

The minute books of the Hendon (United) Synagogue reflect something of the repercussions of this atmosphere of distrust and ill-will in a community that was at once well-to-do, culturally assimilated, and religiously lax. In May 1940 in Hendon the Board of Management refused to allow a special sermon to be preached to refugees because it did not want 'to encourage gatherings of German people' – even though they were Jews! At the 1940

Annual General Meeting of this synagogue the much-respected warden, S. Cohen, berated the community on account of its poor response to appeals for funds to aid the refugees: 'Committees had been set up for the relief of refugees, but the Hendon Synagogue was not represented, because of its fear at the attempt of collection [of money].' He went on to report that, ironically, attendances at the synagogue were excellent, but only on account of the refugee presence.[111] The Jewish aid organizations themselves pursued a deliberate policy of dispersal of refugees from London.[112]

Much defence literature, by its timidity and condescension, arguably strengthened the antisemitic case.[113] This was, naturally, not intended, but it was inevitable given that the Board of Deputies' Defence Committee had in 1940 determined to occupy itself largely with fighting what it alleged were 'the internal causes of antisemitism'.[114] It identified these initially as the behaviour of refugees and evacuees, but as it became preoccupied with Jewish involvement in the wartime black market it reverted to Neville Laski's theme of Jewish commercial behaviour generally.

In 1938, as a response to Laski's strictures, the Board had established a committee to advise its Defence Committee; in 1940 this advisory committee was reconstituted as a separate but affiliated organization, the Trades Advisory Council (TAC), whose self-defined objective was 'the elimination of friction between Jew and non-Jew in trade and industry'.[115] The TAC's first general secretary was Maurice Orbach, a prominent adherent of Poale Zion and (since 1937) a Labour member of the LCC for St Pancras South-West; in 1945 he was to enter Parliament as MP for East Willesden. Orbach's Zionism was idiosyncratic to say the least (within months of election to Parliament he announced that he would not vote against the Labour government's policy of bringing Jewish immigration to Palestine to an end),[116] but his ideological antipathy to capitalism – especially Jewish capitalism – was not in doubt, and he and his friend Noah Barou, the TAC's acting chairman, both used the TAC as a vehicle from which to launch bitter public attacks upon the wickedness of the Anglo-Jewish business community.[117] By the summer of 1942 an open split had developed between the TAC and the Defence Committee in which it had originated, for Orbach's tirades, coming as they did from one so centrally placed within London Jewry, seemed to verge on the counter-productive.[118]

Orbach, however, survived this controversy, and though he relinquished his LCC seat in 1946 he retained control of the TAC until a year before his death in 1979. The strong Jewish support for him at Willesden at this time represented, both politically and geographically, a halfway house: the Jewish middle-classes who dwelt in this area were attracted not by Labour's Socialism but by its Zionism and its commitment to post-war social reform. Like Whitechapel a generation earlier, Willesden turned out to be merely a staging-post on the way to more distant suburbs. The once considerable Jewish presence at Willesden and Cricklewood had peaked by about 1950, by which time the Brondesbury community was already in decline.[119]

In 1945 both Willesden seats had returned Labour MPs, as had the two each at Ilford, Wembley, Walthamstow, and the South Tottenham constituency. The East End remained solidly Labour and in its heartland to some extent Communist – at least for the moment; as late as 1957 every Communist (there were four in all) elected to Stepney Borough Council was a Jew.[120] In spite of the dominating influence of Irish politicians in Stepney during the war, the borough council elected a Jew as Mayor in 1946 and again in 1951 and 1952; in 1951 there had also been Jewish mayors at Hackney and Finsbury, while in 1956 Jews held the mayoralty at Hackney, Stoke Newington, Finsbury, and Shoreditch.[121] These honours were at once a recognition of the Jewish contribution to Labour politics in east London and a testament to the strong ties that still bound inner-London Jewry to the Labour cause. Certainly in terms of representation upon the LCC the immediate post-war period witnessed a surge in Jewish Labourism, a reflection of Jewish sympathy with the party led nationally by Morrison and Attlee.

The representation of Jewish women is especially noteworthy. The elections of 1937 had brought into the Council chamber Mrs Helen Bentwich (1892–1972), elected then at North Kensington, later at North-East Bethnal Green, and later still at Stoke Newington and North Hackney. Mrs Bentwich (chairman of the Council 1956–7), slapdash, temperamental, and a stark contrast to the calm and methodical Lady Nathan, came from a well-to-do family but had early been drawn to social and trade-union work. Her tenure of the chair of the Education Committee (1947–50) provided the opportunity to play a leading part in planning the replacement of selective entry by comprehensive schools in London in the post-war period.[122] Other Jewish women to be elected to the LCC at this time – all in the Labour interest – included Mrs Irene Chaplin (East Islington from 1946), Mrs Eva Hubback (North Kensington 1946-9), Mrs Lena Jeger (Santo Jeger's wife; South St Pancras 1952-5), and Mrs B. Serota (Brixton from 1954). We should note that Mrs Serota's partner in the Brixton division was Victor Mishcon (born 1915, a solicitor and the son of Rabbi Arnold Mishcon, founder of the Brixton Synagogue), whose election there in 1946 had been followed by a rapid rise through the LCC's committee structure to the chairmanship of the Council 1954-5, and who progressed to an equally distinguished career upon the Greater London Council (Lambeth, 1964-7) before accepting a life peerage in 1978.[123]

On the occasion of the Council's fiftieth anniversary (which had coincided with Samuel Gluckstein's election as deputy-chairman) the *Jewish Chronicle* had commented that the attitude of the LCC towards Jewish interests 'whether in respect of education or in other spheres, has been sympathetic.... Long may it continue its humane and noble work!'[124] To what extent was this optimism justified? Certainly in the decade after Cable Street the Labour-controlled LCC proved accommodating: for instance, in making local orders under the 1936 Shops Act and in providing for the needs of Jewish patients and inmates of hospitals and institutions taken over under the 1929 Local Government Act.[125] It was, however, in the field of education that the advantages of a friendly regime at County Hall were most keenly felt.

In 1938 Leon Simon, chairman of the Zionist Federation's Education Committee, had praised 'the generous and far-sighted' policy of the LCC in making centres available for Hebrew and religious instruction, a theme echoed in 1940 and again in 1945 by Dr Nathan Morris, education officer of the Jewish Religious Education Board.[126] In 1942 the harsh scholarships policy was, to a limited extent, further ameliorated to cater for 'friendly' children of alien nationality (i.e. German, Austrian, and Hungarian).[127] Later that year the Council publicly reaffirmed its commitment to religious instruction in schools, and in the immediate post-war period it offered assistance with the sabbath observance of Jewish pupils at LCC schools, and in the provision of kosher school meals.[128]

Throughout the war, the Jewish community had maintained a close contact with the Board of Education, whose president, R. A. Butler, was responsible for the most far-reaching reforms in educational provision and in the role of the state in this provision since the beginning of the century.[129] Much of the thinking behind what became the Education Act of 1944 did not concern Anglo-Jewry, but the interest of the Chief Rabbi, Dr Hertz, and of the Board of Deputies had been aroused by the proposals to give greater financial concessions to denominational schools.[130] As a result of the war Jewish education in London, and the work of the Jewish voluntary schools, had been severely disrupted. Roughly 14,000 Jewish children had been evacuated, most into non-Jewish homes.[131] For the time being a Joint Emergency Committee for Jewish Education did its best to maintain standards, but it was obvious that a fundamental review of Jewish education in London would have to be undertaken, in the light of falling rolls in the Jewish voluntary schools in the pre-war period and the need to raise large sums of money to erect new buildings.[132]

Dr Hertz believed he had obtained general agreement to a scheme of communal taxation that was to finance a new body to co-ordinate Jewish education within the Greater London area, and in January 1944 he and the Board of Deputies invited Butler (whom the Chief Rabbi referred to as 'an illustrious architect of a bold measure of educational reform') to address an impressive gathering of communal leaders and encourage them to participate fully in the implementation of the proposed new Act.[133] The LCC had, meanwhile, been giving a great deal of thought to the role of the comprehensive school in London education after the war. The Council's detailed proposals, contained in the *London School Plan*, did not emerge until 1947; but even as the legislation of 1944 was passing through Parliament the Council suggested that London Jewry might come into this scheme by consenting to the establishment of a large Jewish comprehensive secondary school, centrally located to serve the needs of the entire community.[134]

In time this idea bore fruit in the shape of the relocation of the Jews' Free School, opened as a large purpose-built comprehensive at Camden Town in 1957.[135] But the wider hopes of Chief Rabbi Hertz (who died in 1946), that the opportunities provided by the 1944 Act might be fully exploited, were not realized. One long-term factor was the antipathy of many lower-middle-class Jewish parents to the destruction of the very grammar schools through which their children were able to gain entry to the universities and the professions. In their day the LCC grammar schools were perceived as a Socialist tool – an instrument whereby those born into the lower orders of society might better themselves. This was the Socialism of Attlee, but even during his premiership it was being superseded by a militant egalitarianism that viewed the grammar schools as socially divisive. Even those Jews who paid lip-service to the idea of a classless society did not want it just yet, however; for the moment they wished to enjoy the fruits of a middle-class existence, and the continued functioning of selective-entry schools with proven academic records was perceived as an integral part of this inheritance. As the East End grammar schools were swept away, Jewish resentment intensified.[136]

Quite apart from such considerations, however, and on the purely religious plane, the London Board of Jewish Religious Education (LBJRE), established in 1946 with Dr Homa as its first chairman, was neither adequately financed nor uniformly supported.[137] The claims of Zionist fundraisers weighed more heavily with the community at this period than did the financial demands of Jewish education; the Council of the United Synagogue had originally pledged that a third of the subscriptions paid by its members would be made over to the LBJRE, but in 1951 this proportion was reduced to a quarter and later to 17 per cent; partly as a result, the early years of the LBJRE were plagued by financial crises.[138] The Zionist Federation, searching for a new role now that the State of Israel had been re-established, determined to embark upon an ambitious school-building programme that competed for resources with that of the LBJRE.[139]

Worse still, attempts to exploit to full communal advantage the opportunities provided by the Butler legislation were and have continued to be dogged by religious differences within London Jewry. The immigration to London of large numbers of strictly orthodox Jews from central Europe during the 1930s and 1940s had given a new and (as it turned out) most prolonged lease of life to the Union of Orthodox Hebrew Congregations, established by Rabbi Victor Schonfeld in 1926 and led, after his death, by his son Rabbi Dr Solomon Schonfeld. Adherents of the Union located themselves in two discrete areas of London, Hackney (mainly Stoke Newington and Stamford Hill) and Hendon (mainly

Golders Green); most felt the United Synagogue to be too liberal and many were not Zionists. Solomon Schonfeld, as principal of the Jewish Secondary Schools Movement (founded 1929) would have no truck with the LBJRE, or with the Zionist Federation; he and his supporters went so far as to claim that the rebuilding and relocation of the Jews' Free School would hinder the progress of their own movement.[140] Dr Schonfeld was quite prepared to accept voluntary-aided status for the schools run by the Movement (pre-eminently the Avigdor Secondary School, Stoke Newington, and the Hasmonean Grammar School, Hendon) but he viewed with suspicion any scheme involving collaboration with a Socialist-controlled LCC.[141]

Although, therefore, the Jewish contingent upon the London County Council continued for the remainder of the Council's life to be overwhelmingly Labour in composition, and though this contingent included some leading personalities in Anglo-Jewry, the ties that bound the Council to the Jews of London were weakened rather than strengthened at this time, as the community relocated itself geographically beyond the boundaries of the LCC and politically in a much less leftwing direction. The profound implications that this relocation was to have for the stormy dialogue that was to take place between London Jewry and the Greater London Council (GLC) will be explored in the next chapter. Here it is necessary to observe a withering of Jewish sympathies at one end of the political spectrum, and signs of strong growth at the other.

East London Communism had rarely been able to break out of its Stepney stronghold, and as the Jews departed the fortress collapsed. The failure of the Communists to win Mile End South-East on the borough council in 1948 was an ominous but obvious portent.[142] The absorption of the small Mile End parliamentary constituency within a new Stepney division led inexorably to the end of Piratin's career at Westminster; he was defeated at the 1950 General Election, coming bottom of the poll.[143] Jack Gaster's tenure of the Mile End division on the LCC had already come to an end. In 1949 and 1952 a handful of Jewish Communists (including Gaster, Max Levitas, another veteran of the pre-war rent strikes, and Solly Kaye, a shop steward in the Transport and General Workers' Union), nominated for the LCC in Hackney South and Stepney, were all defeated.[144] Kaye stood for the LCC in

1958 and 1961, and for the Greater London Council in 1964, but his candidature was little more than symbolic.[145] Whatever sentimental attachment Jews might have harboured towards Communism was killed off by news of Soviet antisemitism (under Stalin), proof of Soviet anti-Zionism (in 1956 and 1967), and disenchantment with the realities of East European totalitarianism.[146] Any attempt to replant the seeds of Jewish Communism in the London suburbs was destined to fail.

Meanwhile, the creation of a petty bourgeoisie among the more affluent Jews of east London had led to the reappearance of Conservative sympathies, sometimes disguised as merely a concern for the defence of the interests of ratepayers against the predatory intentions of Socialism. At the Mile End LCC by-election of 1926 the Conservative candidate, Lieutenant-Colonel John Dodge, boasted the support of none other than the Revd J. F. Stern, minister of the East London Synagogue, a well-known social worker who was, at that time, a Progressive member of Stepney Borough Council.[147] Other Jewish supporters of Dodge included Leonard Silver and S. Raphael, who had resigned as vice-chairman of the Mile End Liberal Association in order to assist in the Conservative campaign against Esther Rickards (over whom Dodge triumphed by 273 votes).[148]

Following this victory, and the defeat of the General Strike a few weeks later, the *East London Observer* announced that 'the Jewish vote ... has now gone over entirely to the modern Conservatism'.[149] This prophecy was of course premature, but it was true that by the end of the year there had been a large and unmistakable defection of Jews from the Mile End Liberal Party to the Conservatives; in 1928 the Conservative candidates for the LCC at Mile End had the support not merely of Stern (by now a vice-president of the Mile End Conservative Association) but also of his clerical colleague the Revd B. Michelson.[150] To the Toryism of the established Jewish gentry was thus added the Toryism of the Jewish *nouveaux riches*. At Mile End in 1937 the Conservatives ran a Jew (Thomas Fligelstone) and a Gentile (Mrs O'Donovan, wife of the former MP); Sir Samuel Gluckstein and Leonard Silver appeared on the platform together in support of them.[151] In 1949 a Jew (T. M. Wechsler) was similarly selected as one of the Conservative LCC candidates at Stepney.[152]

The survival and careful nurturing of a tradition of Jewish

municipal Conservatism in east London was of critical importance in the transmission of this tradition to the suburbs. Even in
an area as strongly working-class as Hackney had become by the
1950s, Jews could be found standing as Conservatives; five Jews
stood in the Conservative interest in the Hackney Borough Council elections of 1953.[153] These were, from the Conservative viewpoint, hopeless seats; but in the Cricklewood ward of Willesden
Henry Berney secured election, and the following year Joe Emden,
a well-known East End Jewish Conservative, was brought in to
help Tom Iremonger woo the Jewish voters at Ilford North.[154]

Antisemitism, however, continued to be the major barrier
standing in the way of a fusion of Jewish voters and Conservative
politics in the London that was fast growing beyond the
boundaries of the LCC at this time. During the 1945 General
Election campaign some Conservative candidates had made no
secret of their desire to see Jewish refugees returned 'to their own
countries'.[155] The final, bloody years of the Palestine Mandate
undoubtedly gave such prejudice a new lease of life. There were no
official Conservative MPs who were Jewish between 1945 and
1955; throughout the 1950s, indeed, it was well known, and freely
admitted by Conservative Central Office, that there was anti-
Jewish prejudice in some local Associations.[156] At the level of local
government, however, the picture was not quite so bleak. In 1930
and again in 1946 a Jew (Herman Courlander) was elected Mayor
at Richmond-upon-Thames; another, J. L. Freeman, became
Mayor of Hendon in 1950 and a third, Emil Grant, served as
Mayor in the neighbouring borough of Finchley, 1952–3.[157] All
were Conservatives.

Towards the end of the 1950s Finchley was the setting for one of
the most notorious instances of institutionalized antisemitism in
post-war Britain. At the borough council elections of 1957 Liberals
alleged that the Finchley Golf Club, 'officered by prominent
Conservatives', was implementing a policy of excluding Jews
from membership.[158] The allegations turned out to be true and
since it was equally true that the Club operated from land leased to
it by the local authority, the matter became at once political.
Prompt action by the Council led to the Club being put on
'probation'.[159] Three years later the question of a Jewish quota (as
distinct from the total exclusion of Jews) arose, this time in
relation to golf clubs at Finchley, Hendon, Stanmore, and

Totteridge. 'We do accept them', the secretary of the Hendon Club was quoted as saying, 'but only a certain number'.[160]

These events were subsequently held to have been responsible for a swing of Jewish voters away from the Conservative Party and towards the Liberals. There is some statistical support for this view, and it is also the case that Liberals did well in Jewish wards.[161] In 1956 there was not one Liberal member of Finchley Council; by the time of the 1959 General Election there were seven, all elected at the expense of the Conservatives. At the 1962 local polls the Liberals advanced still further; Tory control of Finchley was maintained only through the votes of eight Conservative aldermen.[162]

But these victories were essentially the result of protest votes, they owed something to the national Liberal revival at this time, and the momentum they generated was not sustained at the parliamentary level. In 1959 the young Mrs Margaret Thatcher held the Finchley parliamentary constituency for the Conservatives, and at once embarked on a pro-Jewish policy from which she has rarely deviated; at the same time the Middlesex County Council and the Finchley Borough Council (also Tory controlled) passed tough anti-discrimination resolutions, and Hendon Borough Council refused to allow its Town Hall to be used by Mosley's Union Movement.[163] Finchley Liberalism lingered awhile. At the elections for the new Greater London Borough of Barnet, in May 1964, all six Liberal seats were won in the Finchley stronghold; but the four Barnet seats on the Greater London Council were taken by the Conservatives.[164] When the issue of a Jewish 'quota' surfaced again, in 1965 (at the Templars Lawn Tennis Club, Golders Green), the Jewish response was muted and the political impact minimal.[165]

The last Mayor of Hendon, Councillor John Shock, writing at the very end of 1964 in the newsletter of the North-Western Reform Synagogue, took his fellow Jews to task for being 'apathetic towards local government'.[166] This was an overstatement of a case which, none the less, had some substance to it. Anglo-Jewry as a community had taken no part in the establishment of the LCC, and, as a community, took no part in the protracted public debate during the 1950s and early 1960s that culminated in the Royal Commission on Local Government in Greater London (1957–60, chaired by Sir Edwin Herbert) and the passage of the London

Government Act of 1963.[167] Individual Jews, especially those prominent in London government and in party politics, did of course make a contribution, but as citizens, not as Jews.

The reform of 1963, inspired and pushed forward by a Conservative government, had two aims. One, frankly political, was to replace a London County Council that the Conservatives appeared to have no chance of ever again controlling by a much larger Greater London Council, encompassing suburban London beyond the LCC boundary, in which Conservative majorities might once more appear. The other, widely supported across and beyond party divides, was to give the nation's capital a form of local government more or less contiguous with its population and with its geography as they existed after the Second World War. On 9 April 1964 the first GLC elections were held, resulting in the return of thirty-six Conservative councillors and sixty-four Labour councillors, to which were later added eleven Labour and five Conservative aldermen. The 1963 legislation also swept away the old London boroughs created in 1899, and a miscellany of outer-London county boroughs, metropolitan districts, and urban boroughs; in their place thirty-two large Greater London Boroughs were created, while the City Corporation remained intact. These new borough authorities polled for the first time on 7 May 1964.

The LCC (and the former borough authorities) ceased to exist on 1 April 1965. Having ignored the LCC's birth, the *Jewish Chronicle* waxed lyrical at the moment of its death, extolling the part played by Jews in its development, contriving to see in this involvement a bold reflection of ancient rabbinic teachings, and expressing the hope that 'the role of Jews in the new organisation will be as distinguished as it was on the old'.[168] Whether this was to be so remained to be seen. At the very least, however, it was evident that London Jewry would be obliged to enter into that sort of dialogue with the GLC that had, in large measure, become unnecessary so far as the LCC was concerned. For the boundaries of the new Greater London Council contained the largest number of Jews to be found anywhere in the United Kingdom.

Chapter Five

DESCENT INTO WAR

At the time of the GLC's creation by far the greater part of London Jewry was settled outside the LCC's borders; the activities of the Council had ceased to be of direct relevance to them. The establishment of the GLC brought about an entirely new situation, which is summarized in table 5.1:

Table 5.1 The pattern of Jewish settlement in London (1974)

Anglo-Jewry	408,311
London Jewry (GLC area)	259,100
Outer London	184,200
Barnet	58,100
Brent	20,400
Enfield	11,000
Harrow	18,000
Redbridge	29,300
Inner London (LCC area)	74,900

Source: adapted from B. A. Kosmin and N. Grizzard, *Geographical Distribution Estimates of Ethnically Jewish Population of the UK 1974* (Board of Deputies of British Jews, mimeo, 1975).

By the early 1970s almost two-thirds of Anglo-Jewry were residents of Greater London and of these over half lived in the boroughs of Barnet, Brent, and Harrow in the north-west of the capital, and Enfield and Redbridge in the north and north-east. The reorganization of London government had, therefore, presented the community with a situation that, on the surface, resembled that of the 1890s: what was to be its relationship with the new London-wide authority? But the similarity was, in truth, entirely superficial. The duties and responsibilities of the LCC, most notably in the fields of housing and education, had had a direct and immediate impact upon East End Jewry, and the later anti-alienism of the Council had, as we have seen, been partly responsible for the migration of Jews to areas beyond its boundaries.

However, the Jews of suburban Greater London did not have a housing problem, and in any case they were, for the most part, no longer dependent upon or affected by local-authority housing policies. In theory at least, the 1944 Education Act had met the community's needs through state support for denominational schools; that Anglo-Jewry did not exploit to the full the advantages of that legislation was not, of itself, an issue affecting relations with local government. For these reasons, and also as a result of migration to the suburbs, the quarter-century that followed the end of the Second World War had witnessed the gradual disengagement of London Jewry as a community from the affairs of the LCC. There seemed, in consequence, little need to formulate a set of policies with respect to the successor body; none were, in fact, forthcoming.

As we shall see, this omission was to result in the community being caught completely off-guard when confronted (in and after 1981) with a GLC whose ruling majority was, in some respects, overtly hostile to Jewish interests. The situation was, however, made palpably more difficult by a serious imbalance in the nature of Jewish representation upon the new Council.

The bare statistics of Jewish representation upon the GLC at each of the six elections held during the Council's twenty-one-year existence are set out in the Appendix. Originally the GLC consisted of 100 elected councillors, to which were added sixteen nominated aldermen; this latter position was abolished in the early 1970s, and from 1973 the number of councillors was reduced to ninety-two. During the 1970s Jews, though forming only about 3.5 per cent of the total population of Greater London, comprised nearly 8 per cent of the elected Council; even in 1981 this overrepresentation persisted, though not to the same extent. These overall percentages, however, conceal some very important changes of balance in the party-political and constituency profiles of the Jewish contingent at County Hall.

Party control of the GLC alternated, but in an uneven fashion. Labour ruled from the inception of the new Council until May 1967 when, apparently in response to the deep unpopularity of Harold Wilson's Labour government, the Conservatives were swept into power in London, winning eighty-two GLC seats as against Labour's eighteen. The Labour Party recovered somewhat in 1970, but it was not until 1973 that it again won power at County Hall. In 1977, as a result once more of a national swing against a Labour government, control of the GLC was returned to the Conservatives; four years later this control reverted, for the last time, to a Labour administration.

In all, therefore, Labour controlled the GLC for eleven years, the Conservatives for ten. But Anglo-Jewry was singularly ill-placed to make any impact, no matter which party was in power. Jews were neither attracted to the GLC nor excited by it in the same positive way that they had approached the affairs of the LCC or had embraced parliamentary politics. Perhaps this was because the community no longer felt it necessary to seek the status that went with a career in London government; the evidence of social standing and societal assimilation provided by election to County Hall was simply no longer important to London Jewry. We should also note that elective service in local government itself fell somewhat into disrepute nationally at this time, as evidenced by continuing low turnout at local elections.

The decline in the number of Jews elected to the GLC may be regarded as a symbolic reflection of the degree of importance and commitment attached by the community to the new authority. This resulted in a most significant mismatch between the increasingly middle-class reorientation of the community and its representation on the Conservative side at County Hall.[1] In parliamentary terms, the upward social mobility and bourgeoisification of Anglo-Jewry was being mirrored throughout this period by an increase in the number of Jews elected as Conservative MPs.[2] No such parallel development ever took place on the Greater London Council; indeed, the number of Jewish Conservative members of the GLC dwindled until the industrialist Alan Greengross, who sat for Hampstead from 1977 till 1986, found himself the last Jew to sit on the Conservative side in the Council chamber.[3]

On the Labour side Jewish membership also declined but, more significantly, in a way that located what remained of this membership on the moderate wing of the Party. Victor Mishcon's membership of the Council terminated in 1967, as did that of Mrs Serota; Irene Chaplin continued to serve until 1977, when the trade-union organizer Harry Kaye was elected for Dagenham. Mr Kaye and Ellis Hillman (a practising orthodox Jew, first elected to the LCC in 1958, and a member of the GLC for Hackney, and later Central Hackney, from 1965 until 1981) no doubt thought of themselves as leftwing; so they were, but within a terminology more suited to 'old guard' Bevanites than to the trendy new left of the 1970s.

The same comment may justifiably be made of Mrs Gladys Dimson, returned for Haringey 1964-7, Wandsworth 1970-3, and Battersea North thereafter. In 1973 Mrs Dimson became chairman of the GLC's Housing Committee, and marked her elevation to that office with a strong denunciation of the 'immoral behaviour' of some Jewish landlords; but in the course of time she found herself increasingly called upon to defend the reputation of Anglo-Jewry against a party leadership intent on attacking it.[4] Because Jewish Labour councillors on the GLC came to be untypical both of London Jewry and of Labour politics in London, the Jewish community found it progressively more difficult to respond to trends within the London Labour Party in the 1970s, especially in relation to increasing support for anti-Zionist ideologies. This failure had few repercussions at first, but after Labour's 1981 victory at the GLC elections its serious implications became all too evident.

One further characteristic of Jewish membership of the Greater London Council is worthy of comment. In the days of the LCC, areas of high Jewish population had consistently returned Jewish councillors, often specifically and deliberately with an eye to the representation and furtherance of Jewish interests at County Hall; it was not at all uncommon for such councillors to have appealed for 'Jewish' votes at the poll. Throughout the history of the GLC, by contrast, although Jewish representation (more especially on the Labour side) remained relatively high in inner London boroughs such as Hackney and Camden, it was very poor, or even non-existent, in the outer areas of substantial and expanding Jewish population. It is remarkable that Barnet, which contained the largest number of Jews to be found in any London borough, only ever returned two Jewish members of the GLC (Reginald Marks, 1964–77 and Rita Levy, 1972–3, both Conservatives) and that Brent, Enfield, and Redbridge only ever returned one or two each.[5]

The reasons for this can have had little to do with anti-Jewish prejudice which, certainly in London by this time, the Conservative Party had largely overcome; there were, after all, plenty of Jewish borough councillors to be found in the outer-London areas. Because (at least prior to 1981) there were no perceivable Jewish issues to be raised on the GLC, the interest of Jews living in these outer boroughs in the deliberations at County Hall was bound to be minimal; if these Jews had a local-government focus at all, it was directed towards the town-hall and was to be found at borough level. In the fullness of time this too was to bring serious consequences. But for the moment it appeared to be without adverse effects.

The first sixteen years of the GLC's existence confronted London Jewry with very few problems. In 1965 the powers of the LCC's Education Committee were transferred directly to a new Inner London Education Authority (ILEA); the outer boroughs assumed responsibility for their own educational provision. Some concern was expressed within the Board of Deputies over the absence of uniformity in relation to the granting of leave to teachers on Jewish holy days, and its Education Committee expressed a nostalgia for the policy of the LCC ('the ideal authority'), which had allowed leave on full pay for three days a year, with days taken off in excess of three being made up during normal school holidays. This policy was continued by the ILEA but not in the outer boroughs, where Jewish teachers faced a loss both of salary and of pension contributions if they absented themselves for more than three days for reasons of religious observance; a compromise eventually permitted observant Jewish teachers to work for one or two terms after normal retirement age in order to preserve their full pension entitlement.[6]

That this formula was accepted without demur by the Jewish authorities is less an indication of weakness than a reflection of the laxity of orthodox observance then to be seen throughout Anglo-Jewry. The decision of the ILEA no longer to permit schools with large numbers of Jewish pupils to close during the festival of *Shavuot* likewise aroused no comment.[7] In 1973 the Jewish

Educational Development Trust appealed, unsuccessfully, against the Authority's refusal to support the establishment of a voluntary-aided comprehensive school at Ilford; the following year, however, the ILEA did agree to give financial assistance to Jewish students following denominational courses of instruction.[8]

On matters relating to Israel and Zionism the policies of both Conservative and Labour sides at County Hall were at this time above reproach. In June 1966, in his capacity as chairman of the GLC's General Purposes Committee, Victor Mishcon welcomed Hayim Koransky, director of the Education Department in Jerusalem, and the following March Teddy Kollek, Jerusalem's Mayor, was given an official reception.[9] More remarkable was the failure of Arab lobbyists, in July 1971, to persuade the Council to withdraw experts it had sent to Jerusalem to advise on the rebuilding of the Old City captured during the 1967 war. Although these experts had been offered by a Conservative-controlled Council, it was a Jewish Labour councillor, Louis Bondy (Islington), who defended their dispatch; the following November Israel's Minister of Housing, Ze'ev Sharef, met GLC officials to discuss house-building and property management.[10]

There was also significant cross-party support for the plight of Soviet Jewry. In October 1972 Harold Sebag-Montefiore (Conservative, Cities of London and Westminster), the chairman of the Arts and Recreation Committee, boycotted a Russian cultural visit which the GLC itself had sponsored.[11] Two years later Ben Mason, the Jewish vice-chairman of the GLC (now under Labour control) made a well-publicized protest at a meeting attended by representatives of the Moscow municipality.[12] In October 1976, while in Moscow, the members of a GLC delegation stressed that, as individuals, they supported the Campaign for Soviet Jewry.[13] This incident, again, occurred during a period of Labour control at County Hall.

Although, therefore, after 1981 much was to be heard by way of Jewish protests that the GLC had no business formulating and giving expression to foreign policies, it had – in effect – been doing so virtually throughout the whole of its previous existence. For the elected authority that controlled the affairs of London to give advice on the administration of East Jerusalem, and for official, albeit individual, protests to be made by members of the GLC at Soviet treatment of Jews, constituted expressions of preference in relation to international affairs. Anglo-Jewish approval of such preferences was merely thrown into much sharper focus by the abrupt policy reversals experienced in the post-1981 period. But what was reversed was, in truth, a set of policies, not the principle of pursuing foreign initiatives.

It is generally recognized that the Six-Day War (June 1967) marked an ominous turning-point in the history of leftwing antisemitism in Britain.[14] With the capture of East Jerusalem, the West Bank, and Gaza, Israel, hitherto the underdog of the Middle East, could now be regarded as an imperialist, colonial power, ruling by force of arms over a downtrodden Palestinian Arab population. This aspect of Israeli policy can be criticized without questioning the legitimacy of the Jewish State or the justice of its re-establishment in 1948; many Jewish citizens of Israel have done so over the years. However, elements of the left in Britain, as elsewhere in western Europe, used the events of 1967 as an excuse to attack the very fact of Israel's existence and, by implication, the entire basis of the movement for Jewish self-determination (i.e. Zionism); the force of this attack was made all the greater by the resolution of the General Assembly of the United Nations (10 November 1975) equating Zionism with racism. Those who supported the Zionist cause could henceforth be branded as racists, and racism could be portrayed as part of a new 'world Jewish conspiracy' that was already alleged to embrace capitalism and imperialism.[15] However vigorously leftwing anti-Zionists denied that their motives were in any way antisemitic, the reaction of Anglo-Jewry was one of justifiable scepticism and disbelief.

These developments can be treated here merely in the barest outline. But they formed the stark backcloth against which hostilities between Anglo-Jewry and a Labour-controlled GLC were eventually to break out. It is, however, worth observing that anti-Zionism was not confined to the Labour side. In the years immediately following the 1967 war it was the Young Liberals who carried the banner of anti-Zionism with most enthusiasm.[16] In 1970 the Liberals still had four seats on Barnet Borough Council; three of their four representatives were Jews. John Webb, the only non-Jew, deserted to the Tories in November 1970 because he objected to the 'heavily racial and anti-Semitic comments' of the Young Liberals.[17] By April 1972 Councillor Frank Davis had also left the party; he fought a GLC by-election in Barnet as an

Independent, but lost (predictably) to Rita Levy.[18] These developments acted as a brake upon Liberal efforts to build upon their earlier successes in exploiting Conservative embarrassments relating to golf and tennis clubs, and the memory of them continued to affect Jewish perceptions of Liberalism in the 1970s and 1980s.

Another development, of more profound significance, was provided by the growing presence in London of Black immigrant communities, and by the early identification of these communities with Labour politics.[19] The failure of Anglo-Jewry and of Afro-Caribbean and Asian groups to form links with each other in combating racism and Fascism was a function of deep inter-communal distrust, in the blame for which all sides must share.

In inner London in the 1950s and 1960s the fabric of Jewish life visibly crumbled as Black immigrants moved into areas where Jews once lived in large numbers. Black–Jewish relations had their positive as well as their negative aspects. Black leaders acknowledged the helpful attitude of Jews in assisting newer immigrants to obtain employment and housing, and the part played by Jews in furthering the civil rights movement in the USA was freely recognized. At the same time West Indian immigrants often alleged that they were the victims of exploitation by Jewish moneylenders, Jewish employers, and Jewish landlords. The issue of Zionism was also a powerful factor inhibiting contact between Blacks and Jews. Afro-Caribbean and Asian radicals adopted the standard leftwing critique of Zionism, and this critique was bolstered by Islamic sympathy with the plight of the Palestinian Arabs. Moreover, Israel's friendly relations with South Africa could easily be presented as evidence of Jewish support for apartheid.[20]

On the Jewish side, there was a strong (though by no means general) tendency to meet prejudice with prejudice. Many of the respondents in a survey of Hackney Jews in the late 1970s 'attributed the deterioration [of the area] ... mainly to the presence of black people'; Hackney Jews disapproved of the life-style of the Blacks; they were convinced that most crimes in the borough were committed by Blacks; and they resented welfare payments to Black immigrants.[21] In any case, the Jewish community of London was comparatively affluent; many Jews, consequently, found it difficult to identify with the Blacks, and had little sympathy with policies designed to provide statutory protection against racial discrimination.

Some Jewish policy-makers certainly realized that race relations legislation could protect them too; others none the less felt (and feel) uncomfortable in its presence. Additionally, many Jews objected (and object) to being classified as an 'ethnic minority' – at least in public. Beyond these considerations, many in the community blamed the Blacks for the resurgence of racist politics, and for the rise of the National Front. 'To show sympathy to the Black community may be a principle', a Yiddish editorial in the *Jewish Tribune* warned in 1978, 'but is this principle so pure and important that it is worth jeopardising the security of the Jewish public?'[22]

From the 1950s a succession of neo-Fascist and racist organizations, including Mosley's Union Movement, had turned their attention from the Jews to the Blacks. Yet, despite a common interest in opposing racism, the Board of Deputies adhered to the view that its only concern was with Jewish matters narrowly defined. The Race Relations Acts of the 1960s were welcomed by some Jewish leaders and by some leading Jews (especially on the Labour side) such as the MPs Barnett Janner, Sydney Silverman, and Paul Rose, all of whom urged that the scope of the legislation be extended to embrace religion as well as race.[23] Nevertheless, the attitude evinced by the organized Anglo-Jewish community was much less enthusiastic. Anglo-Jewry expressed no view on the Commonwealth Immigration Act of 1962 (the first statutory restriction on the right of Commonwealth citizens to enter Britain). Its response to the 1965 Race Relations Act was more devious. The Board welcomed the Act, noting, however, that it made no reference to creed or religion; but privately an assurance was sought – and obtained, from the Zionist Home Secretary, Sir Frank Soskice – that its terms would permit Jews to make use of it, should they wish, to combat anti-Jewish prejudice.[24] A similar policy was adopted in relation to the race relations legislation of 1968.[25]

The Board of Deputies did condemn Enoch Powell's diatribes against Black immigrants (1968); Victor Mishcon, however (by now a vice-president of the Board) felt compelled to express, publicly, his sadness that so many Jews identified themselves with Powellite views.[26] Few Jewish organizations bothered to reply to a questionnaire sent out by a Board working party on race relations, and although the report that the working party subsequently issued called for greater Jewish involvement in countering colour prejudice, nothing positive emerged.[27]

Worse still, in areas of high Jewish concentration in London, the community came, by stages, to be associated with calls to bring all immigration to a halt. In Redbridge, the Conservative MP for Ilford North, Tom Iremonger, who had made a deliberate and conscious effort to cultivate the support of local Jewish residents, had emerged by the spring of 1968 as a devout restrictionist; between then and 1974 he managed to combine staunch support for Israel with an uncompromising immigration policy.[28] Iremonger lost his seat, narrowly, in October 1974, to the Jewish Labour candidate Millie Miller; but although Mrs Miller seems to have attracted a Jewish vote on purely ethnic lines, her victory did not stem from any new-found Jewish sympathy with the Blacks. Her untimely death led to a by-election (February 1978), the central features of which were the intervention of the National Front and a speech by the Jewish frontbench opposition spokesman Sir Keith Joseph, urging the Jews of Ilford North to support Mrs Thatcher's policy of further immigration control.

The Conservatives won back Ilford North on a swing of 6.9 per cent. Among Jewish voters, however, the swing was just over 11 per cent. Sir Keith's estimation of the mood of Ilford Jewry on the question of Black immigration had been faultless.[29] Moreover, it seemed to echo the Jewish mood elsewhere in London. In April 1977, during the course of a by-election in the Burnt Oak ward of Barnet Council, the Jewish Conservative candidate, Brian Gordon, well known as the vice-chairman of Young Herut and a teacher at the Edgware United Synagogue, was reported as having declared that Britain 'could no longer be the "dustbin" of the world'.[30] When the GLC election for the Hendon North seat was held a few weeks later, Bryan Cassidy, the (non-Jewish) Conservative candidate, declined to disown Gordon, and won the seat with a majority of 7,370.[31] Elsewhere, there was explicit evidence of Jewish sympathy for and identification with National Front policies towards Black immigrants; a few Jews actually joined the Front, and stood on its behalf at parliamentary and local-government contests.[32]

The renaissance of the extreme, racist right was the most serious manifestation of its kind since the days of the British Union of

Fascists forty years previously. At the GLC elections of 1973 the Front had contested only seven seats, but four years later it put up candidates in ninety-one out of the ninety-two seats; in thirty of these the Front, or its offshoot, the National Party, succeeded in pushing the Liberals into fourth place, and in Hackney South and Bethnal Green managed to obtain 19 per cent of the votes cast. At the borough elections of May 1978 the Front polled 13.6 per cent of the Hackney votes, and 10.5 per cent in Tower Hamlets. This resurgence was not confined to London, and extended into the realm of parliamentary election contests; the major reasons for it were almost certainly economic, Black immigrants being made the scapegoats for industrial recession and national decline.[33] By 1979 the renaissance had, in a national sense, passed its peak. But in north-east London the Front continued to do well; at the May 1979 General Election its vote in the boroughs of Tower Hamlets, Newham, and Hackney averaged 3.8 per cent, and in the Hackney South and Shoreditch seat stood at 7.6 per cent.[34]

In the aftermath of the Ilford North by-election, the *Jewish Chronicle* published a letter from the (Labour) president of the Board of Deputies, Lord Fisher of Camden, in which it was made clear that the Board would only campaign against racial discrimination; it would not oppose further immigration control and it would not join the Anti-Nazi League (ANL), formed in November 1977 to counter the rise of the National Front.[35] The refusal of the Board to co-operate with the ANL was largely political in origin. Although run by a steering committee the majority of whose members were of the Labour party, the ANL attracted a following among various Marxist and Trotskyist groups (such as the Socialist Workers' Party) who were outspoken in their attacks upon Zionism and the State of Israel; there was also a fear that the ANL would be successful in attracting Jewish money away from the Board, the Association of Jewish ex-Servicemen and Women (AJEX), and the Council of Christians and Jews.[36] These fears proved totally groundless; the ANL never allowed itself to be used as an anti-Zionist platform, and it never damaged the fund-raising capacity of Jewish organizations. The Board's refusal to treat with it, and the pressure brought by the Board to induce local synagogues to refuse it meeting facilities, merely served to further puzzle and anger Black communities.[37]

The Board of Deputies was, of course, deeply concerned about extreme rightwing groups, but basically it knew them to be anti-Jewish, not because they were anti-Black; it wished to counter their influence and popularity without being drawn into the world of leftwing pro-immigration politics, with which it was not, in any case, sympathetic and which it realized was hostile to Zionism. At the time of the 1977 local-government elections organizations such as AJEX and the Board of Deputies called upon Jews to vote at the polls, in order to prevent National Front success through low turnout.[38] However, it was not easy to fight racism (nor to be taken seriously in fighting racism) while keeping aloof from the Blacks and the major anti-racist lobbies which they patronized. In the immediate aftermath of the 1977 local elections, and as much out of fear as out of conviction, a new stratagem was adopted. The prime movers appear to have been Martin Savitt, chairman of the Board's Defence and Group Relations Committee, and Dr Jack Gewirtz, director of the Board's Defence Department.

In July 1976 Savitt had obtained the Board's approval for his participation in a Rally Against Racism organized by the Indian Workers' Association and a number of West Indian organizations; the Board's Executive Committee urged Jews 'to establish a relationship of goodwill, tolerance and understanding with the Asian and African communities'.[39] Contact was also made with the chairman of the Commission for Racial Equality to discuss what role Anglo-Jewry might play in assisting other ethnic minorities. These initiatives culminated, in 1977, in a decision by the Board's Defence Committee to meet Black leaders, and on 19 June 1977 the Board endorsed a proposal from the Committee that it participate in a new Joint Committee Against Racialism.[40]

These initiatives might in time have borne fruit; they might have led to a co-ordinated Jewish–Black response to neo-Nazi activity, and, especially in London, to a much closer relationship between Jews and the new immigrant groups. But, from the outset, they were bedevilled by a public unwillingness, on the part of certain very important sections of London Jewry, to endorse them, participate in them, and thus give them legitimacy. Dr Gewirtz seemed unable to separate out his devotion to Zionism from his desire to meet and make friends with the Black community. He seemed, indeed, to have expected that, in return for Jewish co-operation, Black antipathy to Zionism would be jettisoned, and to have believed that Blacks would be willing to do this.[41]

An external challenge to the Board's policy came from the British branch of Herut, the rightwing party which came to power in Israel in 1977 as the dominant partner in the Likud coalition government headed by Menachem Begin, Herut's leader. Begin's premiership confirmed the worst fears of the left (in emphasizing as it did Israel's determination to retain control of the West Bank, Gaza, and East Jerusalem), but within Anglo-Jewry it strengthened the hand of Herut in claiming to be an authentic communal voice. The unhelpful remarks about immigrants made by Brian Gordon in April 1977 have already been noted. The previous year British Herut had attacked the decision of the Board of Deputies to participate in the Rally Against Racism; anti-Zionist remarks made at the rally by the Pakistani-born Marxist Tariq Ali added strength to their case.[42]

In response to the National Front's relative success at the GLC elections of 1977, the *Jewish Tribune* advised its readers 'to keep a low profile in their personal and communal affairs', with regard to the fight against Fascism.[43] The *Tribune* circulated widely amongst north London's ultra-orthodox communities, themselves an easily identifiable ethnic group who were consequently often subject to racist attacks. Many of them also lived in close proximity to Black populations. Yet, while supportive of a loose liaison with Asian and West Indian organizations, the *Tribune* pointed to the 'wide gulf of difference in temperament and outlook'. Many Black organizations were accused of being infested with extreme leftwing personnel. The *chassidic* communities in particular, formed in the late 1940s by refugees from Communist oppression, had a well-grounded loathing of all leftwing politics. Indeed, while praising the Board of Deputies' active opposition to the National Front, the *Tribune* attacked it for ignoring the 'overall scourge of communism which is creeping into British society at an alarming rate'. Prominent members of the Board were criticized for being sympathetic to Socialism and for their membership of the Labour Party.[44]

The attack in 1978 by the *Jewish Tribune* on the Board's involvement with Black organizations was a further sign of communal disapproval of this policy. Significantly, the attack was translated by and reprinted in the *West Indian World* almost at once.[45] Shortly afterwards, in a letter to the *Jewish Chronicle*, David Sassoon, Headmaster of the Hillel House (Jewish) School,

Brondesbury Park, confessed that he found it disturbing 'to hear Jewish parents ... refusing to agree to send their children to this or that school simply on the grounds that they don't want their children to mix with those of coloured immigrants'.[46]

There were those in the Anglo-Jewish community who viewed these developments with the utmost concern. The Labour MP Greville Janner, who became President of the Board of Deputies in 1979 (and whose West Leicester parliamentary constituency contains a large Asian community) argued fiercely for more tolerance and more understanding on the part of his fellow Jews. At the end of 1979 he and Dr Jakobovits, Chief Rabbi of the United Synagogue and an ecclesiastical authority of the Board, voiced public criticism of the changes in immigration rules brought in by Mrs Thatcher's Conservative government that discriminated against women and British citizens born outside the United Kingdom.[47] Both Dr Jakobovits and Mr Janner supported the establishment, in 1976, of the Jewish Social Responsibility Council (now the Jewish Council for Community Relations), which aimed to foster better understanding between Blacks and Jews; the Council was, however, poorly supported within Anglo-Jewry, and its major objectives came under sustained communal attack.[48]

Attempts to improve Black–Jewish links were not helped by the public utterances of Rudy Narayan, a loquacious Black barrister and Labour Party member, active in Brixton, who in 1977, in a book entitled *Black England*, appeared to have embraced the idea of a Jewish world conspiracy.[49] In October 1980 Mr Narayan, in an address to the Hackney Council for Racial Equality, accused the Jewish Labour MP for Central Hackney, Stanley Clinton Davis, of being a 'racist'.[50] Although these remarks were repudiated by the Council, the generally negative impression which Blacks – especially of Afro-Caribbean origin – had of Jews was undoubtedly authentic. Blacks, one speaker at the Hackney meeting declared, 'have not had the support from the Jews that we hoped for'.[51] The Jews, on their side, distanced themselves still further from Black concerns, especially after the April 1981 Brixton riots, which Jews generally condemned, and the 1982 Israeli invasion of the Lebanon, which evoked much hostility from Britain's Moslem community.[52]

Even before events in the Lebanon had whipped the anti-

Zionism of the left to fever-pitch, however, prejudice against Israel was already eroding much of what remained of the old relationship between Jews and the Labour Party in London. In September 1979 Councillor Arthur Super, a former Jewish Mayor of Hackney, leaked news of a motion passed, in secret, by the Hackney North and Stoke Newington Labour Party the previous July, declaring its opposition to the very existence of the State of Israel and calling for recognition of the Palestine Liberation Organisation (PLO) as the legitimate representative organ of Palestinian Arabs.[53] Super blamed the affair on a 'small, but virulent, anti-semitic element'; but a year later this element was still very much in control, condemning the 'Zionist State of Israel' and, once more, urging PLO recognition.[54] Moreover, this same 'small' element had appeared, by 1982, to have gained control of the Labour Party's National Executive Committee. In May 1982 the NEC, which had already endorsed Palestinian self-determination and urged the participation of the PLO in peace talks, passed a motion criticizing Israeli policies on the West Bank and the bombing of the Lebanon. Anti-Zionist motions had, by then, become standard items on the agenda-papers of many Constituency Labour Parties; local government as well as national political forums were being commonly used as tools for the implementation of these policies.[55]

These themes, of Black antipathy to Jews and leftwing anti-Zionism, both manifested within the arena of mainstream Labour politics, and of hostility to Blacks and Black preoccupations from a London Jewish community increasingly identifying itself with Thatcherite Conservatism, came together in a particularly dramatic way in the borough of Brent. By the end of the 1970s Brent had one of the highest concentrations of ethnic-minority citizens originating from the New Commonwealth and Pakistan (NCWP). Significantly, of the three Brent parliamentary constituencies, that with the highest NCWP proportion, Brent South (45.7 per cent according to the 1981 census), also had the smallest number of Jews, most of whom were by then concentrated at Brent North (Wembley Park, Kingsbury, Kenton), whose NCWP proportion (23 per cent) was the lowest.[56]

This geographical divide, whereby the Jews had congregated at the northern end of the borough, leaving the southern extremity (embracing the once popular areas of Willesden, Cricklewood, and

Brondesbury Park) to the Blacks, reflected also a deepening political chasm. Remnants of the former close relationship between Jews and the Labour Party still existed. In 1976 the Labour-controlled Brent Council elected a Zionist mayor, Councillor Leonard Snow, and two years later John Lebor, who sat on the National Executive of the Labour Friends of Israel, became leader of the Council.[57]

By 1981, however, Mr Lebor was accusing militant leftists of using the Blacks in order to bring about the deselection of moderates like himself; the Asian Labour Party Alliance (founded in December 1980) was alleged to be pursuing a deliberate policy of enrolling members in order to pack local ward meetings called to choose candidates for the May 1982 borough elections.[58] Lebor, originally selected, was later deselected while on holiday, thus becoming the seventh moderate Labour councillor to suffer deposition.[59] Some Jews were chosen to run for the Labour Party; one of them, Ernest Friedlander, became Mayor, but only after a procedural manoeuvre by the outgoing mayor (Karamet Hussain) designed to maintain Labour in office although they had lost overall control.[60]

The election itself had been marked by a great deal of hostility between the Jewish community and the Brent Labour Party. When the Jewish Labour candidate at Cricklewood, Alf Filer, declared that Israel should become a secular state, Dr Harry Rabinowicz, the local Rabbi, called upon congregants not to vote for him.[61] John Lebor went further, advising electors not to vote Labour at all because (he asserted) about a fifth of all Labour candidates in the borough supported the PLO.[62] Labour's loss of the two Cricklewood seats was especially severe, since its share of the poll, compared with 1978, fell by almost 20 per cent, although, over the borough as a whole, the drop in Labour support was about 11 per cent. Certainly, the controversy did nothing to help Labour, and probably contributed to its poor performance, both in the Cricklewood ward and throughout the borough. In Jewish eyes, the image of leftwing pro-PLO extremism entrenching itself within the Labour Party was reinforced. The condemnation of this extremism by Reg Freeson, the Jewish Labour MP for Brent East (of which Cricklewood was a part) and a former Council leader in the borough, was therefore significant not merely in the local context but (as we shall see) as a bridge to the wider controversy that was already taking place within the ambit of the Greater London Council.[63]

The GLC election of 7 May 1981 brought to power at County Hall a Labour majority different in kind from any that had previously ruled London. During the campaign the party had been led by an acknowledged moderate, Andrew McIntosh (Tottenham), but as soon as the results had been declared the newly-elected Labour councillors chose a new leader, Ken Livingstone (Paddington), a man of the 'hard' left convinced that he, and the party he led, possessed a mandate to confront a Conservative government (very widely supported within Anglo-Jewry) by pursuing policies (especially financial policies) destined to clash with those emanating from Downing Street.[64] In the five years that remained of the Greater London Council the ire of London Jewry was to be directed as much at Livingstone himself as at the Labour Party in the metropolis. This personal antipathy, however, merely served to sharpen and highlight the anti-Zionism that had, as we have seen, already taken root in the Labour Party of Greater London. The antipathy was, in turn, a reflection of the substantial disaggregation of interests now to be observed between Anglo-Jewry and Labour politics.

The story of the deteriorating relationship between Anglo-Jewry and the Labour-controlled GLC resolved itself, essentially, into a series of conflicts over specific subjects. Although many of these related ultimately to the Middle East, the earliest, in chronological terms, concerned the policy of the Inner London Education Authority (also Labour-controlled) towards denominational schools. In October 1980 the Greater London Labour Party had adopted a manifesto declaring that no child ought to be educationally segregated on grounds of sex, religion, or ethnic or socio-economic status. This policy came under attack at once at the Board of Deputies. Contact was made with Sir Ashley Bramall, then Labour leader on the ILEA, in an attempt to clarify the position, and an assurance was apparently obtained as to the status of existing voluntary-aided Jewish schools.[65]

There was, in truth, little to fear in this regard; unless a voluntary-aided school was demonstrably inefficient, its status was, in practice, in no danger. Real difficulties arose over applications by private Jewish schools to be granted entry into the maintained sector. In June 1981 three such schools, run by the ultra-orthodox community in Hackney, applied to the ILEA to become voluntary-aided but were turned down, partly on grounds of cost (which, it was said, would total almost £1 million per annum), partly on grounds of efficiency, but also on grounds of policy and principle.[66] The criticism this evoked from the Board of Deputies and the ultra-orthodox community was to some extent unfairly directed. In 1983 and 1984 the Department of Education and Science, headed by Sir Keith Joseph, rejected appeals from the schools concerned, largely because it was felt they did not meet minimum DES standards; to this extent the view originally taken by a Labour-controlled ILEA was confirmed by a Conservative Secretary of State.[67]

In June 1984 the Labour-controlled Hackney Borough Council attempted to mollify Jewish opinion by making grants in excess of £300,000 to a number of Jewish schools, including those whose applications for voluntary-aided status had been rejected; an additional £400,000 was voted by the borough the following year. These grants were justified by Tony Millward, leader of the Hackney Council, on the grounds that they were part of the Council's overall equal-opportunities policy.[68] Moreover, as early as September 1982 the ILEA had signalled its intention to introduce Judaism into the religious education syllabus of the schools it controlled, as an expression of its commitment to a multi-racial and multi-cultural society.[69] It was as a consequence of this commitment, indeed, that although the *chassidic* schools themselves never received ILEA money, the communities that sustained them were to become the beneficiaries of largesse from a quite distinct and novel GLC source which Labour had established after its 1981 victory. But even when the Livingstone-led authority extended the hand of friendship to Jewish organizations in search of funds, it met with much more criticism than praise.

The establishment by the Labour-controlled GLC of an Ethnic Minorities Unit (EMU) represented the fulfilment of a pledge to give concrete expression to a policy of affirmative action. This policy had wide support within Labour circles; there was nothing specifically 'militant' about it. It was understood that the major clients of the EMU would be found within London's Black population, and that some other ethnic groups, such as the Irish and the Chinese, would be encouraged to apply to it. That Jewish groups would be able to make applications for funds does not seem to have immediately occurred either to the EMU or to the Board of Deputies, the vast majority of whose members (reflecting a view widely held in Anglo-Jewry) recoiled from the idea that they might indeed form an ethnic – as opposed to a narrowly religious – body. To be classed as an *ethnic* minority had (it was privately admitted) some advantages.[70] Against these, however, had to be weighed the supposed disadvantages that might accrue from being associated with the Blacks; it was upon this ground that any suggestion that Jews might appear as a separate category on a future census form, along with other minorities, was steadfastly rejected.[71]

On 1 October 1982 the *Jewish Chronicle* carried an advertisement placed by the EMU, offering grant-aid to Jewish organizations and announcing that a meeting would be held at the West London Synagogue. The meeting was not a success. The choice of venue – a Reform synagogue – was unfortunate. The meeting did not have the imprimatur of the Board of Deputies or any other generally representative Anglo-Jewish body. The EMU's own note of the meeting confessed that 'The majority of people attending claimed that it was an unrepresentative gathering.... Those who participated in the discussion made it quite clear that they ... felt consultations could only succeed with the full involvement and blessing of the Board.'[72]

The EMU's note also referred to criticism made at the meeting of the GLC's Labour leadership 'because of its "anti-semitic" pronouncements about Israel'. These pronouncements will be examined in length in due course. Officers of the EMU were left in no doubt, however, that such pronouncements would be bound to constitute a major obstacle to co-operation with the Board and AJEX. A way round this obstacle now presented itself. The ultra-orthodox communities of Hackney are, for the most part, non-Zionist; some sects are, in fact, anti-Zionist. They did not, therefore, feel especially agitated against those who ruled at County Hall on account of any anti-Israel or pro-Palestinian sentiments. Moreover, since these communities had no representation or desire to be represented on the Board of Deputies, the fact that the Board disapproved of the GLC leadership and its Ethnic Minorities Unit was, quite simply, of no concern to them. What did concern them, however, was the prospect of benefiting financially from the considerable budget put at the EMU's disposal.

The major representative organ of the Hackney ultra-orthodox sects is the Agudas Israel organization, part of a world movement which 'opposes assimilation and different interpretations of Jewish nationhood'. With its British headquarters at Stamford Hill, Agudas Israel is excellently placed to articulate the needs of its members, whose large families and relative poverty make considerable demands upon its charitable institutions. Following the abortive October 1982 meeting at the West London Reform Synagogue, Agudas Israel Community Services (which had not, of course, attended the meeting) approached the Ethnic Minorities Unit. Representatives of both sides met on 7 December (at the Marcus Samuel Hall of the New Synagogue, Stamford Hill) when, to the accompaniment of loud complaints from Agudas Israel members that the Board of Deputies 'was no longer an effective and fully representative body', a case was made for substantial grant-aid to meet the educational, housing, and welfare needs of Hackney's orthodox community. An earnest request was also made that the GLC bypass the Board (whose representatives were present) when dealing with such applications. Ansel Wong, the EMU's Director, described the meeting as 'fruitful'.[73]

Agudas Israel members did not mind being termed an 'ethnic minority'; this was a small price to pay for the large sums (£26,000 in 1983–4) that the EMU was to give to it. The willingness of this important if idiosyncratic section of London Jewry to accept EMU money seems to have spurred other London-based Jewish organizations to make their own applications. In the years that followed the EMU was to make available sums ranging from £220 to the Jewish Employment Action Group (formed by a group of Jewish professionals in north-west London to fight cases of anti-Jewish discrimination in employment) to £3,321 to the Jewish Social Responsibility Council, £7,920 to the Redbridge Jewish Youth Association, and £12,000 to the Jewish Association for the Physically Handicapped.[74]

Those who led the Board of Deputies at this time viewed these developments with the utmost anxiety. The reason publicly given for this was (in the words of Henry Morris, who had succeeded Martin Savitt as chairman of the Board's Defence Committee) that 'sections of the community were prepared to accept money from politicians whose views on Israel were suspect' – a view endorsed and echoed in the *Jewish Chronicle*.[75] Since the sums being disbursed came, ultimately, from the ratepayers of London, this rationale seems rather lame. The policy of the Conservative government at this time was that the PLO needed to be brought into Middle-East peace discussions, and that there was an unanswerable case for Palestinian–Arab self-determination.[76] Yet the Board did not turn its back on Whitehall, as it was to do against County Hall.

The real reason for the Board's intense irritation with the EMU stemmed from the fear that, through its grant-giving policies, the EMU would give financial muscle – and hence communal and perhaps national status – to groups of which the Board itself disapproved. Such disapproval might be because (like Agudas Israel) such groups ignored the Board's claim to be the representative body of Anglo-Jewry, or because (like the Jewish Employment Action Group) their activities posed a threat to established organs (in this case the Trades Advisory Council), or indeed because (like the Jewish Socialists' Group, JSG) they rejected the Zionism with which the Board itself was now saturated.[77]

By 1981 Zionism had become a critical litmus test of respectability and responsibility in Anglo-Jewish circles. This was not a test applied by the GLC's Ethnic Minorities Unit. The Board had responded positively to an overture from the EMU, and had welcomed a suggestion that applications from Jewish organ- izations for grant-aid be submitted to the Board 'for comments and guidance'. The extension of such a courtesy certainly did not amount to a veto; the EMU remained adamant that the wishes of any group which did not want its application forwarded to the Board would be respected.[78] At the time, however, officers of the Board appear to have believed that it had indeed been given a veto, and made it publicly known that this was the case. More import- antly, officials at County Hall were left with the impression that whatever technical meaning 'comments and guidance' might have, such guidance as the Board might give would indeed be regarded as mandatory.[79] The Board began to receive copies of relevant grant applications, one of which came from the JSG. Board officers advised that the application be refused. Instead, the JSG was awarded grants totalling £22,258 over the financial years 1983–4 and 1984–5.

When news of this development reached the Board, its fury

knew no bounds. Founded in 1976 with the twin objects of combating racism and encouraging leftwing support for Israel, the JSG consisted of about sixty active members. The money it received from the EMU was to be used to fund the Jewish Cultural and Anti-Racist Project, an imaginative programme of events and exhibitions designed to provide a high-profile explicitly-Jewish input into the movement to combat racial discrimination and to foster better Black–Jewish relations by drawing upon 'the radical anti-racist history and immigrant experience within the Jewish community'.[80] Some members and supporters of the JSG were undoubtedly anti-Zionist, although the JSG itself never adopted such an extreme platform. However, as far as Dr Gewirtz was concerned, the JSG was nothing more than 'a handful of Trotskyists, Communists, Bundists [i.e. anti-Zionist Socialists] and other assorted anti-Zionists who are united only in their support of the PLO'.[81] Now, as a direct response to the grants which the GLC was making to the JSG, the Board's Defence Committee announced that it felt it appropriate 'to suspend participation in the work of the Ethnic Minorities Unit and to arrange the Board's presence purely in the role of observers'.[82]

Although the EMU's refusal to accept the advice of the Board in relation to the Jewish Socialists' Group was the occasion for a rupture in relations with the GLC, it should be regarded more in the nature of a final straw than a full-blown *casus belli*. By the autumn of 1983 the Board's Defence Department had been able to compile a formidable list of complaints against the Labour-controlled GLC. Some of these referred to policy decisions taken by committees or officials of the Council; others arose out of statements made by members of the ruling Party, especially Mr Livingstone himself.

As early as June 1982 Dr Gewirtz had complained about a cartoon that had appeared in the *Labour Herald*, of which Ken Livingstone was an editor; the cartoon depicted Menachem Begin, Israel's prime minister, in Gestapo uniform, astride the corpses of Palestinian Arabs, and was entitled 'The Final Solution'.[83] The newspaper itself was said to have links with Colonel Gadaffi's regime in Libya, and with the Workers' Revolutionary Party.[84] The Board referred it to the Attorney General for prosecution under the Race Relations Act, but without success. Later that year the Labour group on the GLC moved a motion attacking an anti-

Irish cartoon in *The Standard* as racist; an attempt by the Conservative opposition to have the *Labour Herald* cartoon similarly condemned was defeated.[85]

The *Herald* cartoon was not only in itself offensive to Anglo-Jewry, but must be seen in the broader context of a string of unhelpful and provocative statements that appeared in the newspaper at this time. The *Herald* referred to Israel as 'a State entirely built on the blood of Europe's Jews, whom the Zionists deserted in their hour of greatest need'. Livingstone was reported as having referred to Israel as a country based on 'racism and the murder of Arabs', and he was accused of deliberately using the *Herald* in order to launch scathing attacks on Israel and Zionism; nor was his comparison of the sufferings of Northern Irish Catholics with the Holocaust sympathetically received in Anglo-Jewish circles.[86]

In 1984 the GLC launched an 'Anti-Racist Year'. The Board of Deputies' Defence Committee agreed to be represented at the opening ceremony at County Hall, but evidently without much enthusiasm for the venture.[87] If it could be argued that Zionism was Racism, the Anti-Racist Year might well be used as a launching-pad for further anti-Israeli propaganda. This fear was, in part, borne out. The pro-PLO Labour Committee on Palestine was already permitted to use County Hall as its base, and in March 1983 the Board had protested to the ILEA about a school essay competition on the theme 'Palestinians – a People without their Land'.[88] Once the Anti-Racist Year had commenced, GLC support for Palestinian groups became more overt. Matters reached crisis point when it became clear that the EMU had decided to make a grant of £3,000 to the Palestine Solidarity Campaign (PSC) in order to enable it, as part of the Anti-Racist celebrations, to hold a conference on what was termed 'Anti-Arab Racism' in London.

The explanation reportedly given by Peter Pitt, chairman of the GLC's Arts and Recreation Committee, that 'since the philosophy of Zionism has been condemned along with apartheid by the United Nations as racist, it is perfectly in order to place Palestinian Solidarity on this anti-racist platform', confirmed the worst fears of the Anglo-Jewish community.[89] The Board of Deputies launched an immediate campaign against the decision to make the grant, and threatened legal action to reverse it.[90] In August, a similar protest against GLC funding, under the auspices of the Arts and Recreation Committee, of a PSC concert, had been rebuffed.[91] The intention of the Ethnic Minorities Unit to support anti-Zionist propaganda (which was interpreted by most in the Jewish community as anti-Jewish propaganda) met with widespread condemnation which crossed party lines. The Conservatives withdrew from the Anti-Racist Year in protest at what they saw as Livingstone's support for terrorists and his anti-Jewish remarks. Anne Sofer, the SDP member for Camden (married to a Jew) argued that the PSC constitution contained no reference to the well-being of London's Arab population, and was concerned only with Middle-East politics. On the Labour side Gerry Ross agreed with the Board of Deputies that the PSC was Trotskyist and racist.[92]

None the less, the conference on 'Anti-Arab Racism' did take place (on 14 October) and was followed, on 7 December, by the hosting of a rally ('Black People's Solidarity with the Miners') in which PLO (and, for good measure, Sinn Fein) sympathizers took part. Ross compared the meeting to 'a Nazi rally'; one speaker had declared that they were in reality PLO representatives while another, from the East London Asian Collective, argued that Sinn Fein and the PLO were in 'the front line of battle'.[93]

In agreeing to allow the December 1984 rally to take place, Livingstone had apparently overruled his own chief whip.[94] More serious divisions within the ruling Labour group emerged following the publication, in the Israeli magazine *Davar* (the organ of the *Histadrut*, the Israeli Labour Federation), of an interview with Livingstone, in which he claimed that the Board of Deputies had been 'taken over by Jews who hold extreme right-wing views' and that Jews 'have been organising here in London, and throughout Britain, into paramilitary groups which resemble fascist organisations'. Livingstone further claimed that progressive Jews supported him. But the GLC chairman, Illtyd Harrington, called his remarks contemptuous, arguing that they made the GLC appear antisemitic and damaged relations with the entire London Jewish community. Gladys Dimson threatened to resign unless Livingstone apologized.[95] On the initiative of Dimson and Ross, the GLC's Labour group (by twenty votes to eight) demanded the withdrawal of Livingstone's 'outrageous accusations'; the following day (18 December 1984) the full Council (twenty-two Labour members either abstaining or being absent) supported a motion proposed by the Conservative leader, Alan Greengross, censuring Livingstone for having allowed County Hall to be used for the Black People's Solidarity Rally earlier in the month.[96]

Before assessing the significance of these developments it is worth noting that it was not only in relation to the Middle East that Anglo-Jewry had come to find itself at odds with the Livingstone-led GLC. The access given to County Hall by extremist and fringe groups of all sorts was, at best, alienating and, at worst, downright offensive. Of particular importance in this regard were a number of incidents that arose out of contacts between the GLC and the USSR. The GLC had supported an Auschwitz exhibition in east London, but had appeared to drag its feet over a Soviet–Jewry exhibition at the Royal Festival Hall. An exhibition portraying Soviet life had caused offence, not least because it coincided with a hunger strike in Russia by the 'refusnik' Anatoly Sharansky. Peter Pitt, the GLC's Arts and Recreation Committee chairman, later wrote to the Campaign for Soviet Jewry admitting that the decision to allow this exhibition to go ahead had been an error.[97] Comments made by GLC chairman Harvey Hinds, following a Concerned Jewish Youth demonstration on the occasion of a visit by the Mayor of Moscow, had led to further communal protests.[98] In April 1983 women members of Poale Zion found themselves barred from an International Women's Day seminar at County Hall, and in June 1984 four Labour members of the Council (including Dimson and Ross) voted with the Opposition to carry an adjournment motion in protest at anti-Zionist remarks alleged to have been made on the GLC's Women's Committee.[99]

The events of late 1984 marked a watershed of devastating dimensions in the relationship between Anglo-Jewry and the Greater London Labour Party. Of Livingstone's *Davar* interview, Gerry Ross had made the stark but utterly realistic assessment that the Labour leader had 'effectively destroyed the bridges ... built up between the GLC and the London Jewish community'.[100] Although Livingstone suffered a reverse on 18 December, he survived a more general motion of censure put down by Greengross on 22 January 1985. Livingstone's amendment to this motion sought to draw a clear distinction between anti-Zionism and antisemitism.[101] The amendment was carried by forty-two votes to thirty-two. It was obvious, therefore, that his position as leader of the GLC, and chair of its Ethnic Minorities Committee, remained basically secure, and that any hope Anglo-Jewry might have entertained of weaning him, and the ruling Labour group, away from its policies on the Middle East must be abandoned.

In respect of his statements to *Davar* the Board of Deputies demanded an apology. None was ever forthcoming. Parallel with his struggle against the Board Livingstone had fought another battle, which must have become more important to him once it had become clear that (following the Conservative victory in the June 1983 General Election) Mrs Thatcher's promise to abolish the GLC along with the other metropolitan counties was bound to pass into law. The days of the GLC were therefore numbered. But Livingstone had parliamentary ambitions, which centred upon the Brent East constituency. With its large Black and Irish populations, and a local Labour Party gradually succumbing to infiltration by the hard left, Brent East was bound to respond positively to the mixture of anti-Thatcherism, anti-Zionism, anti-racism, and support for the IRA which Livingstone had to offer. Reg Freeson managed (but only after much effort, and the intervention of Labour's National Executive Committee) to retain the Labour nomination there in 1983, but in March 1985 he gave up the struggle for reselection.[102] Livingstone narrowly won the nomination as his successor and – in this very safe Labour seat – could therefore be confident of becoming its MP whenever the next election might be called.

Elsewhere in London, the impact upon the Jewish community of leftwing dominance of constituency Labour parties was equally apparent. At Central Hackney, for example, moves were made as early as 1981 to replace the Jewish Labour MP Stanley Clinton Davis, who had publicly criticized Livingstone. Boundary changes following the 1979 General Election meant that his constituency was, in any case, due to disappear; it was clear that he would not be adopted for either of the two remaining Hackney seats.[103] Towards the end of 1982 the *Jewish Chronicle* reported that at a meeting of the Constituency Labour Party at Paddington (which Livingstone represented on the GLC), a suggestion that Israel had no right to exist was greeted with applause.[104] The Chipping Barnet Constituency Labour Party endorsed a pro-PLO motion in March 1986.[105]

By then, relations between London Jewry and the GLC had

more or less completely broken down. Earlier possibilities of collaboration (most notably in the inquiry initiated by the GLC's Police Committee into racial harassment) had been overtaken by mutual hostility and exasperation.[106] In October 1985 a lunch which the GLC intended to give to honour the Jewish contribution to the life of the metropolis was cancelled when it became clear that neither Sir Immanuel Jakobovits (the Chief Rabbi, who was to be guest of honour) nor the Board of Deputies would attend if Livingstone were present.[107] The following month an attempt by the Council's Arts and Recreation Committee to make the sum of £26,990 available to fund a Palestine Week organized by the British Friends of Palestine was only thwarted after a revolt by some Labour councillors (notably Ashley Bramall and the Jewish members Yvonne Sieve and Gerry Ross) ensured the passage (by forty-three votes to thirty-eight) of a Conservative amendment.[108]

Four months later, under the provisions of the 1985 Local Government Act, the GLC was abolished. During the long campaign to save it (one result of which was the Conservative government's acquiescence in the retention of the ILEA), the Council's Labour leadership had made many appeals to ethnic minorities in the capital for help. From London Jewry none was forthcoming.[109] As a community the Jews of London played no part in the lengthy public debates to which the policy of abolition had given rise. Privately, for the most part, they condemned the institution along with the policies of those who had ultimately gained control of it, and there were few among London Jewry who mourned the day (31 March 1986) of its death.

At the level of issues, it is all too easy to interpret the tensions that characterized relations between London Jewry and the GLC after 1981 in terms of Zionism and anti-Zionism, support for and opposition to the PLO, commitment to Israel and hostility to it. That deep differences existed over these matters cannot be doubted, of course. But these differences sprang, in turn, from much more fundamental divergences of outlook. During the 1980s the close relationship of former times between London Jewry and the Labour Party finally fell apart. In moving out from east London into the suburbs the Jews had also moved up, into the ranks of the middle classes. Even in the early 1960s a survey of Jews in Edgware (within the Borough of Barnet) had revealed that over 80 per cent of the sample regarded themselves as middle-class.[110] An analysis of Redbridge Jewry, carried out by the Board of Deputies in 1978, showed that 70 per cent of the Jews there belonged to the professional, managerial, and skilled non-manual occupational classes.[111] These were precisely the groups among which the Conservative Party that Mrs Thatcher led from 1975 was to make some of its most eager converts.

As prime minister since May 1979, Mrs Thatcher has arguably pursued a foreign policy more pro-Jewish than that of any of her predecessors since David Lloyd George. She has managed to include in her governments a relatively large number of Jews (no less than four Jewish members of the Cabinet at one stage), and she and her Party have gone out of their way to support Soviet Jewry. It is true that her government concluded an arms deal with Saudi Arabia (with which Israel is still at war). But she herself visited Israel, and the Foreign Office ended its complicity in the Arab boycott (through the certification of signatures on boycott documents).

More generally, the Conservative themes of self-help and the virtues of the market-place have struck particularly resonant chords within London's Jewish community. And, as the General Election of June 1987 was to show in a dramatic way, the relationship between housing tenure and party allegiance was bound to make Jewry a particularly fertile source of Conservative support.[112] In Redbridge over 90 per cent of Jews are owner-occupiers, and in those parts of Barnet, Brent, Enfield, and Harrow where Jews reside in large numbers, the proportion of owner-occupiers is not less than half, and often much higher.[113]

These themes, the hallmarks of Thatcherite Conservatism, have also been accorded the most eminent rabbinical endorsement. During the 1980s Mrs Thatcher found herself under increasing attack from within the Established Church of England on fundamental questions of social policy, especially in relation to inner-city areas. Her most consistent theological support has come from within the circle of orthodox Jewry. In a pamphlet published by the rightwing Social Affairs Unit in 1985 Rabbi Dr Jonathan Sacks, the Principal of Jews' College, London, contrived to offer thinly-veiled support from the Old Testament for major elements of Conservative domestic legislation; Rabbi Sacks' selected texts (Hugo Young argued) served to confer 'ethical legitimacy on a series of economic policies that Christian churchmen have denounced'.[114] Nowhere were such denunciations more eloquently expressed than in the pages of the report (*Faith in the City*) of the Archbishop of Canterbury's Commission on Urban Priority Areas. It was Sir Immanuel Jakobovits who came to Mrs Thatcher's rescue, exhorting the disadvantaged not to insist upon public help ('self-reliant efforts and perseverance eventually pay off'), and criticizing the Blacks for wishing to change the character of British society into 'a new multi-ethnic form'.[115] These views were themselves controversial, and did not represent the opinions of all orthodox Jews, or even of all orthodox Jewish clergy. But they did accurately mirror a feeling widespread within an Anglo-Jewish community that was rapidly turning its back on the welfare state and its face against collectivism.

The behaviour of London Jewry during the General Election of June 1987 reflected these developments. The attempt by Mr Ephraim Briskman to persuade the Jewish voters of Finchley that 'Judaism is a faith which promotes the concept of caring for everybody. Therefore no member of the Jewish Community should support Mrs Thatcher' was bound to fall upon deaf ears. The leaflet that he distributed (and from which the quotation is taken) was boldly drafted but totally misconceived. Much more significant was the help that Martin Savitt gave to the Conservative Party in Brent East. Shortly after the abolition of the GLC, Livingstone had prophesied that 'elements' from the Board of Deputies would make 'a major attempt to try to defeat me as the parliamentary candidate for Brent East'.[116] So it was. Savitt, by then no longer an honorary officer of the Board, but still a member of its Executive Committee and a vice-chairman of the Zionist Federation, assisted the Conservative candidate, Harriet Crawley, in the drafting of an anti-Livingstone leaflet, because he considered it his 'personal duty to appraise the community about Livingstone', whom he felt was 'a national danger'.[117] The Livingstone candidature was always controversial, and his return to Parliament, on a much reduced Labour vote, entirely predictable. Martin Savitt is, however, entitled to claim a little credit for the narrowness of his victory.

In December 1984 the *Jewish Chronicle* had drawn the attention of the Labour Party to 'the negative impact' that Livingstone was having 'on what has not been an unimportant segment of its Metropolitan support and vote'.[118] Whether, in pointing to the effect of one individual, the paper was being over-dramatic, or simplistic, is difficult to judge. But what cannot be denied is the considerable distancing of London Jewry from the world of Labour politics. During the February 1974 General Election the author began collecting data relating to the voting preferences of Jews in selected north-London constituencies. Some of the results are summarized in table 5.2, and offer support for the view that the trend of Jewish electoral behaviour in north-east and north-west London has been significantly different from that of the total electorates in these areas: in almost all cases, Jews have displayed a higher than average support for Conservatism and a lower than average support of Labour. At Finchley, in 1987, Mrs Thatcher increased her share of the total poll by 2.8 per cent, but her share of the Jewish poll by nearly three times that amount; while the constituency as a whole exhibited a swing of 1 per cent from Conservative to Labour, the Jewish vote there swung heavily (5 per cent) against the trend.

Table 5.2   Jewish Political Preferences in London, 1974–87

	Conservative	Labour	Alliance
	%	%	%
Hendon North (F.1974) (N=150)	59.1	15.9	25.0
Hendon North (O.1974) (N=178)	68.3	21.9	9.8
Ilford North (1979) (N=143)	61.2	34.7	4.1
Finchley (1983) (N=120)	52.4	23.8	23.8
Finchley (1987) (N=205)	60.5	22.0	17.6

Source: G. Alderman, 'London Jews and the 1987 General Election', *Jewish Quarterly*, 34, no. 3 1987, pp.13–16; all percentages are based on those who stated an intention to vote.

The world that London Jewry now inhabits is in very large measure a Conservative world, even where (as in Hackney) Jews happen to live in a Labour environment.[119] In this world there is no longer a place for an elected authority to represent the views of London as a whole, and the borough authorities that remain are increasingly becoming mere agents, directed by a central government in the hands of the Conservative Party. For the moment, at any rate, this is a state of affairs that London Jewry broadly supports.

CONCLUSION

In this study I have attempted to trace the interaction between London government and one distinctive minority group over a period of little less than a hundred years. Until the Black and Asian immigration of the most recent times, only the Irish presence in London was larger than that represented by the Jews. During the nineteenth century the Irish parliamentary vote remained 'strongly organised', and both in the capital and in other major centres of Irish settlement, such as Liverpool, Irish Catholics managed to inject their own special preoccupations into national and municipal politics.[1] The General Election of 1987 saw the return to the House of Commons of the first Afro-Caribbean MPs (Diane Abbott at Hackney North, Paul Boateng at Brent South, and Bernie Grant at Tottenham); their success was built upon solid achievements at municipal level, where Afro-Caribbean and Asian immigrants have not been slow to use the machinery of local government to further communal ends.[2]

By comparison, the impact of London Jewry upon London government seems relatively modest. Success in achieving 'emancipation' at municipal level was indeed used as a springboard to full political equality, in parliamentary terms, but these achievements were seen as ends in themselves. There was no attempt to *use* the organs of local administration in London to further the well-being of London Jewry; indeed the community was proud of the fact that it could cope with such problems as beset it, mainly through poor relief, without recourse to public funds. The mass immigration from eastern Europe in the 1880s and 1890s forced a reconsideration of this policy. Even in the matter of educational provision, it is doubtful whether the Jewish community would have embraced the legislation of 1902-3 so eagerly had the influx of refugees not compelled it to do so.

During and (especially) after the First World War the not inconsiderable electoral force represented by London Jewry remained largely unharnessed, though it might have been used, if not to overturn the discriminatory policies of the LCC in the fields of education, employment, and housing, at least to ameliorate their impact. This road was abandoned – or rather it was never taken. Faced with the twin enormities of Fascism at home and Nazism abroad, communal leaders preferred not to tackle County Hall head on, but to deal with individual cases through discrete contacts, an approach that was broadly maintained after the war. Individual Jews of course recognized that the electoral card could be played, and occasionally it was (as during the parliamentary by-election at Whitechapel in 1930), but officially the power that it represented was eschewed. It is possible, indeed, that the transitory support for Communism in east London amounted to a genuine Jewish reaction to this policy at grass-roots level.

In political terms, the initial appeal of the Progressive coalition for Jewish Londoners was damaged irreparably by the education controversy, while the Municipal Reformers were identified too closely with the discriminatory policies of the period 1914-23 to remain attractive to the Jewish masses of the capital. During the inter-war years Jews supported Labour not so much on ideological or socio-economic grounds, as through a process of elimination. Under Labour control the LCC retained intact some of the worst features of the anti-Jewish policies that had originated with the Municipal Reformers, but the Labour Party still remained the best option then available to the Jews of the metropolis. The changing political sociology of London Jewry after 1945 was bound to result in a diminution of Jewish support for Labour. Yet the approach of the Jewish community to the problem of how best to address the government of London remained the same. Except in times of acute communal disquiet – as over education in 1904, Fascism in 1937, and racism in the 1970s – the preference has always been to work behind closed doors, to create and maintain good relations with local government leaderships – and bureaucrats – and to keep talking even to less palatable regimes at County Hall.

This is what the leaders of Anglo-Jewry have wanted, partly

because they have genuinely believed that nothing more could be achieved by other means, and partly because the pursuit of quiet (sometimes secret) diplomacy has served to preserve an image of social and political assimilation. This view – almost, that all publicity is likely to be bad publicity – was taken to extreme lengths in the 1950s, when the effects of an adverse public image during the last years of the Palestine Mandate were still being felt, and when domestic Fascism remained a major preoccupation. During the 1950s and early 1960s the Board of Deputies and the Trades Advisory Council made many attempts to persuade the LCC not to allow the Union Movement and the British National Party to use LCC schools for their meetings.[3] Although, in isolated cases, Jewish sensitivities were met (usually as an unintended consequence of intervention by the police) the general response was disappointing. Yet, although within Jewish circles grave misgivings were voiced, the matter was not pressed or (for example) made an issue at any LCC election.[4] In 1957 the Board's Defence Committee communicated to Councillor Frank Davis its displeasure that he had seen fit to raise the matter of anti-Jewish discrimination at Finchley Golf Club during the borough-council elections; in July, with the provincial municipal elections in mind, the Committee re-emphasized (privately) its view that Jews should neither be singled out by mention nor appealed to, as Jews, during the campaigns.[5]

Was this policy and approach in the communal interest? Might more have been achieved by adopting a higher profile? In a sense these are unreal questions because they are unanswerable: we do not know what might have been. We are, however, entitled to raise some related issues. The political potential of Jewish membership of the London County Council was never exploited to the full. 'The community', the *Jewish Chronicle* told its readers in 1965, 'may take pride in the part played by Jews in its [the LCC'S] development'.[6] It is true that the contribution of individual Jews to the work of the LCC was distinguished. But very little of this effort was directed towards helping fellow Jews. Henry Gordon, Nettie Adler, and Morry Davis were the exceptions that proved the rule. Mrs Helen Bentwich spoke frankly when she declared that Jewish members of the Council had never 'allowed their Jewishness to influence their voting on any projects'.[7] But her explanation for this – 'if Jewish members have always given disinterested service ... then the Council itself ... has "always leaned over backwards to be good to the Jews"' - is clearly at fault. During its history there were many occasions upon which the LCC was distinctly and deliberately hostile to Jewish interests. Mrs Bentwich herself, when chairman of the Council's Education Committee, gave (according to the testimony of the then president of the Board of Deputies) 'no satisfaction' on the matter of allowing the Union Movement to meet on LCC school premises.[8]

The attitude that Helen Bentwich and others characterized as 'disinterested' may well have been derived from altruism; most Jews who gained election to the LCC were highly acculturated, with a strong sense of public duty (and, perhaps, of the social acceptance and civic status that would be gained thereby); like their Prussian co-religionists, they served in local government because that was what their commitment to public life obliged them to do.[9] 'The part which Jews played in the Council', Norman Bentwich wrote, 'was remarkable ... no consideration of religion or race affected either the [Jewish] electors or the Councillors.'[10]

But this attitude was also rooted in fear: to adopt too strident and too salient a profile was (it was argued) likely to be counter-productive. Perhaps for this reason, Anglo-Jewry never bothered to formulate an explicit and coherent local-government policy, other than to deal with problems as they arose, by the time-honoured methods of backstairs diplomacy and appeals for communal self-restraint. The limitations inherent in these expedients became all too obvious after 1981. Lulled into a false sense of security by the good relations that had been evinced by GLC administrations hitherto, and increasingly disinterested (through its drift towards Conservatism) in the anti-Jewish and anti-Zionist threads within the new fabric of militant urban Labour politics, London Jewry discovered too late that the old methods would no longer work. Friendly armchair discussions did not impress the hard left, while the total - and deliberate - failure to create a specifically ethnic representation of the community at County Hall resulted in chronic weakness in the Council chamber, from which rescue could only come at the hands of the Conservative opposition in the short term, and, in the long term, outright elimination of a beast that could no longer be controlled or reasoned with.

The progressive weakening of local-government autonomy and

initiative by Conservative administrations since 1979 is thus regarded in many Anglo-Jewish quarters with scarcely-concealed satisfaction. The dangers seem, at the time of writing, to have been hardly appreciated. It is all very well to call in national government to remove otherwise insoluble municipal difficulties. What is to happen if and when the national government itself falls into less accommodating hands?

NOTES

1 LONDON JEWRY AND LONDON GOVERNMENT BEFORE 1889

1 L. P. Gartner, *The Jewish Immigrant in England, 1870–1914* (Allen & Unwin, London, 1960).

2 C. Holmes, *Anti-Semitism in British Society 1876–1939* (Edward Arnold, London, 1979); V. D. Lipman, *A Century of Social Service 1859–1959: The Jewish Board of Guardians* (Routledge & Kegan Paul, London, 1959).

3 I am thinking of works such as: B. Gainer, *The Alien Invasion* (Heinemann, London, 1972); J. A. Garrard, *The English and Immigration 1880–1910* (Oxford University Press, London, 1971); G. C. Lebzelter, *Political Anti-Semitism in England 1918–1939* (Macmillan, London, 1978); and J. White, *Rothschild Buildings* (Routledge & Kegan Paul, London, 1980). However, J. Bush, *Behind The Lines: East London Labour 1914–1919* (Merlin Press, London, 1984) displays throughout an acute awareness of the importance of London's municipal politics.

4 P. Thompson, *Socialists, Liberals and Labour: The Struggle for London 1885–1914* (Routledge & Kegan Paul, London, 1967), especially pp. 27–31.

5 K. Young, *Local Politics and The Rise of Party* (Leicester University Press, Leicester, 1975), p. 19; on Jessel, who was chairman of the London Municipal Society 1903–15, trustee 1915–24, and president 1924–51, see *The Times*, 2 November 1950, p. 6, and *J[ewish] C[hronicle]*, 10 November 1950, p. 8.

6 Sir G. Gibbon and R. W. Bell, *History of the London County Council 1889–1939* (Macmillan, London, 1939); W. E. Jackson, *Achievement: A Short History of the London County Council* (Longman, London, 1965).

7 On the development of Jewish communities in the provinces, see generally *Birmingham Jewry 1749–1914* (Birmingham Jewish History Group, 1980); C. Roth, *The Rise of Provincial Jewry* (Jewish Monthly, London, 1950); A. Newman (ed.), *Provincial Jewry in Victorian*

Britain (Jewish Historical Society of England, London, 1975); and Bill Williams, *The Making of Manchester Jewry 1740–1875* (Manchester University Press, Manchester, 1976).

8 G. Alderman, *The Jewish Community in British Politics* (Oxford University Press, Oxford, 1983), pp. 23–8.

9 E. M. Tomlinson, *History of the Minories* (Smith, Elder & Co., London, 1907), p. 310.

10 C. Roth, *A History of the Jews in England* (2nd edn, Clarendon Press, Oxford, 1949), p. 252.

11 On which see M. C. N. Salbstein, *The Emancipation of the Jews in Britain* (Associated University Presses, London, 1982), pp. 126–31.

12 *Birmingham Jewry*, p. 25.

13 Peel Papers, British Library, Add[itional] MS 40535, fols 245–9: Salomons to Peel, 8 and 20 November 1843.

14 Peel Papers, Add. MS 40442, fols 263–4.

15 L. Simmonds, 'Six Lord Mayors', *JC*, 28 October 1960, pp. 21–2.

16 *JC*, 3 February and 27 October 1882.

17 Alderman, *Jewish Community*, p. 9.

18 J. Jacobs, *Studies in Jewish Statistics* (D. Nutt, London, 1891), pp. 11–13.

19 Lipman, *Century of Social Service*, p. 1.

20 ibid., p. 11; J. Jacobs, *Statistics of the Jewish Population in London, etc. 1873–1893* (Russo-Jewish Committee, London, 1894), p. 9.

21 Lipman, *Century of Social Service*, pp. 8–10.

22 Jackson, *Achievement*, p. 4.

23 Gibbon and Bell, *History of the LCC*, pp. 36–7.

24 S. E. Finer, *The Life and Times of Sir Edwin Chadwick* (Methuen, London, 1952), p. 502.

25 Gibbon and Bell, *History of the LCC*, p. 55.

26 Tower Hamlets Central Library, Stepney, Local Collection file 321.1: handbill in German, [March] 1884, signed by Abraham Benabo, 284 Commercial Road: *E[ast] L[ondon] O[bserver]*, 29 March 1884, p. 3. A further example of the antisemitism to which vestries in east London were prone is given in *London*, 25 October 1894, p. 686 (referring to the Whitechapel Board of Works).

27 On Marks and Levy see D. Owen, *The Government of Victorian London 1855–1889* (Harvard University Press, Cambridge, Mass., 1982), pp. 268 and 319.

28 The final volume of the Metropolitan Board of Works' *Handbook and Diary* (1888), pp. 78–82, lists all members of the Board since its foundation. These included a William Nathan (member for Limehouse 1872–80), whose surname might be said to be 'Jewish'. There is no explicit evidence that John Runtz (Hackney, 1867–88), who was heavily implicated in the financial scandals that surrounded the Board's last years, was a Jew. But the *JC*, 21 November 1890, p. 14, saw fit to report on the unveiling in Hackney of a drinking fountain, as a testimonial to the efforts of Runtz and a colleague in acquiring Clissold Park 'for the people'; Rabbi Professor Sir H. Gollancz was

present at the ceremony. Joseph d'Aguilar Samuda (Poplar, 1861–5) was a convert to Christianity: see Alderman, *Jewish Community*, p. 36. The *JC*, 25 January 1856, p. 461, recorded Lewis Davis (Plumstead) as having been returned as one of the forty Commissioners of the Board.

29 Lipman, *Century of Social Service*, pp. 63–5.
30 Gibbon and Bell, *History of the LCC*, p. 29.
31 H. Marks and W. R. Lawson, *The Metropolitan Board of Works: A Brief Account of the Disclosures Which Have Led to the Appointment of a Royal Commission to Investigate the Charges Brought Against It. Reprinted from the Financial News* (London, 1888). On Marks see *JC*, 29 December 1916, p. 6, and D. Porter, 'A trusted guide of the investing public: Harry Marks and the *Financial News* 1884–1916', *Business History*, vol. 27 (1986), pp. 1–17.
32 W. A. Robson, *The Government and Misgovernment of London* (Allen & Unwin, London, 1939), p. 60.
33 ibid., pp. 73–7.
34 J. Lloyd, *London Municipal Government. History of a Great Reform, 1880–1888* (P. S. King & Son, London, 1910), p. ix; on Cohen see *JC*, 12 November 1909, p. 8.
35 *Parliamentary Debates*, 3rd ser., vol. 323 (1888), cols 1663–4, 19 March 1888.
36 L. Kochan, 'Jews on the move', *Listener*, 27 May 1971, p. 677.
37 V. D. Lipman, 'The structure of London Jewry in the mid-nineteenth century', in H. J. Zimmels, J. Rabbinowitz, and I. Finestein (eds), *Essays Presented to Chief Rabbi Israel Brodie* (Jews' College, London, 1967), p. 255.
38 S. Fyne, 'London's Jewish population', *JC*, 14 October 1955, p. 34; see also S. Waterman and B. Kosmin, *British Jewry in the Eighties* (Board of Deputies of British Jews, London, 1986), p. 6.
39 Lipman, *Century of Social Service*, p. 75.
40 ibid., p. 81
41 Robson, *Government and Misgovernment of London*, p. 84; on Rosebery and his marriage to Hannah Rothschild see C. Bermant, *The Cousinhood* (Eyre & Spottiswoode, London, 1971), pp. 153–64.
42 *Parliamentary Debates*, 3rd ser., vol. 328, cols 991–2, and vol. 329, col. 704 (10 and 27 July 1888); on Goldsmid (who gave the bill a cautious welcome) see Alderman, *Jewish Community*, pp. 32 and 42.
43 The reports of the two Select Committees are summarized in V. D. Lipman, *Social History of the Jews in England 1850–1950* (Watts & Co., London, 1954), pp. 135–7.
44 ibid., p. 104
45 White, *Rothschild Buildings*, pp. 11–20.
46 C. Hershon, 'The evolution of Jewish elementary education in England with special reference to Liverpool' (unpublished PhD thesis, University of Sheffield, 1973), p. 23.
47 ibid., p. 50.
48 Gartner, *Jewish Immigrant*, p. 224.
49 ibid., pp. 227–8.

50 Lipman, *Social History*, p. 152.
51 H. B. Philpott, *London at School: The Story of the School Board, 1870-1904* (Fisher Unwin, London, 1904), p. 113.
52 *JC*, 14 July 1882, p. 13.
53 Gartner, *Jewish Immigrant*, pp. 226-7.
54 *JC*, 17 February 1888, p. 5.
55 *JC*, 26 October 1888, p. 11.
56 L. Cohen, *Some Recollections of Claude Goldsmid Montefiore 1858-1938* (Faber, London, 1940), p. 45. Cohen errs in believing that Montefiore was 'elected twice' to the School Board; he was never elected to it at all.
57 *JC*, 30 November 1888, p. 5; see also 7 December 1888, p. 7, where a correspondent alleged that Montefiore's defeat was due to the apathy of Jewish voters. His victorious opponent was the Socialist Annie Besant: see A. H. Nethercot, *The First Five Lives of Annie Besant* (Hart-Davis, London, 1961), p. 280.
58 On Raphael see *JC*, 26 September 1924, p. 50, and *The Times*, 26 September, p. 1; on Magnus see *JC*, 1 September 1933, p. 10.
59 *JC*, 20 November 1891, pp. 4-5.
60 *JC*, 30 October 1891, pp. 7-8.
61 Alderman, *Jewish Community*, pp. 36-41.
62 G. Alderman, *Modern Britain 1700-1983* (Croom Helm, Beckenham, 1986), p. 141.
63 Alderman, *Jewish Community*, pp. 42-3.
64 ibid., pp. 44-5.
65 H. Pelling, *Social Geography of British Elections 1885-1910* (Macmillan, London, 1967), pp. 42 and 44.
66 *ELO*, 22 September 1900, p. 3.
67 *ELO*, 6 July 1895, p. 5, and 20 July, p. 6; *Reynolds's Newspaper*, 14 July 1895, p. 1.
68 *JC*, 12 October 1900, p. 7.
69 S. J. Curtis and M. E. A. Boultwood, *An Introductory History of English Education Since 1800* (4th edn, University Tutorial Press, London, 1966), pp. 75-6.
70 ibid., p. 163; there was a distinct hypocrisy in the nonconformist view, because no objection was raised to Treasury grants to board and voluntary schools, even though such grants were of course made from moneys derived from general taxation.
71 For the Progressive Party on the School Board see Thompson, *Socialists, Liberals and Labour*, p. 96.
72 To make matters worse, the trade-union lobby within the Progressive camp was, by the mid-1880s, pressing strongly for the Board to adopt a policy whereby trade-union rates of pay would be enforced upon its contractors. This policy was implemented in 1888, even though the Board was under Tory control: ibid., p. 99.
73 W. S. Smith, *The London Heretics 1870-1914* (Constable, London, 1967), p. 192; B. Simon, *Education and the Labour Movement 1870-1920* (Lawrence & Wishart, London, 1965), pp. 143-51; Nethercot, *The*

First Five Lives of Annie Besant, pp. 276-86.
74 *JC*, 4 December 1891, pp. 5-6.
75 Hershon, 'Jewish elementary education', pp. 114-15.
76 Young, *Local Politics*, p. 51.
77 Robson, *Government and Misgovernment of London*, p. 75.
78 S. Buxton, *A Handbook to Political Questions of the Day* (8th edn, John Murray, London, 1892), p. 180.
79 ibid., p. 181.
80 Gibbon and Bell, *History of the LCC*, pp. 86-7; Jackson, *Achievement*, p. 10.
81 On the sweating system in London see J. A. Schmiechen, *Sweated Industries and Sweated Labour: The London Clothing Trades 1860–1914* (Croom Helm, Beckenham, 1984).
82 See, for example, Thompson, *Socialists, Liberals and Labour*, p. 119.
83 Buxton, *Handbook*, p. 185; note the force of the adjective 'undue' in this quotation.
84 *Morning Post*, 10 July 1894, quoted in Young, *Local Politics*, p. 61.
85 *The Times*, 8 November 1894, p. 4.
86 Gibbon and Bell, *History of the LCC*, pp. 90-1.

2 LONDON JEWRY IN THE PROGRESSIVE ERA

1 J. F. B. Firth and E. R. Simpson, *London Government under the London Government Act 1888* (Knight & Co., London, 1888), p. 10; and see above, chapter 1, p. 19.
2 Central Zionist Archives (Jerusalem), Records of the Central Zionist Office, Vienna: Z1, file 243: J. de Haas to Herzl, 17 September 1900.
3 J. White, *Rothschild Buildings* (Routledge & Kegan Paul, London, 1980), p. 271; see also G. Alderman, *The Jewish Community in British Politics* (Oxford University Press, Oxford, 1983), p. 74. The *E[ast] L[ondon] O[bserver]*, 26 August 1905, p. 7, carried a report that the Conservative agent at Mile End had objected to the presence on the electoral register of unnaturalized Jews.
4 See, for example, the *Idisher Ekspres*, 20 February 1907, p. 4. On the naturalization fee see Alderman, *Jewish Community*, pp. 74 and 78.
5 *ELO*, 20 July 1895, p. 6.
6 H. Pelling, *Social Geography of British Elections 1885–1910* (Macmillan, London, 1967), pp. 42 and 44.
7 London County Council, *London Statistics*, vol. V (1894–5), p. 200.
8 ibid.
9 Alderman, *Jewish Community*, p. 183, n. 74.
10 These calculations are based on the statistics given in K. Young, *Local Politics and the Rise of Party* (Leicester University Press, Leicester, 1975), p. 223.
11 London County Council, *London Statistics*, vol. XVIII (1907–8).
12 On Jewish performance at parliamentary elections, see Alderman, *Jewish Community*, pp. 173-5.
13 See, for example, *J[ewish] C[hronicle]*, 21 December 1888, p. 12.

14 On Abrahams see *JC*, 26 July 1895, p. 17; *The Stage*, 21 October 1915, p. 16; and P. Hartnoll (ed.), *The Concise Oxford Companion to the Theatre* (Oxford University Press, Oxford, 1972), p. 406.

15 *JC*, 22 January 1892, p. 7; *The Times*, 4 March 1897, p. 14. The question of Saturday polling for LCC elections had first been raised in 1891, when the Council's General Purposes Committee had decided that the 1892 election should be held on the Jewish Sabbath, notwithstanding pleas from Benjamin Cohen and Sir Thomas Fardell, the Moderate councillor for Paddington South: *JC*, 11 December 1891, pp. 6, 8, and 10. Of this decision the *ELO*, 9 January 1892, p. 5, wrote: 'In the extremity of its Radicalism, and the desire to perpetuate it, the London County Council has done a grievous wrong to the Jewish electors of the Metropolis.' The Moderates were always more sympathetic to the Jewish viewpoint on this matter than were the Progressives, who consistently refused to consent to a change of the day on which the normal triennial LCC elections were held. The Jewish community had to wait until the Moderates came to power for the convention of Thursday polls to be established (1913).

16 *The Times*, 18 March 1897, p. 10. On Lawson see Alderman, *Jewish Community*, pp. 71–2. According to the *ELO*, 20 February 1897, p. 5, Lord Rosebery was approached to stand for the Progressives, but declined the offer.

17 *The Times*, 2 March 1897, p. 5; *ELO*, 4 February 1897, p. 6.

18 *ELO*, 6 March 1897, p. 5; 13 March 1897, p. 5.

19 *The Times*, 9 March 1897, p. 7; 11 March 1897, p. 7. The reason for the Irish support is unclear.

20 *The Times*, 11 March 1897, p. 7.

21 *ELO*, 27 February 1897, p. 7.

22 *JC*, 11 January 1889, p. 5.

23 G[reater] L[ondon] R[ecord] O[ffice], *LCC Minutes*, 23 July 1889: Report of the H[ousing of the] W[orking] C[lasses] C[ommittee].

24 *JC*, 12 April 1889, p. 6.

25 Sir G. Gibbon and R. W. Bell, *History of the London County Council 1889–1939* (Macmillan, London, 1939), p. 366

26 GLRO, *LCC* Minutes, 2 August 1889: Report of the HWCC. See also LCC/MIN/7322: HWCC Presented Papers 1889–92 (Bundles A.12–24): Report of the Sub-Committee on Bell Lane Area, Whitechapel, 29 July 1889; Stuart Samuel was chairman of this sub-committee.

27 Jewish Board of Guardians, *Annual Report 1889*, p. 22.

28 Jewish Board of Guardians, *Annual Report 1890*, p. 75.

29 Leon and Moss were also members of the Asylums Committee, and Leon of the Theatres and Music Halls, Special Water, and Public Control Committees; Benjamin Cohen was a valued member of the Local Government and Taxation Committee.

30 GLRO, LCC/MIN/7256: Minutes of the P[ublic] H[ealth and] H[ousing] C[ommittee], General Sub-Committee meeting, 4 November 1892; and see Jewish Board of Guardians, *Annual Report 1892*, p. 83. On the 1891 Act see J. A. Schmiechen, *Sweated Industries and Sweated*

Labour: The London Clothing Trades 1860-1914 (Croom Helm, Beckenham, 1984), p. 139.

31 Jewish Board of Guardians, *Annual Report 1893*, p. 81; *JC*, 19 January 1894, p. 6. A major difficulty in enforcing the then existing legislation was that sweatshop masters found it easy to evade the regulations. This, in turn, was facilitated by the dearth of inspectors and, more generally, by the economic system which made sweating such a viable proposition. The low pay which was such a central feature of the system was not tackled until the passage of the Trade Boards Act of 1909; see Schmiechen, *Sweated Industries*, pp. 160-79.

32 *JC*, 14 December 1894, p. 5.

33 GLRO, LCC/MIN/7257: Minutes of the Public Health and Housing Committee, 26 November 1894; the reports on Whitechapel and Mile End are in LCC/MIN/7343: PHHC Presented Papers 1893-4 (Bundles E59 and E64). See also Jewish Board of Guardians, *Annual Report 1894*, p. 80, and Letter Book 1880-90: LCC to Board of Guardians, 12 November 1894.

34 GLRO, LCC/MIN/7257: Minutes of the Public Health and Housing Committee, 4 February 1895.

35 *JC*, 14 February 1894, p. 5. In reply to the LCC the Whitechapel Board declared that 'influential members of the Jewish Community can to a great extent remedy the evils of which their Sanitary Committee complain, by using such personal influence in aiding their education, that these people may use, instead of abuse, the Sanitary Conveniences provided for them, and to which they have not hitherto been accustomed': Jewish Board of Guardians, Letter Book 1880-90: Board of Works, Whitechapel District. Reply ... December, 1894.

36 Jewish Board of Guardians, Letter Book 1880-90: Report of the Sanitary Committee on Representations received from London County Council ... 4 December 1894.

37 P. J. Edwards, *History of London Street Improvements 1855-1897* (London County Council, London, 1898), p. 199.

38 A. Morrison, *A Child of the Jago* (Methuen, London, 1896).

39 *The Times*, 9 November 1898, p. 6.

40 ibid., 7 December 1898, p. 12.

41 ibid., 21 December 1898, p. 12.

42 GLRO, LCC Minutes, 28 March 1899; *JC*, 4 August 1899, p. 13. See also L. H. Montagu, *Samuel Montagu First Baron Swaythling* (Truelove & Hanson, London, 1913), p. 53.

43 GLRO, LCC Minutes, 28 July 1903; *JC*, 27 November 1903, p. 12.

44 GLRO, LCC Minutes, 14 May 1907. See also generally LCC/MIN/7260-7265: HWCC Minutes 1899-1905 (especially Estates Sub-Committee) and LCC/MIN/7381: Presented Papers (1901-6), and R. Thorne, 'The White Hart Lane Estate: an LCC venture in suburban development', *London Journal*, 12 (Summer 1986), pp. 80-8.

45 GLRO, HSG/GEN/2/2: Printed Papers of the HWCC, 28 April and 5 May 1909. Leading Jews, including the Chief Rabbi, N. L. Cohen, and Stuart Samuel, were involved in the Mansion House Council on the

Dwellings of the Poor, whose attentions at this time were necessarily occupied with the East End. In its Report for 1903-4 the Council noted with approval (p. 10) the increased tendency of foreigners to move to the outer areas, where housing was cheaper and better: Jewish Board of Guardians, Letter Book 1900-10: Mansion House Council to Board of Guardians, 7 November 1904. By this date the Sanitary Committee of the Board of Guardians was being routinely consulted by the LCC and borough authorities on housing matters, and its own work consisted 'almost exclusively in checking the spread of disease – mainly consumption – among the Jewish poor': *Annual Report 1905*, p. 27.

46 Schmiechen, *Sweated Industries*, p. 163.
47 *JC*, 14 April 1897, p. 16.
48 ibid.
49 GLRO, LCC Minutes, 21 February 1893: Adjourned Report of the Public Control Committee; Montagu, *Samuel Montagu*, p. 72.
50 Gibbon and Bell, *History of the LCC*, pp. 637-8; see also GLRO, LCC Minutes, 19 November 1901: Report of the Public Control Committee.
51 GLRO, LCC Minutes, 12 March and 2 May 1899: Report of the Industrial and Reformatory Schools Sub-Committee.
52 GLRO, LCC Minutes, 4 July 1905: Report of the Education Committee; Jewish Welfare Board, Minutes of Meetings of the Council of the Jewish Association for the Protection of Girls and Women, especially 12 December 1904 and 1 November 1905. See also V. D. Lipman, *A Century of Social Service 1859-1959: The Jewish Board of Guardians* (Routledge & Kegan Paul, London, 1959), p. 252.
53 GLRO, LCC/MIN/7381: Presented Papers of the Public Health and Housing Committee 1901-2 (Bundle 65): Memo from Dr Murphy, 27 March 1901.
54 ibid., 1903-4 (Bundle 1): Memo from the Housing Department to the Chairman of the Public Health and Housing Committee, 23 February 1903; *Parliamentary Debates*, 4th ser., vol. 118, col. 197 (18 February 1903).
55 On these events see Alderman, *Jewish Community*, pp. 68-73.
56 C. Bermant, *Point of Arrival: A Study of London's East End* (Eyre Methuen, London, 1975), p. 145; *JC*, 5 May 1905, p. 25. On Straus (1867-1933, Liberal MP for Mile End 1906-10) see *JC*, 22 February 1907, p. 18, and 1 September 1933, p. 12.
57 B. Gainer, *The Alien Invasion* (Heinemann, London, 1972), p. 279, n. 59.
58 *ELO*, 27 October 1900, p. 8; the Moderate campaign was conducted by Geoffrey Powell, Evans-Gordon's election agent.
59 *JC*, 1 March 1901, p. 18.
60 On Brandon, an 'intimate friend' of Sarah Bernhardt, see *JC*, 8 March 1907, p. 9; and on A. L. Cohen (1836-1903) see *Jewish Year Book*.
61 *The Times*, 16 October 1901, p. 8.
62 *JC*, 25 October 1901, p. 16.
63 *ELO*, 23 November 1901, p. 8.

64 ibid., 30 November 1901, p. 8. I can find no trace of an anti-alien motion having been defeated by the LCC in 1902, as J. A. Garrard asserts, in *The English and Immigration 1880-1910* (Oxford University Press, London, 1971), p. 38.

65 Alderman, *Jewish Community*, p. 77; as I argue there, the main impact of the 1905 legislation was psychological.

66 V. D. Lipman, *Social History of the Jews in England 1850-1950* (Watts & Co., London, 1954), pp. 157-60; A. Newman, *The United Synagogue 1870-1970* (Routledge & Kegan Paul, London, 1976), pp. 59-65.

67 E[*ast*] L[*ondon*] A[*dvertiser*], 16 February 1901, p. 8; 23 February, p. 5. In spite of Jewish support the Progressives lost a seat at Stepney, and the Moderates lost ground at Mile End.

68 GLRO, LCC/MIN/7260: Minutes of the HWCC, 17 May 1899: letter from the Edmonton branch of the Gas Workers' Union, 11 May.

69 On 'rich Jew' antisemitism see C. Holmes, *Anti-Semitism in British Society 1876-1939* (Edward Arnold, London, 1979), pp. 66-70.

70 *JC*, 30 October 1903, p. 20.

71 Lord Rothschild had supported restrictionists such as David Hope Kyd at Whitechapel and Evans-Gordon at Stepney in 1900, while Chief Rabbi Adler had refused to condemn the 1905 Act and, in private, gave it qualified support: Alderman, *Jewish Community*, pp. 68 and 187.

72 The election address of Micholls and Williams is to be found in *London County Council Election 1901 Addresses in Alphabetical Order of Constituencies sold by W. Durrant of three Saint Andrews St Holborn Circus London E.C.*, in the British Library.

73 On the 1902-3 Acts generally see S. J. Curtis and M. E. A. Boultwood, *An Introductory History of English Education since 1800* (4th edn, University Tutorial Press, London, 1966), pp. 162-9.

74 C. Hershon, 'The evolution of Jewish elementary education in England with special reference to Liverpool' (unpublished PhD thesis, University of Sheffield, 1973), p. 129; *JC*, 6 May 1904, p. 8.

75 *JC*, 10 April 1903, pp. 19-20. It was the opinion of Robert Blair, the LCC's Education (Executive) Officer, in 1906 that twenty-four Board schools which the Council had taken over were 'largely attended' by Jewish children; most were in the East End but one (Sigdon Road) was in central Hackney: GLRO, EO/GEN/6/2: Report of the Education (Executive) Officer, 14 February 1906.

76 *JC*, 1 May 1903, p. 20. Jewish parents could of course withdraw their children from such acts of worship.

77 Hershon, 'Jewish elementary education', pp. 133-4.

78 *JC*, 1 May 1903, p. 20.

79 *JC*, 28 October 1904, p. 8.

80 *Parliamentary Debates*, 4th ser., vol. 122, cols 1845-7 (26 May 1903).

81 *The Times*, 22 December 1903, p. 10; *ELO*, 23 January 1904, p. 5.

82 *Parliamentary Debates*, 4th ser., vol. 125, cols 1451-9 (22 July 1903): speech of Dr Macnamara, Liberal MP for Camberwell North. See also London Municipal Society, *LCC Election 1904 Facts and Figures for*

Conservative Speakers and Candidates (London Municipal Society, London, 1904), pp. 3 and 29-31.

83 On Gordon see *JC*, 3 March 1916, p. 10, and 15 December 1939, p. 22.

84 *JC*, 4 March 1904, pp. 3 and 6; *ELA*, 20 February 1904, p. 8, and 5 March, p. 8; *ELO*, 6 February 1904, p. 5. For an earlier example of Jewish–Catholic co-operation (at the London School Board election of 1891 at Chelsea) see *JC*, 30 October 1891, pp. 7-8. In 1906 an alliance of Irish cultural societies in London requested the LCC to allow Irish Gaelic and Irish history to be taught in Council schools frequented by children of Irish parents; the claim was based largely upon the practice in Jewish schools, where Hebrew and Jewish history were taught: GLRO, EO/GEN/6/2: Report of the Education (Executive) Officer, 26 April 1906; EO/GEN/6/70, No. 811a: Report of Education Advisor, 28 March 1906.

85 Speaking at Stepney, where he won a seat for the Moderates, the Earl of Malmesbury pointed out that 'Voluntary schools did not only mean Church schools, but those belonging to chapels and synagogues (Applause)': *ELO*, 20 February 1904, p. 5.

86 On Nettie Adler see *JC*, 21 April 1950, p. 16, and *The Times*, 17 April 1950, p. 7.

87 On Hermann Adler's Toryism see Alderman, *Jewish Community*, pp. 43-4.

88 On Hermann Adler's conflicts with East End Jews see B. Homa, *A Fortress in Anglo-Jewry* (Shapiro, Vallentine, London, 1953), *passim*, and the same author's *Orthodoxy in Anglo-Jewry 1880-1940* (Jewish Historical Society of England, London, 1969), pp. 18-21.

89 *ELA*, 12 March 1904, p. 8.

90 In Gordon's own view his victory was due 'more largely to the Gentile than to the Jewish vote, which was hopelessly divided': *ELO*, 12 March 1904, p. 5.

91 *ELO*, 19 March 1904, p. 5.

92 Alderman, *Jewish Community*, pp. 76-7.

93 *JC*, 24 April 1908, p. 11; 1 May, p. 13.

94 *The Times*, 11 May 1906, p. 8; see also B[oard of] D[eputies of British Jews], C13/1/6: Minutes of the Law and Parliamentary Committee, 16 May 1906: Report on the Education Bill.

95 *JC*, 4 May 1906, p. 40. See also J. M. Stevens, 'The London County Council under the Progressives, 1889-1907' (unpublished MA thesis, University of Sussex, 1966), pp. 31-2.

96 London Board of Jewish Religious Education, Minute Book of the Jewish Voluntary Schools Association 1897-1907: Meeting of the Governing Body, 14 May 1906. GLRO, LCC Minutes: Report of the Education Committee 29 May 1906 (deputation from the Jewish Voluntary Schools Association, 15 May); see also EO/GEN/6/4: Education Officer's Department Reports No. 4 (1907): Report submitted to the Day Schools Sub-Committee, 22 January 1907: 'The deputation began by remarking that, since the schools had been taken over by the Council, a very considerable loss of time for Jewish and

Hebrew instruction had ensued.'
97 GLRO, LCC Minutes, 27 February and 16 July 1907: Reports of the Education Committee.
98 GLRO, LCC/MIN/3691: Minutes of the Non-Provided Schools Sub-Committee vol. 2 (1906), meeting of 22 January 1906.
99 GLRO, EO/GEN/6/69: Report of the Day Schools Sub-Committee, 23 March 1906; *JC*, 11 May 1906, p. 10.
100 *ELA*, 2 March 1907, p. 5.
101 On Stettauer see *JC*, 17 December 1909, p. 20; 25 July 1913, p. 12; 1 August, p. 15.
102 *H[ackney and Kingsland]* G*[azette]*, 16 February 1907, p. 3; 18 February, p. 3; 20 February, p. 3; 25 February, p. 4; 1 March, p. 3.
103 *Idisher Ekspres*, 22 February 1907, p. 4.
104 The letter, dated 26 February, is printed in *HG*, 1 March 1907, p. 3.
105 This strongly-held conviction is reflected in various letters sent by leading members of the House of Rothschild to their French cousins in Paris, copies of which are in the Rothschild Archive, London; see, for example, XI/130A/0: Nathaniel Mayer Rothschild to French cousins, 2 November 1906 (commenting on borough council elections) and XI/130A/1: same to same, 6 March 1907 (on LCC elections).
106 *Idisher Ekspres*, 20 February 1907, p. 4.
107 *Arbeter Fraint*, 1 March 1907, pp. 1–2.
108 On Isadore Salmon (1876–1941), who became chairman of the catering firm of J. Lyons & Co., honorary catering adviser to the British Army, and Conservative MP for Harrow 1924–41, see *The Times*, 17 September 1941, p. 7, and *JC*, 19 September 1941, p. 8. On David Davis (1877–1930) see *JC*, 18 April 1930, p. 10. The remaining Jewish Municipal Reformers elected in 1907 were Jocelyn Brandon and Frank Goldsmith (St Pancras South).
109 *JC*, 8 March 1907, p. 8.
110 *JC*, 15 March 1907, p. 10.
111 *The Times*, 8 April 1908, p. 12: speech of Lord Rothschild at a dinner to raise funds for the Jewish Religious Education Board; 27 November 1908, p. 11: speech of Chief Rabbi Adler. See also *JC*, 27 November 1908, p. 16.

3 MUNICIPAL REACTION AND THE RISE OF LABOUR

1 Sir G. Gibbon and R. W. Bell, *History of the London County Council 1889–1939* (Macmillan, London, 1939), pp. 104 and 188.
2 ibid., pp. 375–89.
3 W. E. Jackson, *Achievement: A Short History of the London County Council* (Longman, London, 1965), pp. 24–5; G. Alderman, *Modern Britain 1700–1983* (Croom Helm, Beckenham, 1986), p. 221.
4 W. E. Jackson, *Achievement*, p. 27.
5 For the reaction of M. H. Davis, the (Jewish) Labour Leader of

Stepney Borough Council, at the commencement of the 1934 LCC election campaign, see *E[ast] L[ondon] A[dvertiser]*, 24 February 1934, p. 5.

6 K. Young, *Local Politics and the Rise of Party* (Leicester University Press, Leicester, 1975), p. 139.

7 *Daily Telegraph*, 10 March 1928, p. 12.

8 Gibbon and Bell, *History of the LCC*, pp. 109–10.

9 An additional factor was that, as a result of the 1918 Act, the task of compiling the electoral registers resided henceforth with local authority officials, and not as hitherto with the political parties; this was of some benefit to the Labour Party, whose officers were least experienced in this type of work. See J. Bush, *Behind the Lines: East London Labour 1914–1918* (Routledge & Kegan Paul, London, 1967), p. 80.

10 *H[ackney and Kingsland] G[azette]*, 19 February 1919, p. 3.

11 G. Alderman, *The Jewish Community in British Politics* (Oxford University Press, Oxford, 1983), p. 194. n. 121.

12 *E[ast] L[ondon] O[bserver]*, 14 February 1925, p. 3.

13 *ELO*, 21 February 1925, p. 3.

14 H. Pelling, *Social Geography of British Elections 1885–1910* (Macmillan, London, 1967), pp. 33 and 38.

15 *Daily Telegraph*, 29 December 1909, p. 12; 20 January 1910, p. 8.

16 On Oscar Warburg see D. Farrer, *The Warburgs* (Stein & Day, New York, 1975), p. 226 and *J[ewish] C[hronicle]*, 3 June 1947, p. 6.

17 *HG*, 16 February 1910, p. 6; 23 February, p. 5; 25 February, p. 1. For Benn's friendship with Nettie, see A. G. Gardiner, *John Benn and the Progressive Movement* (Ernest Benn, London, 1925), p. 101.

18 *HG*, 7 March 1910, p. 5.

19 *Hackney Spectator*, 4 March 1910, p. 5.

20 G[reater] L[ondon] R[ecord] O[ffice], LCC Minutes, 4–5 and 11–12 April 1911: Report of the Education Committee. At this time the Education Committee had six Jewish members (five plus one co-opted); this was the largest number of Jews on any LCC committee.

21 *JC*, 5 March 1913, p. 4.

22 *HG*, 7 March 1913, p. 5.

23 V. D. Lipman, 'The Booth and New London Surveys as source material for East London Jewry (1880–1930)', in A. Newman (ed.), *The Jewish East End 1840–1939* (Jewish Historical Society of England, London, 1981), pp. 46–7.

24 S. Rowson, 'A contribution to the study of the vital and other statistics of the Jews in the United Kingdom', *Journal of the Royal Statistical Society*, vol. lxviii (1905), p. 256.

25 V. D. Lipman, *Social History of the Jews in England 1850–1950* (Watts & Co., London, 1954), p. 99.

26 ibid., pp. 168–9.

27 H. L. Trachtenberg, 'Estimates of the Jewish population of London in 1929', *Journal of the Royal Statistical Society*, vol. xcvi (1933), p. 96.

28 Lipman, *Social History*, p. 169.

29 See G. Alderman, 'The anti-Jewish riots of August 1911 in South Wales', *Welsh History Review*, vol. vi (1972), pp. 190–200, and 'The Jew as scapegoat? The settlement and reception of Jews in South Wales before 1914', *Transactions of the Jewish Historical Society of England*, vol. xxvi (1974–8), pp. 62–70.

30 See generally C. Holmes, *Anti-Semitism in British Society 1876–1939* (Edward Arnold, London, 1979), ch. 8.

31 The fullest treatment of this episode is in Holmes, *Anti-Semitism*, pp. 126–31. See also C. Bermant, *Point of Arrival: A Study of London's East End* (Eyre Methuen, London, 1975), pp. 222–30.

32 *JC*, 7 August 1914, p. 5; C. Roth, *The Jewish Chronicle 1841–1941* (Jewish Chronicle, London, 1949), facing p. 105.

33 *JC*, 11 September 1914, pp. 5, 7, and 11; *ELO*, 1 May 1915, p. 7.

34 *JC*, 1 October 1915, p. 6.

35 Holmes, *Anti-Semitism*, p. 128.

36 Bush, *Behind the Lines*, p. 167.

37 *ELO*, 19 August 1916, p. 4. On the activities of the FJPC see Bush, *Behind the Lines*, pp. 176–81.

38 *ELO*, 5 August 1916, p. 4.

39 Bush, *Behind the Lines*, p. 168.

40 Holmes, *Anti-Semitism*, p. 135.

41 *ELO*, 3 March 1917, p. 4.

42 Bush, *Behind the Lines*, pp. 181–2. These followed disturbances at Leeds in June; see Holmes, *Anti-Semitism*, pp. 130–1.

43 GLRO, LCC Minutes, 27 October 1914, p. 673.

44 GLRO, LCC Minutes, 22 December 1914, pp. 1024 and 1028. The motion to refer back was opposed by three Jewish Municipal Reformers, D. Davis, I. Salmon, and P. Simmons.

45 GLRO, LCC Minutes, 26 January 1915, p. 105; 27 April 1915, p. 677. In 1917 a further four firms were removed: LCC Minutes, 28 January and 1 May 1917.

46 GLRO, LCC Minutes, 4 April 1916, p. 306; the Council agreed that exceptional cases might be excluded from the operation of this rule.

47 *JC*, 24 January 1919, p. 5; *Morning Post*, 8 April 1919, p. 6.

48 On these events generally see G. Alderman, *The Jewish Community in British Politics* (Oxford University Press, Oxford, 1983), pp. 98–101.

49 *JC*, 16 November 1917, pp. 5–6.

50 *Morning Post*, 23 April 1919, p. 6; *JC*, 2 May 1919, pp. 14 and 21. See generally D. Cesarani, 'Anti-alienism in England after the First World War', *Immigrants and Minorities*, vol. 6 (1987), pp. 5–29.

51 Quoted in Holmes, *Anti-Semitism*, p. 149. On the *Protocols*, which purported to give details of a Jewish conspiracy to achieve world domination, see the authoritative work by Norman Cohn, *Warrant for Genocide* (Penguin, Harmondsworth, 1970).

52 B[oard of] D[eputies of British Jews], E3/42 (I), 'Notes of interview between Sir Stuart M. Samuel, Bart, accompanied by Mr Charles H. L. Emanuel, and Mr Cyril Cobb, and Sir Robert Blair', 14 November 1917.

53 BD, E3/42 (I): Cobb to Emanuel, 24 November 1917.
54 GLRO, LCC Minutes, 19 March 1918.
55 GLRO, LCC Minutes, 15 April and 13 May 1919.
56 GLRO, LCC/MIN/6273: Minutes of the General Purposes Committee, 19 May, 13 and 20 October, and 3 November 1919.
57 GLRO, LCC/MIN/6273: Minutes of the General Purposes Committee, 28 June 1920.
58 GLRO, LCC Minutes, 6 July 1920, pp. 26–9.
59 BD, C13/9.
60 BD, C13/9: Memorandum, undated but circa January 1933.
61 Adler, 'Jewish life and labour in East London', in Smith (ed.), *The New Survey*, vol. vi, pp. 272–3.
62 *JC*, 20 March 1925, p. 19.
63 This was the conclusion of a legal opinion obtained by the Board of Deputies in 1917; see BD, A3: Report of the Law and Parliamentary Committee, 9 January 1918. The opinion is in E3/42 (I).
64 BD, A19: Minutes of Meeting of Board of Deputies, 15 March 1925; *JC*, 20 March 1925, pp. 9 and 19.
65 BD, E3/94: Adler to Emanuel, 14 July 1920; Emanuel to Adler, 22 October 1920.
66 *HG*, 9 February 1925, p. 2. See W. Ray, *A Lecture on London Education* (London Municipal Society, 13 November 1924) [GLRO].
67 *HG*, 21 January 1925, p. 4.
68 BD, E2/2: Letter (destination unknown but marked 'Shire and Rubens') from Emanuel, 3 February 1925: 'Miss Nettie Adler ... who has been of great service to the Board on many educational questions affecting disabilities of Jewish students is putting up for Election for the L.C.C.'
69 *HG*, 8 February 1928, p. 4; and see generally the issues of this paper for 15, 22, and 24 February.
70 *HG*, 6 March 1928, p. 5.
71 *HG*, 9 March 1928, p. 5. Ray called Nettie's 'an immoral victory'.
72 *HG*, 18 February 1931, p. 5; 25 February, p. 5.
73 *HG*, 9 February 1934, p. 5.
74 On the decision of Harry Nathan and Barnett Janner to join Labour see Alderman, *Jewish Community*, p. 114.
75 H. Montgomery Hyde, *Strong for Service: The Life of Lord Nathan of Churt* (W. H. Allen, London, 1968), pp. 81–3.
76 *ELO*, 21 May 1927, p. 3.
77 *ELO*, 27 October 1928, p. 4.
78 *ELO*, 10 November 1928, p. 2.
79 *ELO*, 5 January 1929, p. 4.
80 *ELO*, 9 May 1931, p. 2.
81 *ELO*, 14 November 1931, p. 5; on Miriam Moses, formerly a member of the Whitechapel Board of Guardians and the first woman to be appointed a Justice of the Peace in Whitechapel, see *ELA*, 18 March 1922, p. 3 and *JC*, 2 July 1965, p. 35.
82 Hyde, *Strong for Service*, pp. 112–17. See also *ELO*, 4 August 1931,

pp. 4 and 6.

83 On Eleanor Nathan generally see *JC*, 9 June 1972, p. 42.

84 C. T. Husbands, 'East End racism 1900–1980', *London Journal*, vol. 8 (1982), p. 12. In 1937 the Fascists Raven-Thompson and Clarke each polled over 3,000 votes in the LCC elections in Bethnal Green North-East; the Fascists did not fight in the South-West division.

85 Husbands, 'East End racism', p. 19.

86 *JC*, 4 July 1952, p. 25. See also *ELA*, 4 July 1952, p. 8 and 25 July 1952, p. 8. The *ELA*, 15 April 1949, p. 9, commented on the strength of his personal support in Bethnal Green.

87 Nettie's article, 'A call to the Jewish community', was published in *JC*, 9 December 1932, p. 20. The support which it aroused can be followed in the *JC*, 16 December, pp. 7 and 14; 23 December, p. 6; 30 December, p. 10; 6 January 1933, p. 15. See also *ELO*, 17 December 1932, p. 4; 24 December p. 6; 31 December, p. 4; 7 January 1933, pp. 4 and 6; 14 January, pp. 4–6; 21 January, p. 6. Nettie's original outburst was aimed at the Ellen Street slums in St George's, Stepney.

88 Rt Hon. Sir P. Harris, *Forty Years In And Out of Parliament* (Andrew Melrose, London) [1947]

89 *JC*, 4 July 1952, p. 25.

90 P. Thompson, *Socialists, Liberals and Labour: The Struggle for London 1885–1914* (Routledge & Kegan Paul, London, 1967), p. 283.

91 On Lieberman see Alderman, *Jewish Community*, pp. 47–9.

92 E. Mendelsohn, *Class Struggle in the Pale: The Formative Years of the Jewish Workers' Movement in Tsarist Russia* (Cambridge University Press, Cambridge, 1970), pp. 22, 110–11.

93 Alderman, *Jewish Community*, p. 53.

94 G. Alderman, 'The political impact of Zionism in the East End of London before 1940', *London Journal*, vol. 9 (1983), p. 35.

95 O. I. Janowsky, *The Jews and Minority Rights 1898–1919* (Columbia University Press, New York, 1933), pp. 42–6; N. Levin, *Jewish Socialist Movements, 1871–1917* (Routledge & Kegan Paul, London, 1978), p. 411.

96 E. Tcherikower (ed.), *The Early Jewish Labour Movement in the United States*, trans. A. Antonovsky (Yivo Institute, New York, 1961), p. 188.

97 E. Silberner, 'British Socialism and the Jews', *Historica Judaica*, vol. xiv (1952), p. 38.

98 L. P. Gartner, *The Jewish Immigrant in England, 1870–1914* (Allen & Unwin, London, 1960), p. 132.

99 Alderman, *Jewish Community*, p. 47.

100 C. Holmes, 'The Leeds Jewish tailors' strikes of 1885 and 1888', *Yorkshire Archaeological Journal*, vol. 45 (1973), p. 165; J. Buckman, 'The economic and social history of alien immigration to Leeds, 1880–1914' (PhD thesis, University of Strathclyde, 1968), p. 322.

101 *JC*, 4 October 1889, pp. 7–8.
102 Thompson, *Socialists, Liberals and Labour*, p. 104; B. Barker, *Labour in London: A Study in Municipal Achievement* (Routledge, London, 1946), p. 54.
103 *Arbeter Fraint*, 16 December 1892, quoted in Gartner, *The Jewish Immigrant*, pp. 130–1.
104 J Lestchinsky, *Der Idisher Arbayter (in London)* [Yiddish: 'The Jewish worker (in London)'] (Vilna, 1907), pp. 31–2.
105 Alderman, *Jewish Community*, pp. 63–4.
106 Gartner, *The Jewish Immigrant*, pp. 139–40; Buckman, 'Alien immigration to Leeds', pp. 245 and 340.
107 Bush, *Behind the Lines*, p. 186.
108 *ELO*, 1 June 1918, p. 13.
109 On Tobin see *ELA*, 28 January 1922, p. 3.
110 K. Harris, *Attlee* (Weidenfeld & Nicolson, London, 1982), p. 42.
111 Alderman, *Jewish Community*, pp. 66–7.
112 J. Bush, 'East London Jews and the First World War', *London Journal*, vol. 6 (1980), p. 149.
113 Bush, 'East London Jews', p. 153; Alderman, *Jewish Community*, p. 105.
114 *ELO*, 9 November 1912, p. 2. Lyons stood in the Central Ward and came bottom of the poll; a Philip Kalisky, who may have been Jewish, stood unsuccessfully in the St George's North Ward in the same election.
115 *Di Tsait*, 6 March 1919, p. 3; Bush, *Behind the Lines*, p. 211. For a reference to Sharp's Yiddish election leaflets see *Eastern Post*, 8 March 1919, p. 4. On Sharp generally see *ELA*, 1 April 1922, p. 3.
116 On Valentine see *ELA*, 1 April 1922, p. 3.
117 *JC*, 6 November 1903, p. 33.
118 *JC*, 26 February 1904, p. 30. On the early history of Poale Zion in England see G. Shimoni, 'Poale Zion: A Zionist transplant in Britain (1905–1945)' in P. Y. Medding (ed.), *Studies in Contemporary Jewry*, vol. 2 (Indiana University Press, Bloomington, 1986), pp. 227–9.
119 S. Levenberg, *The Jews and Palestine. A Study in Labour Zionism* (Poale Zion, London, 1945), pp. 204–5; J. Gorny, *The British Labour Movement and Zionism 1917–1948* (Cass, London, 1983), pp. 7–10. Labour's sympathetic attitude towards Zionism at this time had a significant impact on the fortunes and membership of Poale Zion: see S. A. Cohen, *English Zionists and British Jews: The Communal Politics of Anglo-Jewry, 1895–1920* (Princeton University Press, Princeton NJ, 1982), p. 251. See also Shimoni, 'Poale Zion', pp. 232–3.
120 Levenberg, *The Jews and Palestine*, pp. 205–6.
121 Alderman, *Jewish Community*, p. 97.
122 ibid., p. 89.
123 *London Statistics*, 1913–14 and 1922.
124 *JC*, 17 November 1920, p. 25.

125 The *ELO*, 25 November 1922, p. 2, thought it worthy of comment that 'a Roman Catholic Labour candidate should succeed in a pronounced Jewish division'.
126 *ELO*, 15 December 1923, p. 2.

4 COUNTY HALL UNDER LABOUR: A FRIENDSHIP UNFULFILLED

1 On Frankel see *E[ast] L[ondon] O[bserver]*, 10 November 1928, p. 5; 17 November, p. 3; *E[ast] L[ondon] A[dvertiser]*, 26 November 1945, p. 7; and *The Times*, 24 May 1988, p. 16. On Homa see *J[ewish] C[hronicle]*, 5 April 1940, p. 8; G. Alderman, *The Jewish Community in British Politics* (Oxford University Press, Oxford, 1983), pp. 115 and 206. In 1949 and 1952 Homa topped the poll in the LCC elections at Hackney South, and there seems little doubt that he attracted a certain personal, Jewish following in the division.
2 On Jeger see *ELO*, 18 December 1929, pp. 5–6; *JC*, 2 October 1953, p. 9; and *The Times*, 25 September 1953, p. 8.
3 Lord Morrison of Lambeth, *Autobiography* (Odhams, London, 1960), pp. 145 and 151; B. Donoghue and G. W. Jones, *Herbert Morrison* (Weidenfeld & Nicolson, London, 1973), p. 256. On Silkin, Minister of Town and Country Planning from 1945 to 1950 (when he took a peerage), see *JC*, 17 May 1972, p. 36.
4 On Davis see *ELA*, 24 January 1925, p. 5; 15 November 1930, p. 4; 11 February 1932, p. 3; 28 December 1935, p. 3. I am grateful to Mr Thomas Reif of London, who befriended Davis in his last years and who was an executor of his will, for providing me with additional information about him.
5 His assets at death totalled £157,368 before tax (see *JC*, 21 November 1986, p. 28). There is a sketch of Davis's background in the obituary of his father which appeared in *ELA*, 30 March 1940, p. 1. See also G. Alderman, *The Federation of Synagogues, 1887–1987* (The Federation of Synagogues, London, 1987), chs 3 and 4.
6 This was the phrase employed by the late Dr Stanley Chazen (who knew Davis well in the 1930s), in conversation with the author on 29 August 1985. Dr Bernard Homa has recalled being asked by Herbert Morrison to intervene after Davis had demanded money from the owners of an East End public house as the price for attending to some LCC matter for them: interview with the author, 15 September 1987.
7 Federation of Synagogues, Minute Book No. 3.
8 Federation of Synagogues, Minute Book No. 3: Special Board Meeting, 19 July 1933; Alderman, *Jewish Community*, p. 121.
9 *ELO*, 1 May 1920, p. 5.
10 *ELA*, 15 November 1930, p. 4; *ELO*, 1 April 1939, p. 6. Sullivan had unsuccessfully nominated Davis as Mayor in 1922 (*ELO*, 11 November 1922, p. 3), and Davis nominated Sullivan as Mayor in

1926 (*ELO*, 13 November 1926, p. 3; 9 April 1927, p. 4). The similarity of political outlook between Davis and Long is noted in A. R. J. Kushner, 'British antisemitism in the Second World War', (unpublished PhD thesis, University of Sheffield, 1986), p. 279. In his speech on accepting the mayoralty in 1937, Long confessed that he owed 'a good deal of my political education to two people, Councillor Davis and ex-Councillor Jack Sullivan': *ELA*, 13 November 1937, p. 1.

11 C. Holmes, *Anti-Semitism in British Society 1876–1939* (Edward Arnold, London, 1979), p. 212.

12 *ELA*, 27 February 1937, p. 1. In 1938 Davis attempted to block the appointment by the Board of Deputies of Councillor Henry Solomons, of Stepney, as the first secretary of the London Area Council of its Defence Committee. Solomons was a man of emphatic left wing tendencies, and Davis appears to have objected to his alleged Soviet sympathies: BD, C6/3/16/5 and 10.

13 *ELO*, 2 July 1938, pp. 1 and 7; *JC*, 8 July 1938, p. 40.

14 *ELA*, 26 November 1938, p. 1; Federation of Synagogues, Minute Book No. 3, Meeting of General Council, 30 June 1938. For early signs of the split on the Borough Council see *ELA*, 12 December 1936, p. 5; 19 December, p. 3; 2 January 1937, p. 4.

15 *The Times*, 5 February 1938, p. 4. The *JC* of 26 February 1937 had run an article sub-titled 'Jewish councillors support Mosley'.

16 I base this statement on interviews (conducted in November and December 1985) with Mr A. B. Olivestone and Mr J. L. Cymerman, lifelong activists in the Federation and early opponents of the Davis regime.

17 Federation of Synagogues, Minute Book No. 3, Special Meeting of General Council, 13 June 1939.

18 *ELA*, 22 October 1938, p. 8; 13 May 1939, p. 1.

19 K. Brill (ed.), *John Groser: East London Priest* (Mowbray, Oxford, 1971), pp. 151–3; for an earlier instance of alleged corruption (relating to the Stepney Public Cleansing Committee) see *ELA*, 1 December 1936, p. 5.

20 *ELA*, 2 December 1940, p. 1; Tower Hamlets Central Library, Minutes of Stepney Borough Council, pp. 1998–9: Extraordinary Meeting 9 November 1940.

21 Kushner, 'British antisemitism', p. 242.

22 *The Times*, 25 November 1944, p. 2; *ELO*, 1 December 1944, pp. 1 and 2.

23 B[oard of] D[eputies of British Jews], E3/42 (I): Davis to Emanuel, 5 April 1925. Davis attacked the education policy of the Municipal Reformers in his 1934 LCC campaign: *ELA*, 24 February 1934, p. 5.

24 *ELO*, 16 August 1924, p. 3.

25 *ELO*, 1 November 1924, p. 3.

26 BD, E3/42 (I): Emanuel to Davis, 14 and 30 April 1925.

27 BD, A3/2: Minutes of Meeting, 21 March 1926: Joint Report of the Education and Law and Parliamentary Committees; E2/54: letters

to Davis, 13 July and 21 August 1931.

28 BD, A20: Minutes of Meetings, 14 February and 26 March 1926; 16 January 1927.

29 BD, E3/42 (I): Letters from Birmingham, Leeds, Liverpool, Manchester, and Sheffield, January and February 1927; note compiled by the Secretary, 1 February 1927.

30 BD, E3/42 (I): Percy Cohen to E. M. Rich (LCC Education Department), 12 December 1926.

31 BD, E3/42 (II): Adler to Rich, 15 July 1928; A22: Minutes of Meetings, 17 June and 15 July 1928.

32 G[reater] L[ondon] R[ecord] O[ffice], LCC Minutes, 17 July 1928, pp. 150–1; the letter is in BD, E3/42 (I); see also GLRO, Minutes of the Education Committee, 11 July 1928, p. 331. In April 1956 a recommendation by the then Education Officer of the LCC, John Brown, that the restrictions upon aliens being granted scholarships be – to all intents and purposes – rescinded, was vetoed, apparently on the personal authority of the outgoing chairman of the LCC, Norman Prichard; Mr Brown's report was simply not presented to the full Council: GLRO, EO/HFE/3/2: Report by Education Officer, 11 April 1956, and handwritten marginal note dated 17 April 1956.

33 GLRO, EO/STA/2/2: Memorandum from Education Officer, 25 February 1927.

34 BD, E3/94: Lord Jessel (President, Municipal Reform Society) to Osmond d'Avidgor Goldsmid (President, Board of Deputies), 28 November 1928.

35 BD, E3/94: Report of the LCC's General Purposes Committee, 23 and 30 January 1928; LCC to Board of Deputies, 28 December 1928; GLRO, LCC/MIN/3467: Minutes of the General Purposes Sub-Committee of the Education Committee, 30 January 1928, pp. 11–12; ELO, 8 December 1928, p. 6.

36 JC, 21 December 1928, p. 9.

37 ELO, 21 April 1928, p. 4.

38 ELO, 2 March 1935, p. 5.

39 BD, A26: Minutes of Meeting, 15 January 1933 (Report of Aliens Committee); see also ELO, 20 January 1933, p. 6, and JC, 24 February 1933, p. 14.

40 BD, A26: Minutes of Meetings, 14 May and 23 July 1933 (Reports of Aliens Committee).

41 ELO, 21 July 1934, p. 5. BD, B4/LO2 contains correspondence between the Board, Dayan Gollop (of the Hampstead Synagogue), Lady Spielman, Sir Isadore Salmon, and the LCC (September 1938 – January 1939) relating to the continued refusal of the County Council to admit alien children to its Central schools.

42 ELO, 2 March 1935, p. 5.

43 ELO, 23 March 1935, p. 5; 22 June, p. 4. Davis's attitude had been made clear (but in the privacy of the Law and Parliamentary Committee of the Board of Deputies) as early as 14 February 1933,

when he advised against action on the housing front: BD, C13/1/11, Minutes of the Law and Parliamentary Committee.

44 A. Sharf, *The British Press and Jews under Nazi Rule* (Oxford University Press for Institute of Race Relations, London, 1964), p. 155.

45 There is some discussion of the social and economic characteristics of the Nazi-inspired German-Jewish emigration in H. Pollins, *Economic History of the Jews in England* (Associated University Presses, London, 1982), pp. 205–8.

46 *ELO*, 7 October 1933, p. 6.

47 *ELO*, 6 July 1935, p. 6; 16 July 1938, p. 2.

48 Kushner, 'British antisemitism', p. 437, n. 173.

49 S. Salomon, 'The Jewish Defence Committee', p. 85, in Neville Laski Papers, Mocatta Library (University College London), AJ33/158.

50 W. F. Mandle, *Anti-Semitism and the British Union of Fascists* (Longman, London, 1968), pp. 57–8. At the borough council elections later that year not a single BUF candidate was returned.

51 For details of the BUF campaign see Holmes, *Anti-Semitism*, p. 194, and *JC*, 12 March 1937, p. 20. The *JC*'s special correspondent noted that in North-East Bethnal Green the BUF had managed to attract many small traders, who apparently resented Jewish competition, and that, had the election been fought on the parliamentary franchise, the BUF vote would have been larger. For a report of an antisemitic disturbance outside Santo Jeger's surgery see *HG*, 8 April 1936, p. 5.

52 R. Skidelsky, *Oswald Mosley* (Macmillan, London, 1975), pp. 394–6.

53 *East London Pioneer*, 5 December 1936, in BD, E3/245.

54 All these papers are in BD, E3/245.

55 J. A. Gillespie, 'Economic and social change in the East End of London during the 1920s' (unpublished PhD thesis, University of Cambridge, 1984), p. 270.

56 Concern at the growth of antisemitism within the trade union movement continued, however, and in November 1939 the Board's Defence Committee authorized an investigation of this phenomenon; the replies from a wide variety of trade unions are in BD, E2/150.

57 *JC*, 7 July 1911, p. 3; 14 July, pp. 17–19; 28 July, p. 11; 24 November, p. 16. See also BD, B2/18/1.

58 J. Wigley, *The Rise and Fall of the Victorian Sunday* (Manchester University Press, Manchester, 1980), pp. 115–16. See also GLRO, LCC/MIN/9833, Presented Papers of the Public Control Committee, 8 December 1933, and LCC/MIN/9626, Minutes of the Public Control Committee, 1 March, 25 October, and 6 December 1935.

59 See the defence of Sunday trading by Councillor J. Kosky in the Stepney Borough Council, *ELA*, 14 May 1932, p. 4.

60 BD, A/22, Minutes of Meeting, 17 February 1929 (Report of Law and Parliamentary Committee). See also Public Record Office, HO45/13812.

61 BD, E3/115 (1): Note of interview between B. A. Levinson (Chairman, Law and Parliamentary Committee), and B. H. Gibbens (Public Control Dept, LCC), 24 October 1934. It was alleged that some Jewish barbers had two shops, one of which they opened on Saturdays and the other on Sundays: *ELA*, 21 January 1933, p. 5. The probability that this would happen had been noted by the Home Office as early as October 1930, and in July 1932 the LCC's Public Control Department confessed to the Home Office that in most cases referred to it no action could be taken: Public Record Office, HO45/16612.

62 A memorandum concerning this meeting is in BD, E3/115 (1).

63 BD, E3/115 (1): Secretary, Board of Deputies to Editor, *ELO*, 10 November 1932; BD, E3/115 (2): typescript note of meeting between Neville Laski and others and a deputation of representatives of hairdressers and shop assistants, 30 July 1935.

64 BD, E3/115 (2): Report by the Chief Officer, LCC Public Control Department, 3 December 1935; and see *Daily Herald*, 11 February 1936, p. 15.

65 For the origins of the 1936 Act see *Report of the Committee of Inquiry into Proposals to Amend the Shops Acts* [hereafter *Auld Report*], Cmnd 9376 (Her Majesty's Stationery Office, London, 1984), pp. 2 and 90.

66 *Parliamentary Debates*, 5th ser., vol. 308, cols 2178–93 (21 February 1936), and vol. 311, cols 483–7 and 2090–1 (24 April and 8 May); *ELA*, 29 February 1936, p. 3.

67 BD, E3/115 (2): Homa to L. L. Cohen (Chairman, Law and Parliamentary Committee), 22 April 1934.

68 The working of these provisions is discussed in G. Alderman, 'One law for the Jews: an unacceptable face of British public administration' (paper presented to the Political Studies Association's Workshop on United Kingdom Politics, Oxford, 1983), pp. 3–5, and G. Alderman, 'Jews and Sunday Trading: the use and abuse of delegated legislation', *Public Administration*, vol. 1x (1982), pp. 99–104.

69 *Auld Report*, p. 2; see also *JC*, 19 November 1937, p. 14.

70 Neville Laski Papers, Mocatta Library, University College London, AJ33/90: typescript note by Laski, 14 October 1936. On 11 April 1937 Laski admitted to a plenary session of the Board that 'anti-semitism is not only due to malice and evil sources, but may unfortunately also be ascribed to a tiny minority of individuals in our midst who refuse to recognise that because of our unique position in every country, the bad conduct of one Jew may and often does reflect on the whole community': BD, A/29: Minutes of Meeting.

71 BD, E3/82 (1): Rabinowitz to Laski, 19 May 1937.

72 BD, B4/EA28: N. Laski to L. L. Cohen, 26 October 1936.

73 *JC*, 19 May 1939, p. 18.

74 M. Rose, *The East End of London* (Cresset Press, London, 1951), p. 266.

75 *ELO*, 1 January 1938, p. 2.

76 P. Piratin, *Our Flag Stays Red* (new edn, Lawrence & Wishart, London, 1978), pp. 32–49. On Shapiro, elected as a Communist councillor at Stepney in 1945, see *ELA*, 18 January 1946, p. 5.

77 On the Jewish People's Council see G. C. Lebzelter, *Political Anti-Semitism in England 1918–1939* (Macmillan, London, 1978), pp. 140–2, 152–3. The view that the JPC was merely a Communist 'front' organization, put forward in (for example) Holmes, *Anti-Semitism*, p. 193, and Skidlesky, *Mosley*, p. 403, is not shared by the present author.

78 Alderman, *Jewish Community*, p. 118.

79 Piratin, *Our Flag*, pp. 33–49.

80 H. Srebrnik, 'Communism and pro-Soviet feeling among the Jews of East London, 1935–45', *Immigrants and Minorities*, vol. 5 (1986), especially p. 287; E. R. Smith, 'East End tailors, 1918–1939: an aspect of the Jewish workers' struggle', *Jewish Quarterly*, vol. 34, no. 2 (1987), pp. 26–9. On Elsbury (who in the 1920s sat as a Labour member of Bethnal Green Borough Council) see Alderman, *Jewish Community*, p. 116; Gillespie, 'Economic and social change', pp. 77 and 339–40; *ELO*, 12 November 1927, p. 5; on Cohen, Gillespie, 'Economic and social change', p. 336.

81 W. Zuckerman, *The Jew In Revolt* (Secker & Warburg, London, 1937), p. 74.

82 Piratin, *Our Flag*, p. 17; *JC*, 8 January 1937, p. 16; 15 January 1937, p. 17.

83 Interview in November 1978 with a former official of the Stepney Communist Party. For Frankel's attitude see *ELO*, 12 and 19 September 1936, p. 1, and *Parliamentary Debates*, 5th ser., vol. 317, cols 161–5.

84 B. Litvinoff, *A Peculiar People* (Weidenfeld & Nicolson, London, 1969), p. 158.

85 D. Cesarani, 'East End Jewry between the wars' (Lecture given to the Jewish East End Project, 1986), pp. 1–2.

86 G. Alderman, 'The political impact of Zionism in the East End of London before 1940', *London Journal*, vol. 9 (1983), pp. 35–8.

87 House of Lords Record Office, Lloyd George Papers, G/26/1/34: typescript minute from Jones, 27 November 1930.

88 *Young Zionist*, December 1932, p. 137.

89 J. Jacobs, *Out of the Ghetto* (ed. and published by J. J. Simon, London, 1978), p. 208.

90 *ELA*, 6 January 1940, p. 5.

91 Tower Hamlets Central Library, Minutes of Stepney Borough Council, p. 2756, 24 November 1943; *ELA*, 26 November 1943, p. 1.

92 BD, E2/54: S. Brotman (Secretary, Board of Deputies) to Davis, 20 February and 20 March 1940.

93 *ELA*, 1 December 1944, p. 1.

94 *JC*, 21 March 1947, p. 16; 7 November 1947, p. 20; *ELA*, 7 November 1947, p. 1. A correspondent to the *JC* noted that Jewish councillors had voted against the Hackney resolution; eventually the LCC acted by approving a motion which was forwarded to the Home Secretary: *JC*, 10 October 1947, p. 5. For evidence of the secret part played by the Board of Deputies in initiating these motions see BD, C6/3/1c/9: memorandum dated October 1947. On the impact of the Union Movement see C. T. Husbands, 'East End racism 1900–1980', *London Journal*, vol. 8 (1982), pp. 14–15, and *H[ackney and Kingsland] G[azette]*, 23 March 1949, p. 3.

95 BD, C6/1/2/4: Report of the North London District Committee of the Defence Committee, 23 February 1948. See also the oblique criticism of Jewish members of the LCC made by the President of the Board, Dr A. Cohen, at its meeting on 20 November 1949 (speaking on the report of the Defence Committee) in BD, A/35, and the undated memorandum in C6/10/25.

96 H. Hopkins, 'Painting the East End red', *John Bull*, 11 January 1947, pp. 14–16. In December 1947 the Jewish Communist Alan Blatt won a by-election in the Spitalfields East Ward of Stepney Council, and there was another Jewish Communist victory (A. L. Steinberg) at Spitalfields West the following year: *ELA*, 12 December 1947, p. 1; 27 February 1948, p. 1.

97 On Gaster see C. C. Aronsfeld, 'Communists in British Jewry', *Jewish Monthly*, vol. 1 (1947), p. 33; H. Pelling, *The British Communist Party* (A. & C. Black, London, 1975), p. 77; *ELA*, 18 January 1946, p. 1. Gaster was the only Jewish Communist ever to sit on the LCC.

98 Kushner, 'British antisemitism', pp. 70–1 and 231; *ELO*, 21 April 1928, p. 4; 1 December 1928, p. 6. Nettie Adler had noted in 1934 that the number of pupils attending the Jews' Free School had declined from a maximum of 3,500 to just 1,737: N. Adler, 'Jewish life', in H. L. Smith (ed.), *New Survey*, p. 270.

99 Adler, 'Jewish life', in H. L. Smith (ed.), *New Survey*, p. 287.

100 *The Times*, 20 October 1936, p. 13.

101 Kushner, 'British Antisemitism', pp. 229 and 234.

102 *H[ampstead and] H[ighgate] E[xpress]*, 12 October 1945, p. 1; 2 November, p. 5.

103 *Sunday Express*, 26 May 1946, p. 2. Boyd was elected for the Belsize ward as a candidate for the 'Municipal Electors' Association' – a euphemism for the local Conservative party. There appears to have been some behind-the-scenes lobbying by the Board of Deputies to obtain the Council's repudiation of the petition: see BD, C6/1/2/3: Minutes of the Metropolitan Area Committee of the Defence Committee, 8 November 1945.

104 *HHE*, 6 October 1939, p. 1.

105 *HHE*, 29 October 1943, p. 2.
106 *HHE*, 7 July 1944, p. 6; *JC*, 19 February 1943, p. 5.
107 *Kilburn Times*, 9 June 1944, p. 3.
108 *JC*, 20 January 1939, p. 29; A. J. Sherman, *Island Refuge: Britain and the Refugees from the Third Reich 1933–1939* (Elek, London, 1973), p. 219.
109 BD, C2/3/3/10/2: Liverman to Brotman, 14 May 1940. On Liverman (a member of the Liberal Party) see *Jewish Year Book* and *JC*, 11 March 1949, p. 5.
110 BD, C2/2/6.
111 G. Alderman, *The History of the Hendon Synagogue 1928–1978* (The Hendon Synagogue, London, 1978), pp. 6–7.
112 B. Wasserstein, *Britain and the Jews of Europe 1939–1945* (Oxford University Press for Institute of Jewish Affairs, Oxford, 1979), p. 92.
113 Kushner, 'British antisemitism', pp. 549–50.
114 BD, C6/2/6: Defence Committee Memorandum, 1940.
115 Trades Advisory Council, *Forty Years of Service* (London, 1980).
116 Alderman, *Jewish Community*, p. 129.
117 M. Orbach, 'Noah Barou and the Trades Advisory Council', in H. D. Infield (ed.), *Essays in Jewish Sociology, Labour and Co-operation in Memory of Dr Noah Barou 1889–1955* (Thomas Yoseloff, London, 1962), pp. 31–3.
118 *JC*, 31 July 1942, p. 8. For Orbach's career after 1945 see Alderman, *Jewish Community*, pp. 129, 132, 139, and 200; and *JC*, 4 May 1979, p. 23.
119 A. Newman, *The United Synagogue 1870–1970* (Routledge & Kegan Paul, London, 1976), pp. 218–19.
120 *JC*, 11 January 1957, p. 9.
121 *JC*, 15 November 1946, p. 15; 30 March 1951, p. 5; 25 May 1951, p. 1; 1 June 1951, p. 5; 9 May 1952, p. 9; 25 May 1956, p. 5; *ELA*, 15 November 1946, p. 1.
122 On Helen Bentwich see *JC*, 24 October 1947, p. 6; 5 May 1972, p. 37; *The Times*, 5 May 1972, p. 14; R. J. D'Arcy Hart, *The Samuel Family of Liverpool* (Routledge, London, 1958), p. 4. There is an excellent comparison of Mrs Bentwich and Lady Nathan by Mrs Irene Chaplin in *The Times*, 10 June 1972, p. 14.
123 Mrs Serota was created Baroness in 1967, and Mrs Jeger in 1979. On the social and educational reformer Eva Hubback (who 'married out') see D. Hopkinson, *Family Inheritance* (Staples Press, London, 1954). On Mishcon see *Jewish Year Book* and *JC*, 19 February 1954, p. 1.
124 *JC*, 24 March 1939, p. 12.
125 *JC*, 18 June 1937, p. 18; 19 November, p. 14; BD, E2/105.
126 *JC*, 3 June 1938, p. 15; 9 August 1940, p. 1; 18 May 1945, p. 10. See generally B. Steinberg, 'Jewish education in Great Britain during World War II', *Jewish Social Studies*, vol. 29 (1967), pp. 27–63, esp. p. 45.
127 *ELO*, 24 July 1942, p. 2; 28 January 1944, p. 1; GLRO, Minutes of

the Education Committee, 22 January 1941, p. 91; 3 December 1941, pp. 164–5; LCC Minutes, 16 May 1944, p. 455.

128 *ELO*, 11 December 1942, p. 3; *JC*, 4 June 1948, p. 16; 11 March 1955, p. 8; 29 April 1955, p. 12. In 1957 the LCC agreed to make grants available to students studying at Jews' College, London: *JC*, 24 May 1957, p. 6.

129 Kushner, 'British antisemitism', p. 465.

130 *JC*, 10 March 1944, p. 10; 12 May, p. 10. The 1944 Act also gave the Jewish authorities the right to arrange special religious instruction ('withdrawal') classes in secondary schools: BD, A/33: Report of the Education Committee, 12 November 1946.

131 S. S. Levin, 'The changing pattern of Jewish education', in S. S. Levin (ed.), *A Century of Anglo-Jewish Life 1870–1970* (United Synagogue, London, 1970), p. 69. The experience of evacuation generally is dealt with in M. Ford, 'The arrival of Jewish refugee children in England, 1938–1939', *Immigrants and Minorities*, vol. 2 (1983), pp. 135–51.

132 By June 1939 the number of pupils attending Jewish voluntary schools had declined to 3,000: Levin, 'Changing pattern', p. 68.

133 *ELO*, 14 January 1944, p. 1; BD, E2/32.

134 *JC*, 27 October 1944, p. 10.

135 *JC*, 8 February 1957, p. 23; 7 March, p. 6; J. Moonman, *Anglo-Jewry – An Analysis* (Joint Israel Appeal, London, 1980), p. 40.

136 For the controversy surrounding the fate of the Grocers' Company's School, Hackney Downs (maintained by the LCC since 1905 and of which Dr Homa was Chairman of the Governors) see G. Alderman, *The History of Hackney Downs School* (The Clove Club, London, 1972), p. 74.

137 *JC*, 8 November 1946, p. 6.

138 Levin, 'Changing pattern', p. 70; Moonman, *Anglo-Jewry*, p. 39. It is fair to add that other synagogal bodies in London also failed to meet their obligations.

139 Moonman, *Anglo-Jewry*, pp. 25 and 40.

140 *JC*, 7 October 1983, p. 21.

141 *JC*, 28 June 1946, p. 14; *HG*, 24 January 1955, p. 1. In 1959 the LCC's Education Committee accepted the advice of its Education Officer, that county council maintenance of the Avigdor school be terminated. This decision (effected the following year) brought to a head several years' disquiet at the behaviour of Dr Schonfeld, whose attempt in 1954 to dismiss the headmaster had resulted in civil litigation: GLRO, EO/PS/1/82: Papers of the Education Officer's Department concerning 'Avigdor School'. See also *JC*, 17 July 1959, p. 7; 13 May 1960, p. 20; 27 May, p. 12.

142 *ELA*, 24 September 1948, p. 1.

143 *ELA*, 3 March 1950, p. 1.

144 *ELA*, 15 April 1949, p. 8; *JC*, 21 March 1952, p. 8.

145 On Kaye see *ELA*, 25 February 1955, p. 9.

146 Alderman, *Jewish Community*, pp. 161–2.

147 *ELO*, 13 March 1926, p. 2. On Stern see R. Apple, 'United Synagogue, religious founders and leaders', in S. S. Levin (ed.), *A Century of Anglo-Jewish Life 1870–1970* (United Synagogue, London, 1970), p. 24.

148 *ELO*, 10 July 1926, p. 2.

149 *ELO*, 9 October 1926, p. 2.

150 *ELO*, 27 November 1926, p. 2; 25 February 1928, p. 3.

151 *ELO*, 4 July 1936, p. 5.

152 *HG*, 14 January 1949, p. 3; Wechsler had represented Holborn 1934–49 and was an Alderman of the LCC 1949–52.

153 *JC*, 1 May 1953, p. 25; 25 May, p. 11. Out of a total of fifty-one Jews elected to London borough councils in 1953, no less than twelve were Conservatives.

154 *ELA*, 22 January 1954, p. 10. Emden unsuccessfully fought West Ham South at the General Election of 1955. For Iremonger and the Jewish vote at Ilford North see Alderman, *Jewish Community*, pp. 140, 144, 148–9, and 202.

155 *JC*, 29 June 1945, p. 5. In November 1945 Louis Levy resigned from the Conservative Party in Golders Green after alleging that his failure to secure election to the Borough Council had been due to the failure of the local party to support him during the campaign: *H[endon] T[imes]*, 9 November 1945, p. 1.

156 A. Ranney, *Pathways to Parliament* (Macmillan, London, 1965), p. 117; B. Glanville, 'The British Jews', *Queen*, 1 March 1961, p. 53.

157 *JC*, 15 November 1946, p. 15; 24 March 1950, p. 6; 21 March 1952, p. 7; *Richmond Herald*, 14 November 1931, p. 10; 3 November 1934, p. 6; 16 November 1946, p. 4. The first Jew to be elected to Hendon Urban District Council was Alderman A. A. Naar, an active Zionist and a member of the Executive of the English Zionist Federation, who was twice Mayor of Hendon and a member of Middlesex County Council: *JC*, 24 June 1949, p. 6.

158 B. Donoghue, 'Finchley', in D. E. Butler and A. King, *The British General Election of 1964* (Macmillan, London, 1965), pp. 241–53; *JC*, 3 May 1957, p. 10. See also BD, C6/1/2/5: Minutes of the Metropolitan Area Committee of the Defence Committee, 10 July 1957.

159 *JC*, 11 October 1957, p. 25.

160 *HT*, 1 April 1960, p. 6.

161 Donoghue, 'Finchley', pp. 250–2.

162 *HT*, 18 May 1962, p. 13.

163 *HT*, 11 November 1960, p. 9; 31 August 1962, p. 4; *JC*, 24 October 1960, p. 11.

164 *HT*, 17 April 1964, p. 12; 15 May 1964, p. 14.

165 *HT*, 11 June 1965, p. 1; 18 June 1967, p. 8.

166 *HT*, 11 December 1964, p. 1.

167 W. E. Jackson, *Achievement: A Short History of the London County Council* (Longman, London, 1965), pp. 230–41.

168 *JC*, 9 April 1965, p. 7.

5 DESCENT INTO WAR

1 The evidence for this reorientation may be found in G. Alderman, *The Jewish Community in British Politics* (Oxford University Press, Oxford, 1983), pp. 136–7, and S. Waterman and B. Kosmin, *British Jewry in the Eighties* (Board of Deputies of British Jews, London, 1986), pp. 44–7.

2 Alderman, *Jewish Community*, pp. 174–5.

3 On Greengross, twice Mayor of Holborn and at one time National Chairman of the Trades Advisory Council, see *J[ewish] C[hronicle]*, 20 June 1986, p. 8.

4 On Mrs Dimson see *JC*, 4 May 1973, p. 25 and 4 April 1986, p. 1. Her impact on GLC housing policy is discussed in K. Young and J. Krauser, *Strategy and Conflict in Metropolitan Housing* (Heinemann, London, 1978), pp. 154–9.

5 See table 5.1. Peter Otwell (Labour, 1964–7) and A. A. Berney (Conservative, 1967–73) sat for Brent, Ben Mason (Labour, 1973–7) represented Edmonton, and A. Kinzley (Conservative, 1977–81) was returned in Ilford North; no Jew was ever returned to the GLC for Harrow.

6 B[oard of] D[eputies of British Jews], Minutes of Meetings 20 June and 18 July 1965, 23 January 1966: Reports of the Education and Youth Committee.

7 *JC*, 11 December 1965, p. 15.

8 *JC*, 28 September 1973, p. 11; BD, Minutes of Meeting 21 April 1974: Report of Education and Youth Committee. See also *J[ewish] T[ribune]*, 15 March 1974, p. 1.

9 *JC*, 3 June 1966, p. 11; 17 March 1967, p. 11. In April 1967 the GLC hosted a reception in honour of Judge Joseph M. Proskauer, honorary president of the American Jewish Committee; the Israeli Ambassador, A. Remez, was also present: *JC*, 7 April 1967, p. 11.

10 *JC*, 23 July 1971, p. 5; 10 September, p. 44; 15 October, p. 9; 5 November, p. 7.

11 *JC*, 20 October 1972, p. 8. Sebag-Montefiore (a member of a well-known Sephardi family) was supported by Sir Louis Gluckstein, now no longer a member of the GLC, but President of the Royal Albert Hall, where the Russian visitors were to perform.

12 *JC*, 7 June 1974, p. 19.

13 *JC*, 8 October 1976, p. 6. This support was reinforced through letters handed over in Moscow by Lord Ponsonby (GLC chairman) and Alderman Frank Abbott (on behalf of the Conservative opposition leader on the Council, Horace Cutler).

14 The origins and development of leftwing antisemitism in Britain are explored in S. Cohen, *That's Funny You Don't Look Anti-Semitic* (Beyond the Pale Collective, Leeds, 1984).

15 ibid., pp. 38–49.

16 On the antisemitism of the Young Liberals, the part played in it by the activist and anti-apartheid campaigner Peter Hain, and the

consequent resignation from the Liberal Party of Professor (now Lord) Max Beloff, see *JC*, 7 April 1972, p. 5 and 29 December, p. 6.

17 *H[endon] T[imes]*, 13 November 1970, p. 1; *JC*, 14 November, p. 1.

18 *HT*, 14 April 1972, p. 1; *JC*, 7 April 1972, p. 5; 6 October, p. 11; 13 October, p. 10; 27 October, p. 10.

19 See generally M. Anwar, *Race and Politics: Ethnic Minorities and the British Political System* (Tavistock, London, 1986), especially ch. 5.

20 J. Rose, 'Black views on Jews', *JC*, 28 October 1977, p. 8; *W[est] I[ndian] W[orld]*, 11 June 1976, p. 6; *A[sian] T[imes]*, 13 April 1984, p. 21; 25 January 1985, p. 11; *C[aribbean] T[imes]*, 20 September 1985, p. 27. For some discussion of the problems caused to the Anglo-Jewish community by the activities of what the Board of Deputies termed 'unethical landlords' (1972) see H. Pollins, *Economic History of the Jews in England* (Associated University Presses, London, 1982), pp. 229–30. See also M. Coren, 'When underdog bites underdog', *New Statesman*, 15 March 1985, pp. 16–17.

21 Y. Ginzberg, 'Sympathy and resentment. Jews and coloureds in London's East End', *Patterns of Prejudice*, vol. 13, nos 2–3 (March–June 1979), pp. 39–42.

22 The editorial was reprinted in the *WIW*, 2 February 1978, p. 1.

23 See especially the speech of Barnett Janner on the 1965 bill: *Commons' Debates*, 5th ser., vol. 170, cols 955–62 (7 April 1965).

24 L. M. Waldenburg, 'The history of Anglo-Jewish responses to immigration and racial tension, 1950–70' (unpublished MA (Economics) thesis, University of Sheffield, 1972), pp. 37–9, 57–8. Soskice (later Lord Stow Hill), a warm supporter of Israel, was a Christian born of Jewish parents; see *JC*, 5 January 1979, p. 20. It is worth recording that in May 1965 the Conservative MP for Hendon North, Sir Ian Orr-Ewing, announced that he had decided not to vote against the Labour government's Race Relations Bill after having received 'well-argued Jewish representations': *HT*, 21 May 1965, p. 10.

25 Waldenburg, 'Anglo-Jewish responses', pp. 58–9. See also *JT*, 4 July 1975, p. 4; 19 September, p. 4.

26 Waldenburg, p. 59.

27 ibid., pp. 60–4. The report, *Improving Race Relations – A Jewish Contribution*, was published in 1969.

28 *Ilford Recorder*, 23 March 1968, p. 18; 11 April, p. 56; 2 December 1970, p. 3; 31 January 1974, p. 1.

29 These events are dealt with at length in Alderman, *Jewish Community*, pp. 147–9.

30 *JC*, 15 April 1977, p. 9.

31 *HT*, 21 April 1977, p. 3; 28 April, p. 12.

32 Alderman, *Jewish Community*, pp. 164–7.

33 See generally M. Walker, *The National Front* (Fontana, London, 1977), and D. Butler and D. Kavanagh, *The British General Election*

of 1979 (Macmillan, London, 1980), pp. 418–19.

34 M. Steed, 'The National Front vote', *Parliamentary Affairs*, vol. 31 (1978), pp. 287–9. At the General Election of October 1974 the Front's vote in contested seats stood at 2.9 per cent; by May 1979 it had fallen to 1.3 per cent.

35 *JC*, 10 March 1978, p. 20. On the ANL see G. Alderman, 'Fighters against the Front', *JC*, 6 October 1978, p. 25. On Lord Fisher of Camden, president of the Board 1973–9 and (1953) the first Jewish Mayor of Stoke Newington, see *JC*, 19 October 1979, p. 24.

36 BD, Minutes of Meetings 19 February, 19 March, and 16 April 1978: Reports of the J[ewish] D[efence and] G[roup] R[elations] C[ommittee]. The Board was also unhappy with the ANL's policy of taking to the streets in campaigning against the National Front.

37 BD, Minutes of Meetings 19 March and 16 April 1978: Reports of the JDGRC. In January 1979 Lord Fisher met the ANL's secretary, Paul Holborrow, in an attempt to reach an accommodation with it; co-operation proved impossible: *JT*, 26 January 1979, p. 2.

38 *JC*, 22 April 1977, pp. 1 and 4.

39 BD, Minutes of Meeting 25 July 1976: Report of the Executive Committee; M[anchester] J[ewish] T[elegraph], 24 September 1976, p. 36.

40 BD, Minutes of Meeting 19 June 1977: Report of the JDGRC. For details of the Joint Committee Against Racialism see *JC*, 25 May 1977, p. 6.

41 For example, in 1976 Dr Gewirtz wrote to the *WIW* complaining that it had published an unsigned letter attacking Israel and Zionism: BD, Minutes of Meeting 25 July 1976: Report of the JDGRC.

42 BD, Minutes of Meeting 25 July 1976: Report of the JDGRC; *MJT*, 30 July 1976, p. 3. On Ali see *The Times*, 4 May 1978, p. 16. Savitt alleged that Ali's intervention had breached assurances that the Middle East would not be mentioned at the rally (held at Trafalgar Square) and he made it clear, in a letter to the rally organizer, that those who attacked Zionism also attacked Anglo-Jewry.

43 *JT*, 13 May 1977, p. 4; see also 11 November 1977, p. 1.

44 *JT*, 29 April 1977, p. 4; 3 June, p. 4.

45 See above, n. 22, and BD, Minutes of Meeting 19 March 1978: Report of JDGRC.

46 *JC*, 3 March 1978, p. 18.

47 *JC*, 7 September 1979, p. 10; 7 December, p. 14. See also *MJT*, 14 November 1980, p. 1: speech by Janner declaring that 'an attack on any minority was an attack on Jews'.

48 *The Times*, 16 June 1980, p. 16.

49 R. Narayan, *Black England* (Doscarla Publications, London, 1977), esp. ch. 9, 'The Jewish example'.

50 *HG*, 10 October 1980, p. 40; see also *JC*, 24 October 1980, p. 20 (leader on Narayan) and 12 December, p. 18 (letter from A. Super).

51 *HG*, 10 October 1980, p. 40.

52 *JC*, 27 November 1981, p. 21; 4 December, p. 22; 11 December, p. 22; 18 December, p. 16; 8 January 1982, p.16. Anglo-Muslim reaction to events in the Lebanon may be sampled in the *Slough Observer*, 24 September 1982, p. 5; *Lancashire Evening Telegraph*, 27 September 1982, p. 3; and the *CT*, 11 June 1982, p. 8; 18 June, p. 8; 5 November 1982, p. 22.

53 *JC*, 25 September 1979, p. 6; *HG*, 25 September 1979, p. 6.

54 *JC*, 23 November 1979, p. 22; 11 July 1980, p. 22.

55 *JC*, 7 May 1982, p. 10; 28 August, p. 6.

56 Anwar, p. 165; the NCWP proportion in Brent East was 29.9 per cent.

57 *JC*, 2 June 1978, p. 7.

58 *HT*, 12 March 1981, p. 3; *Observer*, 15 March 1981, p. 4.

59 *HT*, 9 April 1981, p. 2; 16 April, p. 1; *JC* London Extra, 17 April 1981, p. 1.

60 *The Times*, 26 May 1982, p. 1. As a result of the local elections, the Brent Council consisted of thirty-three Labour members, thirty Conservatives, and three Liberals.

61 *JC* London Extra, 26 March 1982, p. 1.

62 ibid., 30 April 1982, p. 1.

63 ibid., 2 April 1982, p. 1.

64 For qualitative and quantitative discussion of Anglo-Jewry's strong support for Thatcherite Conservatism by this time see G. Alderman, 'Anglo-Jewry: the politics of an image', *Parliamentary Affairs* (1984), pp. 160–92 and the same author's 'London Jews and the 1987 General Election', *Jewish Quarterly*, vol. 34, no. 3 (1987), pp. 13–16.

65 BD, Minutes of Meeting 11 January 1981.

66 *The Times*, 21 October 1981, p. 2. The three schools were the Yesodey Hatorah Girls' and the Lubavitch Boys' and Girls' primary schools; these had a total of about 800 pupils on their rolls. There was also a fear that the granting of voluntary-aided status to these schools would encourage similar applications from the Muslim community.

67 *JC* London Extra, 4 November 1983, p. 1; *JC*, 16 March 1984, p. 4. The ILEA had also taken the view that the surplus primary school capacity in Hackney did not merit voluntary-aided status for the Jewish schools concerned. That such surplus capacity existed was true, but the surpluses were to be found in secular state schools, not in Jewish denominational ones.

68 *JC* London Extra, 27 December 1985, p. 1. A central part in obtaining these grants was played by Rabbi Avroham Pinter, elected a Labour member of the Borough Council in 1982.

69 *JC* London Extra, 10 September 1982, p. 1.

70 Notably that, by being so classified, Jews could claim the protection of the 1976 Race Relations Act.

71 See the evidence given by the Board of Deputies to the Home Affairs Select Committee of the House of Commons on 7 February 1983, printed in the HC 33–x (session 1982–3), pp. 372–80 and in vol. 2 of the main report (HC 33–II), pp. 370–8.

72 GLC Ethnic Minorities Unit internal memorandum, 'Consultation with the Jewish Community' (D/372/104).
73 ibid.; *JC*, 17 December 1982, p. 6; *JT*, 10 December 1982, p. 3. The meeting was attended by some seventy persons, including Councillor H. J. Lobenstein, the well-known and strictly orthodox Jewish member of the Conservative opposition on Hackney Borough Council, on whom see Alderman, *Jewish Community*, pp. 159–60 and 206.
74 G. Alderman, 'Two cheers for the GLC', *JC*, 28 March 1986, p. 27.
75 BD, Minutes of Meeting 19 December 1982; *JC*, 17 December 1982, p. 18.
76 *The Times*, 18 March 1980, p. 5.
77 On the JSG's attitude to Zionism and the Anglo-Jewish leadership see *AT*, 31 August 1984, p. 7.
78 Letters to the author from Councillor P. Boateng, 26 January 1983 and from Mr Henry Morris, 4 March 1987, and to Mr Morris from the author, 18 April 1983, following the author's interview with Mr Ansel Wong of the EMU. See also *JC*, 29 December 1986, p. 14: letter from Mr R. Kalman, vice-chairman, JDGRC.
79 BD, Minutes of Meeting 19 December 1982: exchange between the author and Mr Morris. See also *JC*, 2 May 1986, p. 6: interview with Livingstone.
80 *CT*, 31 January 1986, p. 11.
81 *JC* London Extra, 21 October 1983, p. 1. The JSG believes, in common with many on the left of Israeli politics, that there should be direct negotiations with the PLO; but it is equally committed to Israel's existence: *JC*, 4 November 1983, p. 16: letter from Dr S. L. Ogin.
82 BD, Report of the JDGRC, December 1983.
83 *Labour Herald*, 25 June 1982, p. 7; *The Times*, 3 July 1982, p. 1; BD, Report of the JDGRC, July/September 1982. The *Labour Herald* also numbered among its editors Ted Knight, leader of Lambeth Council.
84 BD, Report of the JDGRC, June 1983, referring to an item on BBC Television's 'Money Programme'. See also the article by Dr Gewirtz in *JC*, 3 January 1986, p. 9.
85 GLRO, Minutes of the GLC 23 November 1982, pp. 214–15.
86 *Labour Herald*, 19 March 1982, p. 14; *JC*, 17 December 1982, p. 18. See also *Ilford Recorder*, 3 October 1983, p. 7, and the articles by Dr Gewirtz, *JC*, 3 January 1986, p. 9, and G. Alderman, *JC*, 28 March 1986, p. 27. Livingstone's reference to Israel as a country based on racism was made at a Trafalgar Square rally called to support the PLO: *JC*, 13 August 1982, p. 3.
87 BD, Report of the JDGRC, February 1984.
88 *JC*, 13 August 1982, p. 3; 11 March 1983, p. 5.
89 *JC*, 17 August 1984, p. 1. See also Anne Sofer writing in *The Times*, 1 October 1984, p. 12.
90 *JC*, 28 September 1984, p. 5.

91 BD Press Release, 16 August 1984.
92 BD, Minutes of Meeting 23, September 1984: speech by M. Savitt. *JT*, 24 August 1984, p. 1; 10 October, pp. 3–4.
93 BD, Report of a Joint Meeting of the Executive and Law, Parliamentary and General Purposes Committees, 7 December 1984. *JT*, 13 December 1984, p. 1.
94 *JC*, 28 December 1984.
95 *JC*, 14 December 1984, p. 1; *JT*, 13 December 1984, p. 1.
96 *On Board* (Newsletter of the Board of Deputies), January 1985, p. 1; *JC*, 14 December 1984, p. 1; 21 December, p. 1. The *JT*, 20 December 1984, p. 1, reported that the censure had been carried by thirty-six votes to sixteen, with eighteen Labour members abstaining. See also Livingstone's article in *New Socialist*, December 1984, p. 6.
97 *JT*, 24 February 1984, p. 3.
98 *JC*, 8 July 1983, p. 1; *JC* London Extra, 19 August 1983, p. 2 and 28 October, p. 1; *JT*, 24 February 1984, p. 3.
99 *JC*, 8 April 1983, p. 32; 20 July 1984, p. 32.
100 Quoted in *JC*, 14 December 1984, p. 1.
101 GLRO, Minutes of the GLC, 22 January 1985, pp. 9–20. The distinction which Livingstone drew, between anti-Zionism and antisemitism, is, in the author's view, legitimate, and certainly in the period before the Second World War many leading British Jews would have agreed with him. However, in the context of the post-Holocaust Jewish experience the distinction is much harder to make; Livingstone's belief that many British Jews are anti-Zionist is therefore fundamentally flawed (see Anne Sofer in *The Times*, 1 October 1984, p. 12). The overwhelming majority of British Jews would have agreed with the stricture voiced by the Labour MP Greville Janner (president of the Board of Deputies), who after a meeting with Livingstone explained that to call Zionism racism was tantamount to calling Jews racists. (BD, Minutes of Meeting 18 December 1983). At the conference of the National Union of Students held in Blackpool in April 1986 Livingstone declared that 'it is a fundamental mistake to equate Zionism with racism. It is a form of nationalism' (*JC*, 11 April 1986, p. 1). His views appear, therefore, to have undergone a fundamental change since 1982: see above, nn. 83 and 84, and *AT*, 6 December 1985, p. 2.
102 *JC*, 15 March 1985, p. 8; *JC* London Extra, 29 March 1985, p. 1; *The Times*, 13 April 1985, p. 1. Freeson's position as co-chairman of Poale Zion had clearly become a disadvantage.
103 *JC*, 21 August 1981, p. 4. In 1985 Clinton Davis became a member of the European Commission, in charge of transport, the environment, and nuclear safety.
104 *JC* London Extra, 31 December 1982, p. 1.
105 ibid., 21 March 1986, p. 1.
106 In 1982 the Board of Deputies had accepted an invitation to give evidence to the Police Committee (chaired by Councillor Boateng), and a team led by Mr Morris and Dr Gewirtz actually did so. The

Police Committee's report – *Racial Harassment in London*, published in 1984 – was unstinting in its praise of the Board and unequivocal in its condemnation of the discrimination and violence from which Jews in London were suffering. The author also gave evidence to the inquiry.

107 BD, Minutes of Meeting 1, 27 October 1985: address by the president, Dr L. Kopelowitz; *JC* London Extra, 25 October 1985, p. 1; 22 November, p. 1. The chairwoman of the Brent East Labour Party subsequently condemned Sir Immanuel as 'rude, bigoted, and narrow-minded': BD, Report of the JDGRC, January 1986.

108 BD, Report of the JDGRC, November 1985; *JC*, 29 November 1985, p. 52; *AT*, 6 December 1985, p. 3. Ross, a member of the GLC's Ethnic Arts Sub-Committee, revealed that the decision to recommend the grant had only been made on the casting vote of the chairman, Peter Pitt (on whom see p. 133 above).

109 *JC* London Extra, 25 November 1983, p. 1. There had indeed been calls from within the community for the GLC to be boycotted and for its abolition to be supported; see, for example, the letter from Brian Gordon (by then honorary secretary of British Herut) in *JC*, 21 December 1984, p. 14.

110 E. Krausz, 'A sociological field study of Jewish suburban life in Edgware 1962–63 with special reference to minority identification' (unpublished PhD thesis, University of London, 1965), pp. 93 and 103.

111 Waterman & Kosmin, *British Jewry*, p. 45.

112 I. Crewe, 'A new class of politics', *Guardian*, 15 June 1987, p. 9.

113 B. A. Kosmin, C. Levy, and P. Wigodsky, *The Social Demography of Redbridge Jewry* (Board of Deputies of British Jews, London, 1979), p. 25; R. Waller, *The Almanac of British Politics* (3rd edn, Croom Helm, Beckenham, 1987), pp. 40–2, 46, 60, and 70.

114 J. Sacks, *Wealth and Poverty* (Social Affairs Unit, London, 1985); *Guardian*, 27 May 1986, p. 23.

115 Sir I. Jakobovits, 'From doom to hope', *JC*, 24 January 1986, pp. 26–8. As early as 1977 Jakobovits had condemned the welfare state for undermining individual responsibility and for encouraging a 'get something for nothing' attitude; the *JT*, 17 June 1977, p. 4, voiced its support for these views. For a critical Black response to Jakobovits see *CT*, 7 February 1986, p. 11.

116 *JC*, 2 June 1986, p. 6.

117 Interview with Savitt, 5 June 1987.

118 *JC*, 21 December 1984, p. 14.

119 Alderman, *Jewish Community*, p. 159.

CONCLUSION

1 J. A. Jackson, *The Irish in Britain* (Routledge & Kegan Paul, London, 1963), p. 123. On Liverpool see P. J. Waller, *Democracy and Sectarianism* (Liverpool University Press, Liverpool, 1981).

2 B. D. Jacobs, *Black Politics and Urban Crisis in Britain* (Cambridge University Press, Cambridge, 1986).

3 The papers are in B[oard of] D[eputies of British Jews], C6/1/2/5: Minutes of the Metropolitan Area Committee of the Jewish Defence Committee, 1950–63.

4 See especially BD, C6/1/2/5: Minutes of the Metropolitan Area Committee of the Jewish Defence Committee, 1 December 1954 (protest of Beatrice Barwell) and C6/10/25: correspondence between the Board and H. Sebag-Montefiore and V. Mishcon, December 1960 and January 1961.

5 BD, C6/1/2/5: Jewish Defence Committee 'Current notes', May 1957; Minutes of the Metropolitan Area Committee, 17 July 1957.

6 *J[ewish] C[hronicle]*, 9 April 1965, p. 7.

7 ibid.

8 BD, C6/10/25: Memorandum (undated).

9 E. P. Hennock, *Fit and Proper Persons* (Edward Arnold, London, 1973), pp. 303–4.

10 N. Bentwich, *My 77 Years* (Routledge & Kegan Paul, London, 1962), p. 310.

Appendix

JEWS ELECTED TO THE LONDON COUNTY COUNCIL

	Progressives/ Liberals	Moderates/ Municipal Reformers/ Conservatives	Labour	Total
1889	5	2	0	7
1892	2	1	0	3
1895	2	3	0	5
1898	2	1	0	3
1901	2	2	0	4
1904	2	2	0	5[a]
1907	2	6	0	8
1910	5	7[b]	0	12[c]
1913	5	6	0	11
1919	3	6[d]	0	9[e]
1922	2	7	0	9
1925	1	6	4	11
1928	3	6	5	14
1931	3	6	5[f]	14[g]
1934	0	6	10	16
1937	0	3	12	15
1946	1	3	10	15[h]
1949	1	2	4	7
1952	0	2	10[i]	12[j]
1955	0	4	11	15
1958	0	4	16	20
1961	0	3	15	18

[a] includes one Independent
[b] 8 from 1911
[c] 13 from 1911
[d] 7 from 1921
[e] 10 from 1921

[f] 6 from 1932
[g] 15 from 1932
[h] includes one Communist
[i] 11 from 1954
[j] 13 from 1954

JEWS ELECTED TO THE GREATER LONDON COUNCIL

	Conservative	Labour	Total
1964	4	13	17
1967	4	4	8
1970	4[a]	7	11[b]
1973	1	8	9
1977	2	6	8
1981	1	6	7

[a] 5 from 1972
[b] 12 from 1972

INDEX

182